Art and human rights

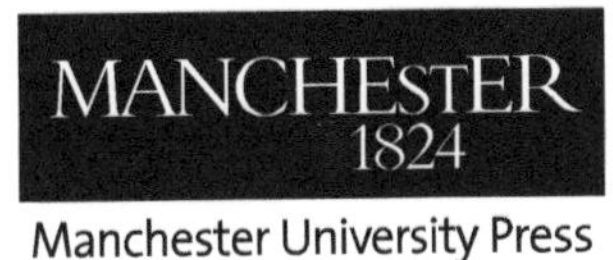

Manchester University Press

rethinking
art's histories

SERIES EDITORS
Amelia G. Jones, Marsha Meskimmon

Rethinking Art's Histories aims to open out art history from its most basic structures by foregrounding work that challenges the conventional periodisation and geographical subfields of traditional art history, and addressing a wide range of visual cultural forms from the early modern period to the present.

Also available in the series

Art, museums and touch   Fiona Candlin

The 'do-it-yourself' artwork: Participation from fluxus to relational aesthetics   Anna Dezeuze (ed.)

The face of medicine: Visualising medical masculinities in late nineteenth-century Paris   Mary Hunter

After the event: New perspectives in art history
Charles Merewether and John Potts (eds)

Photography and documentary film in the making of modern Brazil   Luciana Martins

Women, the arts and globalization: Eccentric experience
Marsha Meskimmon and Dorothy Rowe (eds)

Flesh cinema: The corporeal turn in American avant-garde film   Ara Osterweil

After-affects|after-images: Trauma and aesthetic transformation in the virtual Feminist museum   Griselda Pollock

Vertiginous mirrors: The animation of the visual image and early modern travel   Rose Marie San Juan

The paradox of body, building and motion in seventeenth-century England   Kimberley Skelton

Art and human rights

Contemporary Asian contexts

Caroline Turner and Jen Webb

Manchester University Press

Published by Manchester University Press
Altrincham Street, Manchester M1 7JA
www.manchesteruniversitypress.co.uk

British Library Cataloguing-in-Publication Data
A catalogue record for this book is available from the British Library

Library of Congress Cataloging-in-Publication Data applied for

ISBN 978 0 7190 9064 6 hardback
ISBN 978 0 7190 9957 1 paperback

First published 2016

Typeset by Out of House Publishing

Contents

Illustrations

Cover

Nalini Malani, *Cassandra*, 2009. Detail. 30-panel polytych, acrylic, ink and enamel reverse painting on acrylic sheet. 227.5 × 396cm. Collection Kiran Nadar Museum of Art, New Delhi. Courtesy the Artist.

Plates

Plates can be found between pages 76 and 77.

Photograph Aaron de Souza. Courtesy the Artist and Sherman Contemporary Art Foundation.

Figures

Acknowledgements

Our sincere thanks go first to the artists who are the subject of this book, for significant assistance with our research over many years and for their input to this text, as well as to image editor Ursula Frederick and scholarly editor Glen Barclay.

Many people helped with our research and exhibition projects including: Michelle Antoinette, Scott Brook, Zoe Butt, Alison Carroll, Christine Chinkin, Christine Clark, Costas Douzinas, Debjani Ganguly, Katie Hayne, Elly Kent, Iola Lenzi, Jacqueline Lo, Sophie McIntyre, Marsha Meskimmon, Jacqueline Menzies, Charles Merewether, Andrew Melrose, Anthony Oates, Jodi Parvey, Paul Pickering, Johan Pijnappel, Suhanya Raffel, Claire Roberts, Chaitanya Sambrani, Natalie Seiz, Nancy Sever, Gene Sherman, Zara Stanhope, Martin Stuart-Fox, John White, David Williams, Asia Art Archive, and the staff of the Queensland Art Gallery (in particular Judy Gunning, Cathy Pemble Smith, Chris Saines, Aaron Seeto, Russell Storer and Robyn Ziebell).

We thank all the artists, copyright holders, institutions and photographers who have given their kind permission to reproduce images and whose names appear in our image list. We especially note the assistance of the Queensland Art Gallery, Sherman Contemporary Art Foundation, Museum of Contemporary Art, Sydney (Phoebe Rathmell), Singapore Art Museum (Aimilia Safuan and Chu Chu Yuan), Cai Studio (Stephanie Lee and Lydia Ohl), the Carnegie Museum of Art (Stefanie Brown), Bradford Museums and Galleries (Kathryn Barker), the Guggenheim Foundation (Kim Bush), Seattle Art Museum (Matt Empson), Kimsooja studio, Thavibu Gallery (Jørn Middelborg), Ota Fine Arts (Mr Ota), Mary Boone Gallery (Ron Warren), Peggy Bose, Jan Manton Gallery and Valentine Willie.

Research for this book was supported by the Australian Research Council (ARC) Discovery Project, 'Art and Human Rights' (DP0452961, 2004–7). We thank our fellow Chief Investigators, Pat Hoffie and Margo Neale, and our respective institutions, especially the Humanities Research Centre at the Australian National University and the Centre for Creative and Cultural Research, Faculty of Arts and Design, at the University of Canberra. The

Humanities Research Centre at the ANU supported our conferences *Art and Human Rights* (2003), *Recovering Lives* (2008) and *The World and World-Making in Art* (2011), and a series of exhibitions from 2003 to 2010. Our research was also greatly informed by the Asia-Pacific Triennial exhibitions at the Queensland Art Gallery.

Finally, we thank the staff of Manchester University Press, for their consistent support, excellent advice, and careful shepherding of this text.

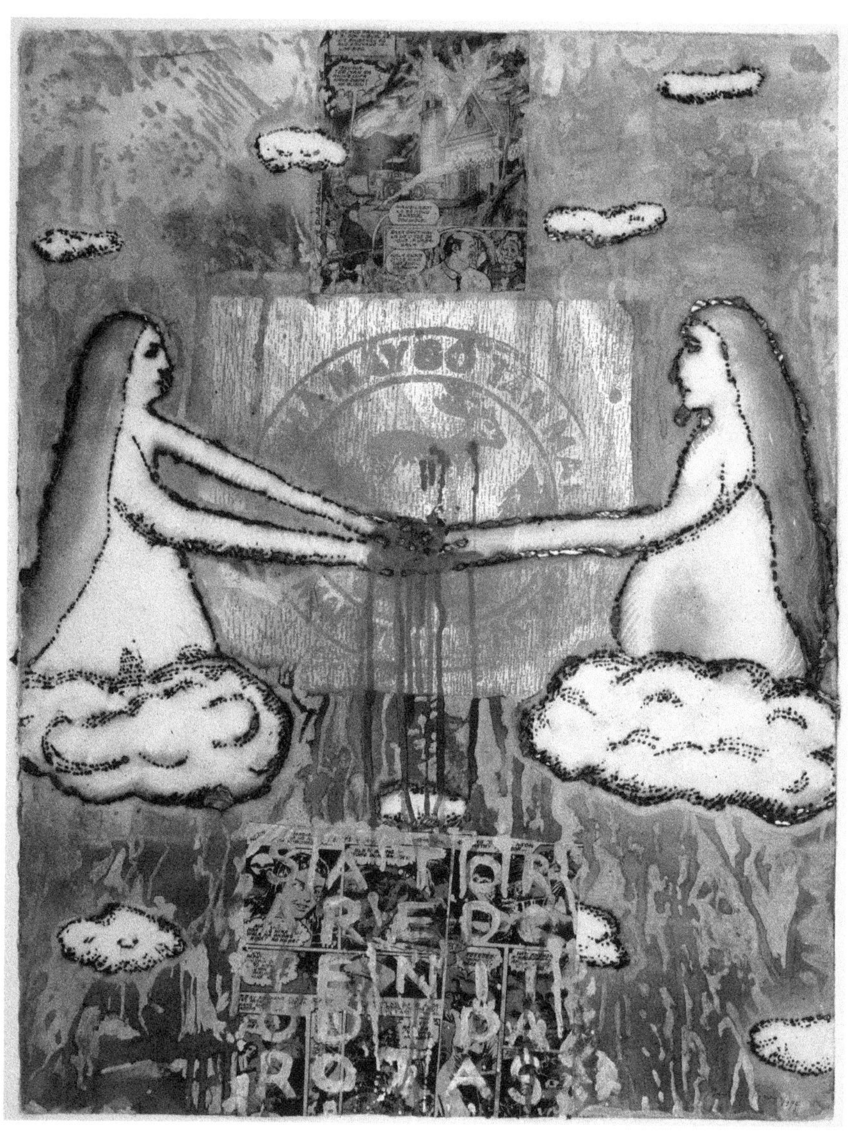

1.1 Santiago Bose, *Let it bleed*, 1994. Collection: Queensland Art Gallery. Purchased 1995. Queensland Art Gallery Foundation Grant. Celebrating the Queensland Art Gallery's Centenary 1895–1995.

Frameworks and contexts **1**

Introduction

This book is concerned with Asian contemporary artists and the connection of their art to human rights. Our definition of 'human rights', drawn as it is from the United Nations Universal Declaration of Human Rights (1948), is very broad and encompasses issues of critical concern to all humanity including poverty, social justice, health and cultural rights.[1] The majority of those we discuss would not see themselves as activists but as artists working for a better future for their communities. We focus on a cohort of artists who came to prominence in the late 1980s and early 1990s, the time when the works of Asian artists began to be seen in large numbers in exhibitions throughout the world, and when geopolitical and economic change forced not only a rethinking of art's histories but also the reconceptualisation of global frameworks for art.

Although the idea of Asia as a continent and as different from Europe was a concept largely developed outside Asia, notably by the ancient Greeks, it is a construction of the world that still dominates geography and social, political and cultural divisions in the twenty-first century. The western world has long been in active dialogue with Asia and its art: western cultural practitioners have appropriated Asian styles and iconography from as far back as records show, with traces of Asian art, architecture and mythology evident, for instance, in ancient Greek culture.[2] Trade and commerce passed between Europe and China via the ancient silk road from Roman times. War also provided routes of exchange – the armies of Alexander reaching the borders of northern India in the fourth century BCE, and the sons of Genghis Khan threatening Venice and Vienna in the thirteenth century CE. Art historian Michael Sullivan, writing about what he calls the meeting of eastern and western art, notes the earlier lengthy cultural exchanges but reads this as intensifying from 1500.[3] The late nineteenth and early twentieth centuries saw a 'rediscovery' of Asian art by many European and American avant garde artists who appropriated elements from those art traditions;[4] Asian artists, too, drew inspiration from western modern art, many studying in western countries.

While the historical arts of Asia have long been collected, exhibited and admired in the west, until comparatively recently western art historians and museum directors showed limited knowledge of Asian modern and contemporary art, artists and art practices, or understanding of ways of thinking about and historicising art outside a western framework. As Charles Green wrote, 'Until recently, even the most basic information on contemporary art from Asia and the Pacific … has not been widely accessible outside of the region.'[5] However, the late twentieth century saw a process of geopolitical change that led to a shift from an art centred in Europe and America, and towards greater inclusion in arts discourses of artists from regions such as Asia and Latin America. Our decision to focus on Asian art in this book is at least in part because of the importance of documenting a key cohort of artists, and a moment in time when Asian art became part of those international art discourses.

Scholars agree that the world of art changed dramatically in the last decade of the twentieth century. This was also a time when the definition of the 'contemporary' changed. Hans Belting wrote in 2009, 'Contemporary art, a term long used to designate the most recent art, assumed an entirely new meaning when art production, following the turn of world politics and world trade in 1989, expanded across the globe. The results of this unprecedented expansion challenged the continuity of any Eurocentric view of art.'[6] The artists we focus on and discuss in this book have helped shape those challenges to a Eurocentric view of art.

Art historian Terry Smith has pointed to a historical shift from Euro-American geopolitical and economic hegemony over the last fifty years. This has occurred at an accelerated pace in recent years, he notes, writing, 'Geopolitical change has shifted the world picture from presumptions about the inevitability of modernisation and the universality of EuroAmerican values to recognition of the coexistence of difference, of disjunctive diversity, as characteristic of our contemporary condition.'[7] At the same time artists and scholars outside Europe and North America were contributing new frameworks for global art expressions. This change to a new global art is much more substantial than artists from the so-called 'periphery' being admitted to a 'canon' of art controlled by the west. There has been a determined move from scholars and artists in Asia to develop what Oscar Ho has referred to as 'languages outside of a Western-dominated art world'.[8]

Key writers and institutions in the 1990s began to make the case that local knowledges and histories, and regional values, need to be understood when exploring Asian art and the concept of an 'Asian' art. Art historian John Clark, however, who has made major contributions to our understanding of concepts of modern Asian art, points to 'the still largely absent discourse of a worlded art history that takes account of Asia'.[9] Clark developed the notion of a modernity in Asian art that emerged parallel to and at the same time as modernity in what he terms 'Euramerica'. As Clark notes, there were Asian artists who achieved distinction in Europe in the nineteenth and early twentieth centuries: for example, Javanese aristocrat Raden Saleh, who studied painting in the Netherlands and whose work was highly regarded in Europe; Juan Luna from the Philippines, who won the gold medal in the 1884 Madrid Exposition of Fine Art, and was later involved in the liberation war against Spain; or Japanese artist Fujita Tsuguharu (or Léonard Foujita), who developed friendships with European artists including Picasso. A significant number of other Asian artists also visited or studied in Europe and the US. Many artists in Asia have embraced the challenges of reconciling the cultural traditions of their own region and locality with international art and art movements.

Chaitanya Sambrani has pointed out that sophisticated traditions of scholarship existed within many Asian nations, but until recently these were largely confined to national boundaries.[10] This is not to say, as Sambrani and Singaporean scholar T. K. Sabapathy emphasised, that there were no historical artistic connections between Asian nations in art.[11] Thai art historian Apinan Poshyananda, too, writes that syncretism has been a key factor in historical cultural formations in the region.[12] The influence of the fountainhead cultures of India and China in historical times has been significant, and Japan has been a major influence in connections with the west since the Meiji Restoration in the nineteenth century. While western colonialism had a major effect, the history of interconnections in the modern era is far more complex. A framework of comparative national art histories has been developed by Asian scholars and curators such as Jim Supangkat, T. K. Sabapathy, Redza Piyadasa, Geeta Kapur, Gulammohammed Sheikh, Salima Hashmi, Akira Tatehata, Apinan Poshyananda, Somporn Rodboon, Fumio Nanjo, Vishakha Desai, Hou Hanru, Kim Youngna, Gao Minglu, Wu Hung, Eriko Osaka, Soyeon Ahn, Alice Guillermo and Patrick Flores, among others, who have been at the forefront of exploring the legacies of the historical and more recent past since the 1990s.[13] The modern art history of individual countries has also been explored by scholars outside Asia, such as Astri Wright, Britta Erickson, Nora Taylor and Alexandra Munroe.

The Asian region has continued in recent years to develop its own forums for art and for creative dialogue between artists, curators and scholars. Art schools and universities were an early and obvious site of dialogue. Museums and art exhibitions have played a significant role in defining this new Asian art, reflexively adjusting their attitudes and practices. Collecting policies have been re-examined, and a number of galleries have deliberately built collections of contemporary Asian art that extend beyond individual nations. Fukuoka in Japan and Brisbane in Australia were very early adopters, showing and collecting contemporary artists from across Asia: the Fukuoka Art Museum and later the Fukuoka Asian Art Museum from the late 1970s, and Brisbane's Queensland Art Gallery from the late 1980s. These collections are now of major international significance in documenting contemporary Asian art.[14] The Singapore Art Museum and the new National Gallery of Singapore have been critical in collecting and showing Southeast Asian art. The Japan Foundation has played a leading role in forming networks in art through its Asia Center in Tokyo in the 1990s, and also conferences and collaborative exhibitions, grants and residencies over an extended period. The New York-based Asia Society has also been a key facilitator. Many of these institutions have also conducted research and mounted exhibitions designed to investigate art movements in Asia, such as *Asian Modernism* (1995–96), which was organised by the Japan Foundation, and travelled widely in Asia and beyond.[15]

Local and regional artist collectives, too, have been integral to the development of contemporary art across Asia, especially, as Christine Clark notes, in areas with lower levels of infrastructure.[16] The Asia Art Archive in Hong Kong, established in 2000, is a major resource for scholarship within the region, and a number of curator and artist networks, and the Asian Art Museum Directors network, have formed in recent years.[17] Artist collectives such as Cemeti Art House in Indonesia, established in 1988 by Nindityo Adipurnomo and Mella Jaarsma and discussed in Chapter 6, have allowed artists to operate within their own countries, and to form links with artists in other nations. Such collectives and networks have provided exhibition venues and workshop spaces, facilitated networking and mentorships, contributed to policy development and arts education, and developed the intellectual frameworks needed to enrich the discourse of art in their regions, and internationally.

These developments have happened alongside the emergence of biennales and triennales that have a major focus on contemporary art from the region, along with an international scope. Key examples are the Indian Triennial (established in 1968), the Bangladesh (1981), Gwangju (1995), Shanghai (1996) and Taipei (1998) biennales; the Asia-Pacific Triennial at the Queensland Art Gallery, Brisbane (1993), the Fukuoka Triennale (1999), the Yokohama (2001) and Guangzhou (2003) triennials; and the Busan (2002), Beijing (2003), Singapore (2006) and Kochi-Muziris (2012) biennales. A World Biennial Forum in Gwangju, South Korea, in 2012 had representatives from all over Asia,[18] and there are now at least 150 biennales worldwide, many of them in Asia. Charles Green and Anthony Gardner have completed a major research project on world biennales and, as Gardner has pointed out, biennales have

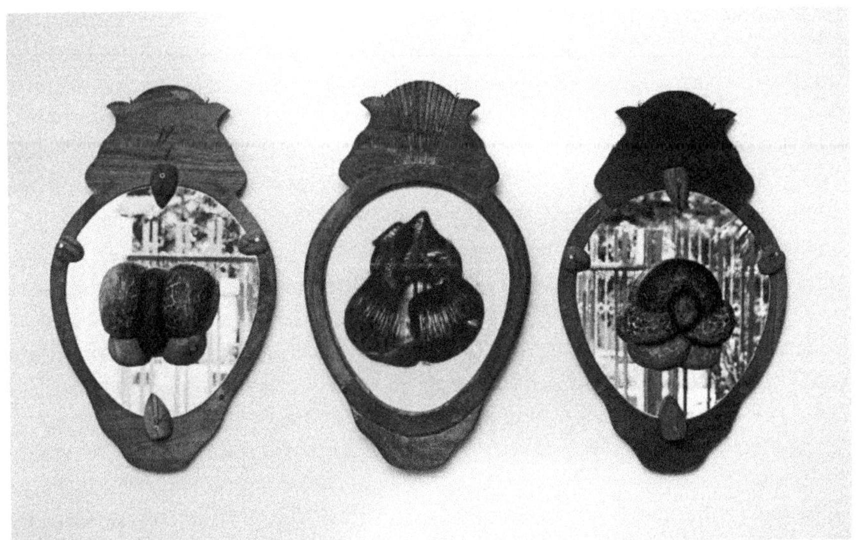

Nindityo Adipurnomo, *Introversion (April the twenty-first)*, 1995–96. Detail. **1.2**
Collection: Queensland Art Gallery. Purchased 1996. Queensland Art Gallery
Foundation.

been one of the main driving forces in production and display of contemporary art over recent decades.[19] These recurring exhibitions have been very significant for the cohort of artists we discuss in ensuring their work can be seen as part of international art practice. Key recurring international exhibitions such as the Venice Biennale and Documenta in Germany, together with the Havana, São Paulo and Sydney biennales, were also early contributors to the exhibition of Asian contemporary art outside the region. The result is that Asian art now enjoys a substantial audience, scholarship and market internationally.

This is the context in which we began investigating and preparing to write this book. Much of the research emerged from a project we completed with artist/academic Professor Pat Hoffie, curator Margo Neale and researcher Christine Clark, with funding supplied by the Australian Research Council. The project began in 2000, sparked by a conversation with international human rights lawyer Christine Chinkin, who at the time was a Visiting Fellow at the Humanities Research Centre (HRC) at the Australian National University. We conducted interviews with artists, curators and scholars in Asia, and undertook extensive analysis of the art produced and the considerable secondary research in the literature of art in Asia, as well as a close reading of exhibitions of Asian art in the various Asian nations, in Australia, Europe and the US. Our research included our involvement with the Asia-Pacific Triennial exhibitions and conferences in the 1990s in Australia, and we have worked with most of the artists discussed in this book through those exhibitions. In addition we organised a number of international conferences, beginning with 'Art and Human Rights' (at the HRC, 2003); contributed to an edited volume with essays by a number of key scholars from the region on art and social change in Asia and the Pacific;[20] and curated a number of exhibitions on the theme over the period 2003 to 2010.[21] We found that many of the artists and arts commentators and museum professionals were concerned with the legacies of colonialism, immigration, multiculturalism and 'the other within' in their own cultures, and with the impact of globalisation and western universalism on both art and culture. We therefore found ourselves exploring their cross-cultural and cross-disciplinary approaches to nationalism and globalisation. This book aims to provide knowledge and insight into art in the region, with particular reference to artists whose focus is how contemporary art might contribute to building a better and more equitable society. The human rights debate is at the heart of this concern, and with it the problem of universality versus cultural specificity.

In no sense could we have tried to cover all the art movements extant in this period, and our focus has been on artists whose work connects to ideas of human rights and social justice. Our cohort comprises a segment of a particular generation of artists who were born, for the most part, post-second world war, came to prominence in the late 1980s and 1990s, and who were part of major transformations that took place throughout Asia in the wake of the collapse of colonial regimes. While not all Asian nations had been colonised, all had to a degree been subjected to western imposition. As well, the defeat and occupation of Japan, and the communist victory in China in 1949, unleashed new and complex forces and ideologies in Asia as new nation states were shaped. Western countries continued to engage with Asia, including through wars in Korea and Vietnam, and in support of regimes like those of Ferdinand Marcos in the Philippines and General Suharto in Indonesia, as part of Cold War political strategy. New and changing geopolitical and economic transformations at the end of the twentieth century saw western influence decrease with the rise, first, of Japan and more recently of China and India, and this, along with the economic and cultural power of nations throughout the Asian region, has led commentators to predict that the twenty-first century will be the 'Asian century'.[22]

While this process has been surprising to many in western countries, it has been described by Kishore Mahbubani as merely a case of the world returning to the historical normality of the place of Asian societies in the global hierarchy.[23] These contexts frame the different worlds of the artists we discuss in the following chapters. Geopolitical and economic change did without question have an effect on interest in Asian art. Japanese artists were included in major international exhibitions beginning in the 1960s and 1970s, at the time when the Japanese economy became the second largest economy in the world (although it has since dropped to third place after China). China's economic rise in recent times has also led to world attention being focused on Chinese artists, a number of whom are now international 'superstars'. Geopolitical and economic transformations have led to an unprecedented growth in the middle classes in Asia, with hundreds of millions of people lifted out of poverty, but with huge inequities still to be resolved. Geeta Kapur, one of the pre-eminent writers on art today, describes the context for Indian (and by extension) many Asian artists as 'a civil society in huge ferment, a political society whose constituencies are redefining the meaning of democracy and a demographic scale that defies simple theories of hegemony'.[24] Alison Carroll, the Founding Director of the Asialink Arts programme in Australia (overseeing nearly eighty exhibitions in twenty years in eighteen countries in Asia), terms the twentieth century in Asia the 'revolutionary century'[25] because of the dynamic changes and restless experimentation in Asian art during the period 1900–2000.

The artists in our cohort have for the most part been educated at universities and art colleges in the new nations formed after 1945 and have thus benefitted from improved economic conditions in their individual nations. Many also studied abroad, including in Europe and the US, and most have exhibited internationally in major exhibitions and biennales, and have made a significant contribution to contemporary art and its discourses. Many have been collected by major museums outside their own countries. In this book we have limited our geographical coverage of Asia to South, Southeast and East Asia, acknowledging that Central Asia and Russia, with areas west of Pakistan – now usually called West Asia – such as Iran, Iraq, Syria to present-day Turkey, also form part of the continent of Asia. We limit the scope in the main because in the 1990s, when debates about an 'Asian' contemporary art were in formation, the largely Islamic countries of West Asia were not generally included in definitions of 'Asia'.

In the remainder of this chapter we address the issue of human rights, including the question of what constitutes a human being, what constitutes rights, and the limits of rights, and provide a background to key issues associated with the investigation of contemporary art in the Asian region, including the debate about and the changing status of Asian values. We look at the contexts for art's connections with human rights in Asia, and the changing approach to art's histories globally. We explore the relationship between local and global issues, and particularly the effects of globalised practices on the production of art and the protection of human rights. Finally, we explain and contextualise our selection of artists for the case studies presented in this book.

In subsequent chapters we explore the work of art and artists in addressing change in the contemporary world through case studies of artists who respond to the challenges of the contemporary moment by engaging with human rights. Of the many themes possible under the rubric of 'human rights', we have selected key terms to categorise the art works and the context of the artists who are the focus of the case studies. While this is by no means either exhaustive or conclusive – the artists collected under one term might, from a different standpoint, equally have been considered under a different term – our analysis of the field indicates that it provides a useful structure in which to examine the topic of this book.

In Chapter 2 we focus on practices that can be categorised as cultural and political activism, exploring this through case studies focused on Wong Hoy Cheong from Malaysia, Dadang Christanto from Indonesia and Vasan Sitthiket from Thailand. Chapter 3 takes up the problem of war and divided societies, with case studies focused on Japanese artist Yoshiko Shimada, Sri Lankan artist Jagath Weerasinghe, FX Harsono from Indonesia, and Dinh Q. Lê from Vietnam and the US. Chapter 4 examines the work of artists in a globalising world, and the effects of that world on cultural identity, discussing the art of Kimsooja from South Korea, Alfredo and Isabel Aquilizan from the Philippines, and Oscar Ho and John Young from Hong Kong. Finally in Chapter 5 we consider the work of artists that can be understood as 'worldmaking', with case studies on Pakistan-based Salima Hashmi, India-based Nalini Malani, Chinese-Australian Guan Wei, and Chinese-born (now American) Cai Guo-Qiang. Each case study examines the art within the specific contexts in which these individuals emerged as artists to provide a general portrait of the environment, as well as a specific focus on their own careers and approach to social and creative practice. Our purpose throughout is to look at developments in key countries in the region, while acknowledging that national boundaries should not be seen as confining our view of artistic practice or confining the artists, many of whom, today, are global travellers.

Human rights

Later in this chapter we discuss the specific links between art and human rights that are our focus in this book. While the artists we discuss in this book are not concerned so much with legal regimes of rights as with issues facing their communities, and with witnessing to and resisting injustice, we need to look at ideas about human rights as they have evolved internationally to develop an international face in the decades following the United Nations Universal Declaration of Human Rights in 1948. This document, developed in response to the atrocities of the second world war, is effectively the doctrine of human rights as natural rights – the rights we have simply by virtue of being alive. It is a reminder that everyone, in any context or culture, needs food and shelter, security, a sense of belonging and self-worth, and the capacity for self-expression. At base it demands two things for everyone: that 'I' survive; and that 'I' be recognised in my totality – in all that makes me human.

Although human rights discourse typically focuses on extreme forms of abuse such as segregation, slavery or genocide, the thirty Articles that make up the Declaration give equal weight to such apparently less extreme issues as the right to hold particular beliefs, or to attend school. Articles 1–19 address the person, and are based on what might be called Enlightenment concepts. They assert that everyone is equal before the law regardless of 'race, colour, sex, language, religion, political or other opinion, national or social origin, property, birth or other status'; everyone has the 'right to life, liberty and security of person', including rights not to be unlawfully imprisoned or tortured; everyone has the right to marry, own property, and enjoy freedom of thought and expression. Articles 20–26 deal with social and economic equity, and are in the tradition of the sorts of concepts that came out of the Industrial Revolution: the right to work, but also to rest; the right to engage in the government of their nation; and the right to belong to a trade union. Articles 27–29 deal with cultural issues: the right to participate in social and cultural life as a member of a national community. Article 30, which wraps up the Declaration, sets out to preserve the authority of its principles.

As a working document, it seems both idealistic and practical, designed to ensure a sound working community across the globe. However, its implementation has been patchy at best, and the beginning of the twenty-first century has seen significant challenges and attacks on the framework of ideas underpinning such legislation and on their implementation. Though we now live in what Norberto Bobbio calls the 'age of rights',[26] at a point in history when, as human rights lawyer Costas Douzinas says, human rights have triumphed in the world, there is barely a month free of manifest abuses. As Douzinas goes on to point out, 'our enlightened age has witnessed the greatest infringements of human rights … This is a paradox, a triumph drowned in disaster.'[27]

It is a paradox that seems to have dogged human communities right across history. Micheline Ishay traces the enactment of rights in law from the Code of Hammurabi to the US Patriot Act, and shows just how fundamental, even universal, are the notion of the common good and the desire to protect human beings.[28] Thus the problem of human rights is not first of all philosophical or ideological, but political: we all agree with rights (in principle) but cannot (in practice) work out how to protect them in the face of competing and contradictory interests.[29] Human rights lawyer Christine Chinkin suggests art can play a role in the transformation and comprehension of legal ideas and the delivery of human rights, and she notes 'it is only too apparent that the language of international human rights is inadequate to ensure delivery of this message'.[30]

One problem associated with the failure to implement this universally shared value may be the fundamental differences between communities. Edward Said writes:

> When we ask ourselves 'Whose human rights are we trying to protect?' … we need to acknowledge frankly that individual freedoms and right are set irrevocably in a national context. To discuss human freedom today, therefore, is to speak about the freedom of persons of a particular nationality or ethnic or religious identity whose life is subsumed within a national territory ruled by a sovereign power.[31]

Responding to Said, we agree that this is an issue, and locate it, in part, in the fact that the terms 'human rights' and 'human' are under-defined and recondite. Before one can even begin to consider what 'human rights' means, it is necessary to clarify what is meant by human. Joseph Slaughter notes:

> From its inception, human rights law has relied on both philosophical inquiry into, and sociological understanding of, the nature of human subjectivity, whether explicitly expressed or implicitly referenced. The nature of our understanding of human subjectivity is central to any thorough discussion of human rights.[32]

In the absence of a shared idea of human subjectivity, it is very difficult to know how human rights legislation can be consistently enacted. Neither 'human' nor 'human rights' has a stable or necessary meaning: they are abstractions, rather than actualities. An individual person is a particularity; 'humanity' is an abstraction, and thus is a floating signifier, a term that has no necessary meaning but plenty of surplus value. The surplus value emerges in situations where decisions must be made about particularities. One problem is whether there is such a thing as an autonomous subject who must be treated as a particular individual with rights; there is a line of postmodern thought that finds this an impossibility, which renders problematic the very concept of human rights.[33]

A second problem is whether everyone is counted as human, and therefore worthy of rights. Human status is universally accorded to all, but in fact applied according to local criteria, with women, people of colour, adherents of certain religions, foreigners, people with mental or physical conditions and so on variously excluded from full social identity. The ASEAN Human

Rights Declaration of 2012 is more precise than is the Universal Declaration, specifically naming 'women, children, the elderly, persons with disabilities, migrant workers, and vulnerable and marginalised groups' as possessing inalienable rights; but there is a sort of loophole in Principle 6, which states: 'The enjoyment of human rights and fundamental freedoms must be balanced with the performance of corresponding duties as every person has responsibilities to all other individuals, the community and the society where one lives.'[34] Does this mean that those who fail to perform their civic duty appropriately are not eligible for rights? The Declaration has yet to be tested. But perhaps the worst off are stateless people, or those who lack identity papers because, as Hannah Arendt insists, 'the right to have rights is citizenship'.[35] Those who lack citizenship belong to nowhere, and are no one's responsibility.

A further problem in this respect is that the Declaration of Human Rights establishes rights in universal terms, but the application of these rights is vested in the sovereign state, which means the legitimacy of the Declaration depends on state consent. It is not clear that nations are able – or that their governments consider themselves able – to preserve their sovereignty and integrity while still holding to a vision of universality. Hans Seigfried writes, 'It would be abominable beyond measure if states cultivated a sense of loyalty to the nation at the expense of the responsibility, allegiance and solidarity we owe to every human being';[36] and yet states typically do just this. Since human rights are applied within nation states, the rights proclaimed on behalf of 'man', or the 'human being', are actually claimed only on behalf of the citizen.

The conundrum here rests on whether human rights should be conceived of as pertaining to the individual or the community; and whether the universalist or the communitarianist approach is more effective. For the universalists, all human rights issues are resolved through the application of universal norms and obedience to categorical imperatives. For communitarians, human rights are created in local contexts. Neither approach is necessarily sound; people have been slaughtered by communitarians in the interests of the community; and universalists have in their turn killed the murderous communitarians, as evidenced by the current conflicts in Afghanistan. Arjun Appadurai, in *Fear of Small Numbers* (2006), analyses culturally motivated violence in the globalised post-1989 world and states, 'We now live in a world, articulated differently by states and by media in different national and regional contexts, in which fear often seems to be the source and ground for intensive campaigns of group violence.' Appadurai points out that in the 1940s and for some time after, many scholars assumed that large-scale collective violence was the product of totalitarian regimes, but that 'the 1990s have left no doubt that liberal-democratic societies, as well as a variety of mixed state forms, are susceptible to capture by majoritarian forces and large-scale ethnocidal violence'.[37]

For Douzinas, the history of human rights is an attempt to close the gap between the abstract and the concrete, between the living and the political animal. It hasn't happened yet and perhaps cannot happen; not within these discourses. Moreover, Douzinas points out, legal codes are not the full story in relation to human rights. He writes:

> There is a poetry in human rights that defies the rationalism of law: when a burnt child runs from the scene of an atrocity in Vietnam, when a young man stands in front of a tank in Beijing, when an emaciated body and dulled eyes face the camera from behind the barbed wire of a concentration camp in Bosnia, a tragic sense erupts and places me, the onlooker, face to face with my own responsibility that does not come from codes, conventions or rules but from a sense of personal guilt for the suffering in the world, of obligation to save humanity in the face of the victim.[38]

Defining Asia and Asian values

Asia, it could be said, does not *in fact* exist except as an artefact of mapmaking and discursive acts. A Japan Foundation forum in 2002 concluded that 'Asia' has always been a form of discourse.[39] Chaitanya Sambrani, in noting that the idea of Asia had until recently, for the most part, been constructed outside the region, points to the work of Anthony Milner and Deborah Johnson on the historical dimensions of this construction,[40] though in recent years ideas about the 'Orient' and 'Asia' have been subjected to new scholarship and analysis.[41] Asia is both an ancient idea and a modern one, often used in counterpoint to Europe or the west.

In the early twentieth century an idea of cultural connections emerged in Asian countries, and Japan, as part of creating its empire during the Pacific War, also extolled the idea of 'Asia for the Asians'. Anti-colonial nationalisms in the modern nation states that emerged from the process of decolonisation also contributed to ideas about Asia, as did geopolitical change at the end of the twentieth century. Milner and Johnson conclude, 'The signification of "Asia" is, in fact, in contest and it is those who would identify themselves as "Asians", who have most recently been at the forefront of the defining process.'[42] One way in which Asian nations have been considered to differ from many of those in the west is in the concept of Asian values: a concept widely associated first with Confucian traditions, and then with the politics of ex-prime minister of Singapore, Lee Kuan Yew, in the late twentieth century. In an interview with Fareed Zakaria in 1994 he announced:

> The expansion of the right of the individual to behave or misbehave as he
> pleases has come at the expense of orderly society. In the East the main object
> is to have a well-ordered society so that everybody can have maximum enjoy-
> ment of his freedoms. This freedom can only exist in an ordered state and not
> in a natural state of contention and anarchy.[43]

This, for Lee Kuan Yew, is an axiom predicated on Asian values, which can be summed up as: discipline; respect for authority; respect for hard work; and respect for one's family. It is a communitarian rather than an individualistic set of values,[44] and one that fits neatly with popular views that identify Asia as both authoritarian and communitarian, and the west as committed to egalitarianism and individuality.

But there are flaws in this logic. First, the idea of Asia as a coherent unit, as we have suggested earlier in this chapter, is problematic. The continent defined by the Greeks as stretching from the shores of present-day Turkey has a population of over half the world's population. The World Values Survey, conducted regularly from 1981, does not support the popular discourse on 'Asia' or on 'Asian values'. What it has found in over thirty years of study is that there are really just two value dimensions that differentiate communities. The first is the traditional/secular divide between societies characterised by a dependence on God, and a greater respect for economic wellbeing than for self-expression, and those with opposite tendencies. The second divide is between wealthy communities, who enjoy the freedom from economic crisis that means they can value self-expression, and poorer communities, whose focus must be on survival.[45] The two areas of division are not neatly organised in terms of shared borders or even, necessarily, shared cultural backgrounds, but rather depend on a variety of factors, including modernisation, democratisation and globalisation. Though analysis of the World Values Survey project data reveals that in many cases a shared cultural background leads to shared contemporary values, this is by no means universally true. Indeed, as Dalton and Ong argue, the data shows very few differences in attitudes held by people in East Asia and in the west about the relative values of democratic and authoritarian government.[46]

While we acknowledge the complexity of reality, and the rather dubious underpinnings of the logic of Asian values rhetoric, it is perhaps reasonable to make the point that the universalist view of human rights that obtains in the west does not necessarily serve the interests of all people everywhere. There is a line of thought that the Asian polity is less sympathetic to universal human rights than is the polity in the west. This emerges in the discourse from time to time; for example, the public announcement of the ASEAN Human Rights Declaration attracted considerable debate about its merits. Amnesty International expressed concern that it failed to meet human rights standards on a number of points. They (and others) drew attention to its General Principle 6, which they read as positioning rights as 'a commodity that must be earned' rather than being 'a birthright of all persons'.[47] Similar concerns were expressed by the United Nations' High Commissioner for Human Rights, Navi Pillay, who drew attention to the process of drafting the Declaration, and observed that '[t]he balancing of human rights with individual duties is not a part of international human rights law'.[48]

Authors of a recent study on Asian values and human rights agree on the need for human rights discourses and protocols that are not purely universalist. Writing about human rights in Islamic cultures, for example, Norani Othman argues that contemporary Muslims evidence a 'concern for human rights that is not grounded in any borrowed "Western" model',[49] and calls for a more nuanced approach, one that does not rely on the universality arguments made either by western human rights activists or by militant Islamic forces.[50] There is evidence of an opening up and greater acceptance of universalist rights, and expanded freedom of expression in some Asian countries. There is also substantial evidence that in western countries there is a gap between discourse and practice when it comes to human rights challenges. Some of the artists in our study produce work that offers fresh understandings of these complex questions and of other differences between cultures, religions, regions and nations, including within Asia, as well as the differences within the complex multicultural societies in which so many people now live.

Art and human rights

At this point we need to interrupt the discussion on context, and touch on the connection between art and human rights. This is not something that is universally agreed on by commentators. After all, art has an 'obligation', according to dominant discourses in the field, to focus on the aesthetic; this demands 'a renunciation of certain functions, particularly political functions'.[51] Such discourses generally insist that art is politically and socially neutral, and economically disinterested. Such disinterest is, though, more in the discourse than in the practice. Artists are necessarily involved in the social, political and economic spheres because art is a mechanism for representing and constituting social relations and social values. The artist Leon Golub observed:

> Everyone knows artists don't change society, but that's too easy a way to put it. Artists are part of the information process. If artists only make cubes, then what the world knows of art will be cubes. If there are artists who are doing

other subject matters … these start to enter into different dialogues regarding
the nature of art and circumstance. It may not change the world, but the contexts and operations of art shift. Art becomes part of the context of experience
in unexpected ways.[52]

The point here is that whether artists choose to focus on their own aesthetic
and maintain a distance from sociopolitical concerns, or engage energetically
in current troubles, they are part of the culture, and in presenting a particular
set of images and attitudes, will necessarily reflect something about the lived
world. Salima Hashmi, whose work we discuss in Chapter 5, states that artists can also 'keep hope alive',[53] while writer Hanif Kureishi insists 'in the end
there is only one subject for an artist. What is the nature of human experience? What is it to be alive, suffer and feel?'[54] What this implies is that there is
a drive within the field of art to explore humanity in all its complexities and
contexts, including human rights contexts, and to bring a critical eye to the
context being explored.

The problem of human rights cannot be solved by art, but art has some
important qualities that can be used to clarify this problem, or at least to
ask better questions.[55] Christine Chinkin has also suggested that there are a
number of ways in which art and formal regimes of human rights do connect through witnessing, resistance, cultural survival, education and even
reconciliation and restorative justice.[56] Art is in an extremely good position
to raise questions of human rights, and of human being more generally,
because it is, in some respects, a national outsider – art owes its allegiance
to art, as much as to national identity – but also because, at least in its
autonomous form, it is a social outsider, distanced from the imperatives
that require allegiance to dominant social paradigms.[57] This is not to say
it is necessarily disengaged; art tends to engage, if in a desultory or erratic
manner. As artist William Kentridge says, 'I am interested in a political
art, that is to say an art of ambiguity, contradiction, uncompleted gestures
and uncertain endings.'[58] Art can perform in this way because it is deeply
invested in the material and the concrete, and thus sidesteps the abstractions, and the universalist generalities, found in both law and philosophy.
In its focus on the material, and the sensible, art can offer a way to suture
the space between lived reality and legal abstractions. Costas Douzinas
addresses this, arguing that 'the subject of law … is constrained, rational,
genderless'; while by contrast, 'the self in art … is free, desiring, with gender
and history'.[59] Because art locates people in all their particularities and complexities, and most importantly, in their materiality, in a material world, it
is perhaps reasonable to assert that art is always at some level politically
engaged: it always locates itself in a time and place, and responds to the
local material context. Chantal Mouffe writes:

> One cannot make a distinction between political art and non-political art, because every form of artistic practice either contributes to the reproduction of the given common sense – and in that sense is political – or contributes to the deconstruction or critique of it. Every form of art has a political dimension.[60]

This places a responsibility on artists who agree with Mouffe's perspective. The artist Hans Haacke, for instance, said in conversation with Pierre Bourdieu that 'in the practical world, the evacuation of the political is tantamount to inviting whoever wants to occupy the vacuum that's left behind':[61] by any measure, this is a call to artists to take on the challenge of the political in their work. For some commentators and art historians, art that connects to social and political issues can be seen to lessen its aesthetic purpose. Donald Preziosi suggests this stems from a perspective on 'art as a second reality alongside the world in which we live day to day, rather than as one of the powerful social instruments for the creation and maintenance of the world in which we live'.[62] So, while not all artists are attached to the view that they should address political actualities, it may be reasonable to say that artists generally are attached to the world: to looking at it, understanding it, and reflecting or representing it in its particularities. For many, this translates into such considerations, and certainly there has been a growing focus on art that records, represents, interprets or challenges human rights abuses. A number of major exhibitions across the twentieth century have made it a feature, and many biennales and triennales include at least some works that draw attention to the problem of human rights.

This is not to suggest that artists should make a career of art that protests against human rights abuses; but many artists at some point in their career do use their work to do precisely this: like Goya, who reported on the Peninsular War in *The Disasters of War* (1810–20), or Picasso, who responded to the atrocities of the Spanish Civil War in *Guernica* (1937), many artists whose work otherwise explores form and colour, or produces images of the environment, will respond in art to a manifest abuse of power. While art cannot necessarily change the world, it can – as Goya, Picasso and many other artists, including in Asia, have shown – protest against injustice, war, racism, oppression, human rights abuses, environmental degradation, cultural loss, poverty and all forms of discrimination and exploitation.

The power of art, we suggest, is to mirror both the failures and the aspirations of humanity, and to highlight our commonalities. The role contemporary artists can play in cultural and social transformation has been shown to be a critical one. Visual artists frequently play an essential role in witnessing, interpreting and communicating, through visual languages that increase cultural understanding of complex issues, bind emergent as well as ancient communities, revive memory and, in confronting trauma, initiate healing. It is unreasonable to suggest that art must be politically engaged; that artists must be always watching for shifts away from an ethical standard and ready to cry out like prophets against it. But it is also unreasonable to pretend that artists are not inflected by the contexts in which they live. Artists make work as responses to the events that have touched them, that have crossed their paths and their consciousness. The ethical dilemma they face is not how they report or record the things around them, but whether they will tell and make enduring images of the stories of their time. This attitude was re-affirmed during a recent roundtable between Indonesian and East Timorese cultural practitioners working on issues of reconciliation, trauma, conflict and divided societies in their two nations after more than twenty years of conflict. Participants noted the significant role of art as a language of communication after war, and also in education and in cultural revival within communities devastated by past conflict.[63] Art is one pathway those working for reconciliation can use to bring people together.

It is not always possible for artists to have their work associated with the concept of human rights within the contexts in which their art is made. We have been highly conscious of this obvious but extremely relevant factor in writing this book and in selecting artists to write about. There were artists and projects we chose not to include in this volume because to frame them as contributing to 'human rights' would do the artists and communities a disservice. There are real sensitivities in some countries to identifying artists' work as being about issues of human rights, even within our broad definition of human rights. This includes, for example, work about cultural and religious themes in areas such as Tibet.[64]

In many countries in Asia in the last few decades there has been significant censorship, and many artists need to conform to that censorship. Artists in Pakistan have faced the possibility that they might need to hide their work.[65] In China a number of highly talented artists left the country in the wake of events at Tiananmen Square in 1989 after a brutal crackdown on the democracy movement, although many have returned in recent years. Dissident artists and writers can face significant penalties in China today. Nobel Peace Prize writer and human rights activist Liu Xiaobo is still, at the time of writing, in gaol. Artist Ai Weiwei, also at the time of writing (in 2015), is unable to travel abroad after having had his passport cancelled, and, while released from detention, is still under what he describes as 'soft detention' in Beijing, although he is able to send works to overseas exhibitions.[66] Ai's challenges to authorities included his campaign with volunteers in China in a citizens' investigation, using social media and blogs to bring to public attention the thousands of children killed in the 2008 Sichuan earthquake and the attempts by authorities to conceal the extent of that death toll.

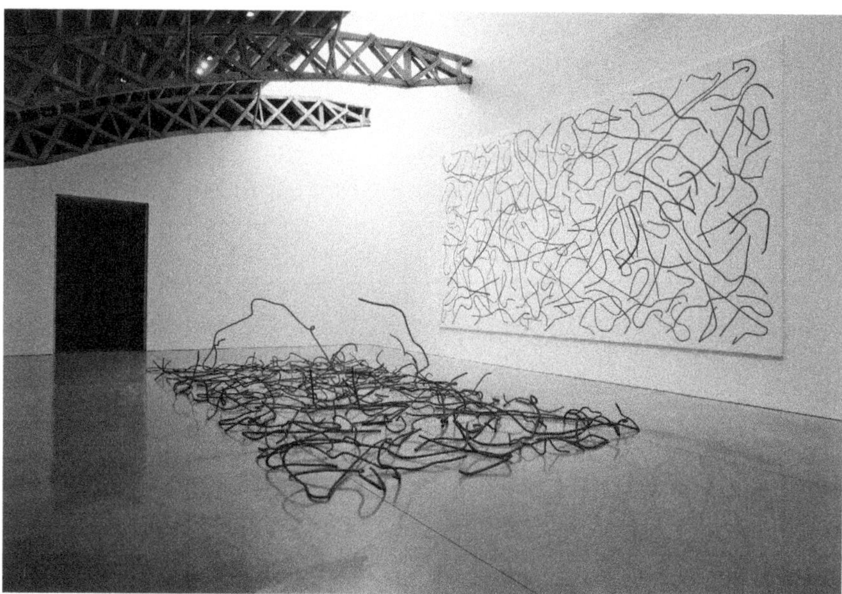

1.3   Ai Weiwei, *Forge*, 2012. Installations at Mary Boone Gallery, New York, 2012.

He has subsequently shown art works about the tragedy outside China as a form of memorial. One example is his installation *Remembering* (2009), where he assembled 9,000 children's backpacks on the façade of the Haus der Kunst in Munich. The backpacks spelled out the Chinese characters for 'She lived happily for seven years in this world' – a quotation from a mother who had lost her child.[67] Another moving work by Ai on this subject is *Forge*, which shows mangled metal bars salvaged and collected from the sites of schools that had collapsed in the earthquake.[68]

Other artists described in this book have also found ways to narrate different and sometimes silenced stories in their home countries, but many would not see themselves as activists. As Golub again states, 'Visual history is important in providing a record of what is going on':[69] and the artists we selected for the case studies, along with many of their contemporaries, are not necessarily illustrating events, but providing a record of events, and new ways of seeing them.

The universal or the specific?

Artists are members of many communities: the community of artists, of course; the local community in which they were born and educated, and the community in which they now live; the nation state of which they are citizens;

and so on. The nation state is, perhaps, the most problematic because of the ways in which it is formulated, and formulates both identity and control of those who live within its border.

The nation state is often viewed as an ancient form of social organisation, but in fact it is really quite recent, dating only from the emergence of the western Enlightenment.[70] The nation state is based on territory rather than on a relationship to a ruler, or an affiliation with a religious organisation; as such it is both highly localised and highly diverse. The boundaries that separate one nation from another are arbitrary and, often, rather fluid – as the history of almost any nation will show. The people who make up that nation are themselves often connected more by the name of their home country than by any other factor, with cultural traditions, language, religious observance and social values often differing markedly within a single nation. It is perhaps not surprising, then, that political leaders seek indicators of nationhood around which the idea of 'us' can be firmed up.

Art is a useful indicator because it can be used to promote the nation with which it is identified, and to represent that nation to itself and to the world.[71] National governments across the globe have established procedures to support and manage the field, instituting national arts funds, national galleries, legislative acts that define and determine what is done with and for art, and policies that spell out where and why support is to be directed to the arts. In Singapore, for example, arts funding is designed to generate 'hallmarks of artistic excellence in and beyond Singapore' which express 'Singapore's cultural identity, values, heritage and aspirations'. Bangladesh's constitution articulates the centrality of art to national culture.[72] Japan's Agency for Cultural Affairs 'strives to promote culture and international cultural exchange', and 'to contribute to the realization of heart-enriching lives for the Japanese people through the comprehensive implementation of measures concerning the promotion of culture and the arts'.[73] In India, the Ministry of Culture's mission 'ranges from creating cultural awareness from the grass root level to the international cultural exchange level',[74] while – following a departmental restructure in 2009 – China's Ministry of Culture adopted a number of new responsibilities, the first of which was 'To organize major international cultural exchange activities'.[75] What emerges from a reading of the government cultural policies and legislation is that art receives significant attention from governments because it is viewed as being capable of expressing a unifying sense of the nation, and of being used to broker international relationships.

Of course, art is rarely just 'for art's sake'; rarely innocent or neutral. Whatever artists may believe themselves to be doing and saying – and however effective and evocative that doing and saying may be – as soon as art enters the community through official commissions and purchases, exhibitions and reviews, it begins to be put to tasks other than the aesthetic, exploratory or communicative. One of the things this does is divide: make real the national boundaries of their area (if it is 'Indonesian' art then it at least seems to be ontologically different from Singaporean art; and by extension Indonesia seems ontologically different from Singapore). But the idea of the nation, especially as represented through instances of 'national art', is highly problematic especially now, when the notion of a permanent, stable and ontologically discrete nation state is being shaken by globalisation and its transformative effects.

John Beynon and David Dunkerley observe that 'globalization might justifiably be claimed to be the defining feature of human society at the start of the twenty-first century',[76] and one that informs the lives of everyone on the planet. People are moving, whether voluntarily or involuntarily, in great numbers around the globe, and crossing borders (legally or illegally), bringing with them stories, languages and cultures that are now juxtaposed, and cohabiting in local spaces. The interweaving of currencies and trade has an even more profound effect on our everyday lives, since in Tokyo, Berlin or New York stock markets impact on us all, while the mass media's movies, television shows and popular music provide are part of everyday life for much of the population of the globe.

It is important, though, not to overstate the effects of globalisation on everyday life or on the practice of artists. 'Global sceptics' argue that much of the 'truth' of globalisation, especially its potential to break down national boundaries and revolutionise ways of thinking and seeing, rests on the deluge of communication technologies. But only a very small percentage of the world's population is actually in the loop of the network society: at the turn of the current century most of the world's population lacked access to telecommunication; and although mobile phones now proliferate across the world, reliable and consistent access to electricity, let alone to networks, is very uneven.[77]

Even if every home across the globe had a telephone line, a computer and an internet service provider, this would not necessitate a transformation or homogenisation of art. Local cultures have always been supremely good at picking up just enough of a colonising or influencing culture to enhance their own practices and world views – as the Catholic Church could attest. Despite its incredibly successful spread across the globe, what it means to be Catholic, and how worship is both conducted and understood, are deeply inflected by local, rather than universal or Vatican, accounts of the same.[78] Any failure to appreciate the importance of the local is an example of what Bourdieu refers to as the 'false universalism of the West', a claim to universalism that is 'no more than a nationalism which invokes the universal (human rights, etc.) in order to impose itself'.[79] There is nothing to suggest that social, political and cultural forms are either constitutive of or inform any kind of universalisation. There are many groups of people throughout the world for whom time and space are still experienced in much the same way as was common in their cultures a century ago. As for the homogenising effects of western culture, this ignores the evidence of local communities transforming hegemonic cultural forms for their own purposes. There are many ways to be human and to enact culture, so while artists may draw on other traditions, they do not necessarily lose their own. Vietnamese artist/writer Đặng Thị Khuê points out that

> [d]irect exposure to and contact with the world's art has widened our artists' views and perspectives, helping them see more clearly the worldwide artistic panorama, and to establish therein a position of their own, an orientation for the development of their own art … Our choice is to accept selectively, as a necessity, the influences of modernist and postmodernist art from the outside world and retain, as a constant value, our original artistic traditions with their spiritual core.[80]

So despite the preponderance and proliferation of global communication, media, economy and cultural forms, there is no totalising force. If anything, the pressure that globalisation brings on the state is equalled by the pressure brought to bear by the (re)-emergence of local interests and identities. As Benjamin Barber observes, the world is being pulled in two directions: one, 'a retribalization of large swaths of humankind by war and bloodshed'; and the other, the pressure to become 'one commercially homogenous global network'.[81]

What do these somewhat depressing ideas and facts mean for creative production in the contemporary world? In fact, not necessarily all that much. First, although art has been used to serve national priorities, artists have generally found ways to make their own work and follow their own aesthetic, regardless of government policy. Next, few artists have seen themselves as necessarily committed to, or purely informed by, a national sensibility. There has always been interchange between artists, across national boundaries. For many artists too, there has been something other than the nation informing their work: local traditions, or the long tradition of art practice, for instance. So despite the formidable effect of globalisation on the lives of everyone, there can be no such thing as a truly global arts culture, because identity and cultural attachment rely on emotional and traditional resonances, and on the specific signifiers of cultural identity to which people can relate. As Held and McGrew write, 'there is no common global pool of memories; no common global way of thinking; and no "universal history" in and through which people can unite'.[82] This absence limits the capacity of global markets and movements to engage the peoples of the world in any genuine or sustained way. While the markets are certainly captured by global capital, and much of the media likewise, the idea that we are seeing a cultural homogenisation, and/or the westernisation of the globe, is not borne out by practice. Curator and critic Hou Hanru made this point in 1999, in discussing the interaction between western and Chinese art:

> After some initial moments of excitement and hope, Chinese contemporary artists' contact with western-dominated global art has been disappointing and frustrating, which has pushed many artists to reconsider their relationship with the international art world. On the one hand, they confirm the necessity to search for a space for expressions which are both personal and universally significant. On the other hand, they recognise that it is now time to restructure the art world and create a genuinely global scene.[83]

The flow of cultural images and ideas is never one way, but more like a spiral – one that, in its movement, always returns on itself. This means that artists can attach to those aspects of global culture that are attractive and valuable, while still adhering to those aspects of local traditions that serve their aesthetic and meaning-making aspirations.

If nations are being fragmented by the effects on the one hand of globalisation, and on the other of localism, and if artists are being pulled about by all these imperatives and yet are forming their own way, how can we understand the work of art in the globalised world? One way is to consider what globalisation theorists call 'cultural hybridisation', the blending of foreign and local to make a new form. This is perhaps more significant in the contemporary work of artists than the purely local, purely national, or purely global, and it enables two-way or multi-way traffic in the flow of cultural ideas and images. With globalisation, clearly, things change; old cultural forms may be swept away, or replaced, or they may absorb and re-form the new cultural products that impinge on their space, and sell them back to the centre. But what does not happen is a unification of cultural forms and values, or an impossible division between them. Rather, what happens is the proliferation of ideas, signification, visions and practices that provide artists with new pressures and tensions, but also new ways of making work.

The remarkable success of contemporary Asian artists in negotiating these complex relationships between local and global, and in attracting the attention of both local and global audiences may, we suggest, be attributed to the qualities of the works themselves. Though in the nineteenth and early twentieth centuries the west had tended to view Asian art merely as raw material that could be appropriated to invigorate their own art, and could be collected as anthropological artefacts, now the art is being viewed and collected *as* art. Major art museums have holdings of works by a growing number of contemporary Asian artists. To cite only a very few examples of the works of Asian artists discussed in this volume, the Guggenheim has acquired work by Wong Hoy Cheong; the Museum of Modern Art in New York holds works by Nalini Malani; Dadang Christanto is represented in the National Gallery of Australia's collection; and the Carnegie Museum of Art in Pittsburgh holds works by Dinh Q. Lê. Both the Guggenheim and Tate Modern are building significant and diverse collections of Asian contemporary art.

What this suggests is that the artists' work has sufficient impact to move audiences, both at home and on the international stage. Jill Bennett's writings on art and affect provide a framework for understanding how these works have been able to capture attention across so many domains. Because the artists have, generally speaking, drawn directly on their own observations and memories, their works operate not only as representations, but also as 'sense memories' that resonate with others. Writing about the art that emerged from responses to the AIDS trauma, Bennett posits that the artistic language employed in the works not only contained the artists' own 'sense memory', but also 'cut across common memory, revealing a kind of truth that eludes the moral organization of common memory'.[84] This references Roland Barthes' notion of the *punctum*: the element in a work that 'pierces me', 'that accident which pricks me (but also bruises me, is poignant to me)'.[85] Much of the work of the contemporary Asian artists has, we suggest, been so keenly received both at home and abroad because it has the capacity to pierce and bruise viewers from different backgrounds, despite their very different cultural knowledges and experiences. Because such works operate at the level of affect rather than direct signification, they provide a space in which viewers can find their own memories, values and empathy suddenly engaged by the trauma, loss, grief and, often, hope with which these works are imbued.

Themes of this book

In this book we have focused on key themes that emerge from conversations with or research into the artists who are the subject of this book, and that link art and human rights in Asian contexts. As we have already suggested, while art cannot necessarily change, let alone rescue, the world, artists can help ask the critical question for human rights – what is it to be human?

There are a number of ways in which art responds to this question, and one of the most common responses is in witnessing to human rights abuses. The Cambodian artists who documented the horrors of the Khmer Rouge genocide in Cambodia from 1975 to 1979 are an example of this. One artist caught up in the murderous project was Vann Nath, who was one of only seven survivors of the secret prison S-21 in Phnom Penh (a former school and now a genocide museum, where his art works about what happened there form part of the display). Like most of the other prisoners, he had little understanding of why he had been arrested. Some 14,000 men, women and children were interrogated, tortured and executed there, but Vann Nath was permitted to survive because he could paint portraits and make busts of the Khmer Rouge leader, Pol Pot. The paintings, films and writing he produced after the overthrow of the regime document its brutality. He has received many international awards for his work, and has been called Cambodia's Goya, but he did not accept that encomium. His obituary in *The Economist* states: 'His principal fear was that young Cambodians would not learn about – or, worse still, would not believe – what he had witnessed. He painted, he said, so that Cambodia would never turn on itself so monstrously again.'[86] Though he died in 2011, he was able to see some of his drawings from his time in S-21 used in evidence during the genocide tribunal that began in Phnom Penh in 2007.[87]

Another Cambodian artist, Bun Heang Ung (who died in 2014), was a student in 1975, at the beginning of his country's descent into genocide. He had to hide his background as a 'bourgeois intellectual',[88] because intellectuals were a particular target of the Khmer Rouge's programme to destroy the old and form a new society based on peasant workers. Cities were evacuated and their occupants sent to the villages to labour in the fields, where many died. Like Vann Nath, Bun Heang Ung lost several members of his extended family, but he survived; unlike Vann Nath, he elected not to remain in Cambodia, but emigrated to Australia where he drew political cartoons – often with a strong human rights focus – for several publications, including the *Far Eastern Economic Review*. He also produced a series of drawings documenting his experiences under the Khmer Rouge, in which he depicts the horrifying conditions of work and life under a regime to which Hannah Arendt's phrase 'banality of evil' may be applied.[89] In 1985 he published a selection of these drawings in *The Murderous Revolution*, with an accompanying text by historian Martin Stuart-Fox, in an attempt to ensure that the violations of human rights committed by the Khmer Rouge would never be forgotten: it remains an important text about these extraordinary events.[90]

Another recurring theme is the importance artists place on the opportunity to work with communities. An example is the late Santiago Bose, one of the founders of the indigenous art movement in the Philippines. He was very much a grassroots activist and educator as well as an artist, and is considered one of the most significant contemporary Philippine artists. Like many artists in the Philippines, Bose grew up between two cultures in Baguio, a city in the Cordillera Mountains of Northern Luzon. The Americans built the city as a military recreation base, but traces of the old rituals and traditions of a pre-Christian past could still be found. Pat Hoffie relates that Bose developed his responses

> to the vast gulf that separated the First World and the Third World, how he was among those intellectuals who were blacklisted by the Marcos regime when martial law was implemented in 1972, and how he focussed his practice on key questions related to community and the connection between art and life.[91]

In such works as *Lies, magicians and blind faith* (1993–95) and *Let it bleed* (1994) (see Figure 1.1), Bose used folk art symbols and indigenous natural materials, such as bamboo and volcanic ash. Although he lived in the US for some years, a key focus of his work was the Baguio Arts Guild, of which he was President for a number of years. This Guild concentrated on community art, including, as Hoffie notes, environmental concerns. It also took on social concerns, such as providing soup kitchens for earthquake victims. Bose says of the connection between art, activism and human rights:

> The artist cannot but be affected by his society. It is hard to ignore the pressing needs of the nation while making art that serves the nation's elite … We struggled to change society, which is difficult and dangerous, and we also sought to preserve communal aspects of life. I too am haunted by visions of hardship, poverty, disenfranchisement of the 'primitive' tribes, but between outbursts of violence and exploitation are also tenderness, selflessness and a sense of community. These will always remain unspoken and unrecognized unless we make art or music that will help to transform society. The artist takes a stand through the practice of creating art.[92]

There are many other examples, from across the region, of artists working with communities to 'take a stand'. Indonesian artist collective Taring Padi, for example, has in recent years joined in projects with East Timorese artists' group Gembel to produce work related to reconciliation between those nations, a project which included Australian artists' collective Culture Kitchen.[93] Htein Lin in Myanmar sees himself as an artist rather than as an activist – like so many artists discussed in these pages. However, having previously belonged to the All Burma Students' Democratic Front, he spent almost seven years in gaol (1998–2004). While in gaol he painted a series of works inspired by his Buddhist beliefs, and these have been exhibited internationally. After his release he went to the UK, but has now returned and is creating art in Yangon,

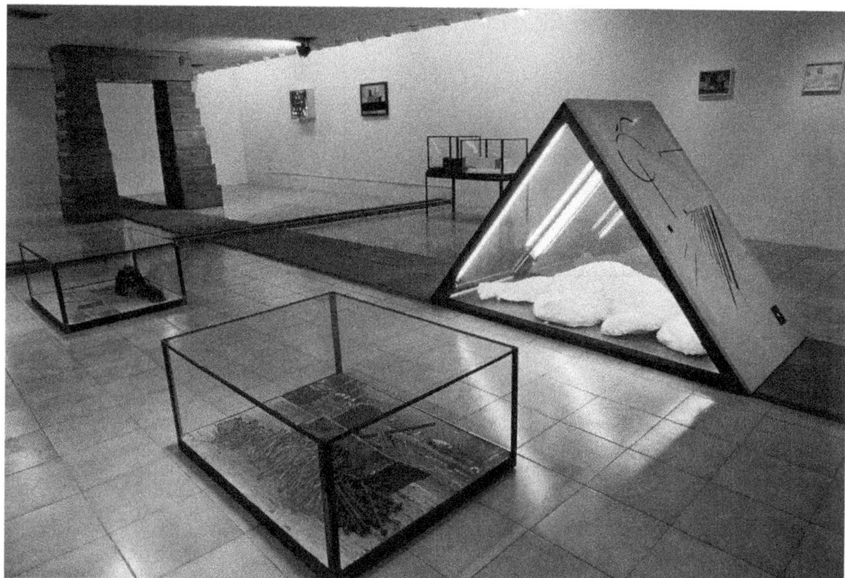

1.4 Vivan Sundaram, *Memorial*, 1993. Installation view AIFACS Gallery, New Delhi. *Mausoleum*, 1993. Steel, glass, neon light with white inlaid marble. At rear *Gateway*, 1993 with painted/rusted etched tin trunks, with neon sign 'Fallen Mortal' inside top trunk.

including performance art and, through projects such as *A Show of Hands*, with former political prisoners.[94]

These projects are often developed away from the great metropolitan centres that have come to typify contemporary Asia. However, many other artists have viewed the cities themselves as critical sites for change. One example is the Aar Paar project in Mumbai and Karachi, a collaboration which began in 2000 and addressed the prevailing tensions between India and Pakistan. Ten artists from each city communicated by email to develop projects which were inserted in the cities in attempts to speak to ordinary people across societies deeply divided on historical, religious and political fault lines, and where the threat of war is ever present.[95]

Related to this is a third recurring theme: artists' involvement in working for social change. Academic and film maker Ma Khin Mar Mar Kyi, for example, had to leave Myanmar in 1990 because of her work with Aung San Suu Kyi.[96] She lived in Thailand, Cambodia and Laos before going to Australia as a political asylum seeker in 1995. She has also worked for many years with Burmese living in vulnerable circumstances on the border between Myanmar and Thailand, where many young women crossing the border from Myanmar to seek work to support their families have been forced into prostitution; this is documented in her film *Dreams of Dutiful Daughters.*[97]

Indian artists, including Gulammohammed Sheikh, Nilima Sheikh, Nalini Malani, Atul Dodiya, Navjot Altaf and Vivan Sundaram, have condemned violence – and especially religious and sectarian violence – in their country. They have participated, for example, in SAHMAT, an organisation of artists, writers, poets, musicians and actors who promote artistic freedom, and democratic and secular values.[98] It was founded in 1989, after the violent death during a street theatre performance of Safdar Hashmi, an actor, playwright, poet and political activist.

Sundaram has been involved with artist protest movements from the 1970s, and has devoted a major part of his work, first as a painter and later in large-scale conceptual installations, to critical issues in society. His art work *Memorial* (1993) was a complex set of philosophical explorations of the theme of memorialising, and his direct response to the destruction of the Babri Masjid Mosque in Ayodhya in 1992, and the violent Hindu/Muslim riots in the weeks and months that followed. A central inspiration of Sundaram's room-sized installation, which involved a number of different sculptural and other elements, was the photograph of an elderly Muslim who had been killed by a mob. Geeta Kapur says of this seminal work of contemporary Indian art that 'Sundaram stretched the ontological possibility of the photo-image … offering not only an elegy and an expiation but a carnal symbiosis between self and other, and thus a personally mediated nemesis for public murder'.[99]

The rest of this book explores how selected artists are doing precisely this: finding ways to make art that accords with their political and ethical ideals. The artists we have chosen for the case studies form a particular and significant cohort from a critical period in Asian art when artists confronted rapid social and political change in the postcolonial and rapidly globalising world of the late twentieth and early twenty-first centuries, but they cannot be representative of all art of that particular generation and time. Contemporary art by its very nature is constantly changing. The selection was necessarily limited, given the many excellent artists currently practising, and different writers might have made a different selection of artists for the case studies. But the scale of a single book does not permit us to include all relevant possibilities, and our choice of artists was predicated on a number of factors – not least, whether we knew them and their work, and would therefore be able to discuss their work with them and incorporate their personal perspectives. We also aimed to include artists from a number of significant Asian countries; those whose work is marked by an engagement with human rights concerns; and those whose work reaches beyond the nation state to engage issues with a global impact, such as environmental crises.

We examine the context and work of these artists under a number of themes within our broad overarching theme of 'human rights', including activism, conflict, globalisation, worldmaking and environmentalism. Our organisation of the material in this way is not intended to suggest that these artists' work and art can be confined to those themes, or that these themes can possibly cover the wide spectrum of art practice in Asia today. The artists we have chosen open a door to the richness and diversity of that art world; and we encourage readers to explore contemporary Asian art and artists more expansively.

Notes

1 Since the UN Declaration of 1948, nine core treaties (and some sixty Human Rights instruments) have been initiated and 'all UN Member States have ratified at least one core international human rights treaty, and 80 percent have ratified four or more'. See http://www.ohchr.org/EN/HRBodies/Pages/HumanRightsBodies.aspx, accessed 9 January 2015, and also the University of Minnesota's Human Rights Library, http://www1.umn.edu/humanrts/research/ratification-index.html, accessed 9 January 2015.

2 Erich S. Gruen (ed.), *Cultural Borrowings and Ethnic Appropriations in Antiquity* (Stuttgart: Franz Steiner Verlag GmbH, 2005).

3 Michael Sullivan, *The Meeting of Eastern and Western Art* (Berkeley: University of California Press, 1989).

4 Partha Mitter, 'Decentering Modernism: Art History and Avant-Garde Art from the Periphery', *The Art Bulletin*, 90:4 (December 2008), pp. 531–48.

5 Charles Green, 'Beyond the Future: The Third Asia-Pacific Triennial', *Art Journal*, 58:4 (Winter 1999), pp. 81–7: 82.

6 Hans Belting and Andrea Buddensieg (eds), *The Global Art World: Audiences, Markets and Museums* (Ostfildern: Hatje Cantz, 2009), p. 39. An important contributor to these changes was the journal *Third Text*, which was first published in 1987 and which from the start has challenged the universalism of Eurocentrism, and provided a venue for alternative aesthetics and perspectives.

7 Terry Smith, 'Worlds Pictured in Contemporary Art: Planes and Connectivities', in Caroline Turner, Michelle Antoinette and Zara Stanhope (eds), *The World and World-making in Art: Humanities Research*, 29:2 (2013), pp. 11–26: 12.

8 Oscar Ho, 'Under the Shadow: Problems in Museum Development in Asia', in Michelle Antoinette and Caroline Turner (eds), *Contemporary Asian Art and Exhibitions: Connectivities and World-Making* (Canberra: ANU Press, 2014), pp. 172–97.

9 John Clark, 'The Worlding of the Asian Modern', in Antoinette and Turner (eds), *Contemporary Asian Art and Exhibitions*, pp. 67–88.

10 Chaitanya Sambrani, 'An Experiment in Connectivity: From the "West Heavens" to the "Middle Kingdom"', in Antoinette and Turner, *Contemporary Asian Art and Exhibitions*, pp. 89–107. See also John Clark, *Modern Asian Art* (Sydney: Craftsman House & Honolulu: University of Hawai'i Press, 1998); Jonathan Hay, 'Double Modernity, Para Modernity', in Terry Smith, Okwui Enwezor and Nancy Condee (eds), *Antimonies of Art and Culture: Modernity, Postmodernity, Contemporaneity* (Durham, NC: Duke University Press, 2009), pp. 113–32.

11 T. K. Sabapathy, 'Developing Regionalist Perspectives in South-East Asian Art Historiography', *Second Asia-Pacific Triennial* (Brisbane: Queensland Art Gallery, 1996), pp. 13–7; T. K. Sabapathy (ed.), *Modernity and Beyond: Themes in Southeast Asian Art* (Singapore: Singapore Art Museum, 1996).

12 Apinan Poshyananda, 'The Development of Contemporary Art of Thailand: Traditionalism in Reverse', in Caroline Turner (ed.), *Tradition and Change: Contemporary Art of Asia and the Pacific* (St Lucia: University of Queensland Press, 1993), pp. 93–106.

13 See www.canberra.edu.au/cccr under 'Resources' for an extensive bibliography of key texts.

14 See http://faam.city.fukuoka.lg.jp/eng/home.html and www.qagoma.qld.gov.au/. Both Fukuoka and Queensland have offered residencies to significant numbers of artists from Asia.

15 *Asian Modernism: Diverse Developments in Indonesia, the Philippines and Thailand* (Tokyo: Japan Foundation Asia Center, 1995).

16 Christine Clark, 'Distinctive Voices: Artist Initiated Spaces and Projects', in Caroline Turner (ed.), *Art and Social Change: Contemporary Art in Asia and the Pacific* (Canberra: Pandanus Books, 2005), pp. 554–68.

17 The Archive has significant online and other resources. See, e.g., 'The And: An Expanded Questionnaire on the Contemporary', *Asia Art Archive*, 'Field Notes', 1 (June 2012), www.aaa.org.hk/FieldNotes/Details/1167; 'All You Want To Know About International Art Biennials', www.aaa.org.hk/onlineprojects/bitri/en/index.aspx.

18 See the Biennial Foundation's World Biennial Forum (2014), www.biennialfoundation.org.

19 Ben Eltham, 'An Interview with Anthony Gardner about Biennales', *A Cultural Policy Blog* (9 January 2011), http://culturalpolicyreform.wordpress.com/2011/01/09/an-interview-with-anthony-gardner-about-biennales/, accessed 14 September 2014.

20 Caroline Turner (ed.), *Art and Social Change: Contemporary Art in Asia and the Pacific* (Canberra: Pandanus Books, 2005).

21 Exhibitions associated with this research include: Caroline Turner and Nancy Sever (eds), *Witnessing to Silence: Art and Human Rights* (Canberra: Drill Hall Gallery and School of Art Gallery, Australian National University, 2003); Pat Hoffie and Caroline Turner (eds), *Future Tense: Security and Human Rights* (Brisbane: Queensland College of Art Gallery, 2005); Caroline Turner and David Williams (eds), *Thresholds of Tolerance* (Canberra: School of Art Gallery, Australian National University, 2007); Nancy Sever and Caroline Turner (eds), *Recovering Lives* (Canberra: Drill Hall Gallery, Australian National University, 2008); Caroline

Turner and David Williams (eds), *Recovering Lives* (Canberra: School of Art Gallery, Australian National University, 2008); Caroline Turner and Nancy Sever (eds), *Dadang Christanto: Wounds in Our Heart* (Canberra: Drill Hall Gallery, Australian National University, 2010).

22 See, e.g., Jeffrey Sachs, 'Welcome to the Asian Century', *Fortune Magazine* (12 January 2004); Glen St John Barclay, 'Geopolitical Changes in Asia and the Pacific', in *Art and Social Change*, pp. 14–29; Greg Austin and Stuart Harris, *Japan and Greater China: Political Economy and Military Power in the Asian Century* (Honolulu: University of Hawai'i Press, 2001); Harinder S. Kohli, Ashok Sharma and Anil Sood (eds), *Asia 2050: Realizing the Asian Century* (New Delhi: SAGE, 2011); and a press briefing from Premier Wen of China: 'Strong China-India Relations to Usher in True Asian Century', *China View* (14 March 2006), http://news.xinhuanet.com/english/2006-03/14/content_4302492.htm.

23 Kishore Mahbubani, *The New Asian Hemisphere: The Irresistible Shift of Global Power to the East* (New York: PublicAffairs, 2008).

24 Geeta Kapur, 'Dismantled Norms: Apropos other Avantgardes', in Turner (ed.), *Art and Social Change*, pp. 46–100: 97.

25 Alison Carroll, *The Revolutionary Century: Art in Asia, 1900–2000* (South Yarra: Macmillan, 2010).

26 Norberto Bobbio, *The Age of Rights*, trans. A. Cameron (Cambridge: Polity Press, 1996), p. 32.

27 Costas Douzinas, 'The End of Human Rights' (public lecture), Humanities Research Centre, Australian National University (10 April 2006).

28 Micheline Ishay, *The History of Human Rights* (Berkeley: University of California Press, 2004).

29 José A. Lindgren Alves, 'The Declaration of Human Rights in Postmodernity', *Human Rights Quarterly*, 22 (2000), pp. 478–500: 496.

30 Christine Chinkin, 'The Language of Human Rights Law', in Caroline Turner and Nancy Sever (eds), *Witnessing to Silence: Art and Human Rights* (Canberra: Humanities Research Centre and Drill Hall Gallery, 2003), pp. 13–15: 14.

31 Edward Said, *Reflections on Exile and Other Essays* (Cambridge, MA: Harvard University Press, 2000), pp. 430–1.

32 Joseph Slaughter, 'A Question of Narration: The Voice in International Human Rights Law', *Human Rights Quarterly*, 19:2 (1997), pp. 406–30: 407.

33 Zühtü Arslan, 'Taking Rights Less Seriously: Postmodernism and Human Rights', *Res Publica*, 5:2 (1999), pp. 195–215: 196.

34 Association of Southeast Asian Nations [ASEAN], *ASEAN Human Rights Declaration* (2012), www.asean.org/news/asean-statement-communiques/item/asean-human-rights-declaration, accessed 12 September 2013.

35 Cited in Chantal Mouffe, interviewed by Rosalyn Deutsche, Branden W. Joseph and Thomas Keenan, 'Every Form of Art has a Political Dimension', *Grey Room 02* (Winter 2001), pp. 98–125: 105.

36 Hans Seigfried, 'We the People/s: Bloody Universal Principles and Ethnic Codes', *Philosophy & Social Criticism*, 27:1 (January 2001), pp. 63–76: 64.

37 Arjun Appadurai, *Fear of Small Numbers: An Essay on the Geography of Fear* (Durham and London: Duke University Press, 2006) pp. 1, 2.

38 Costas Douzinas, *The End of Human Rights: Critical Legal Thought at the Turn of the Century* (Oxford: Hart Publishing, 2000), p. 245.

39 'Under Construction: New Dimensions in Asian Art', Japan Foundation Forum 2002, convened by Yasuko Furuichi (author observations at forum).

40 Chaitanya Sambrani, 'An Experiment in Connectivity'; Anthony Milner and Deborah Johnson, 'The Idea of Asia', in J. Ingelson (ed.), *Regionalism, Subregionalism and APEC* (Melbourne: Monash Asia Institute, 1997), pp. 1–20.

41 Andrew Gerstle and Anthony Milner (eds), *Recovering the Orient: Artists, Scholars, Appropriations* (London: Harwood, 1995); Fuyubi Nakamura, Morgan Perkins and Olivier Krischer (eds), *Asia Through Art and Anthropology: Cultural Translation Across Borders* (London: Bloomsbury, 2013).

42 Milner and Johnson, 'The Idea of Asia'.

43 Lee Kuan Yew, cited Russell Dalton and Nhu-Ngoc T. Ong, 'Authority Orientations and Democratic Attitudes: A Test of the "Asian Values" Hypothesis', *Japanese Journal of Political Science*, 6:2 (2005), pp. 211–31: 212.

44 Molly Elgin, 'Asian Values: A New Model for Development', *Stanford Journal of East Asian Affairs*, 10:2 (Summer 2010), pp. 135–45: 137.

45 Ronald Inglehart and Christian Welzel, *Modernization, Cultural Change and Democracy: The Human Development Sequence* (New York: Cambridge University Press, 2005).

46 Dalton and Ong, 'Authority Orientations and Democratic Attitudes', pp. 213–14.

47 Amnesty International, 'Public Statement: Civil Society Rejects Flawed ASEAN Human Rights Declaration' (15 November 2012), www.amnesty.org/en/library/asset/IOR64/005/2012/en/7eacdb53-76a6-49d8-9466-dc7fdaeccec7/ior640052012en.pdf, accessed 12 August 2013.

48 United Nations Human Rights, 'Statement by the High Commissioner for Human Rights at the Bali Democracy Forum', Office of the High Commissioner for Human Rights (7 November 2012), www.ohchr.org/EN/NewsEvents/Pages/DisplayNews.aspx?NewsID=12752&LangID=E, accessed 12 September 2013.

49 Norani Othman, 'Grounding Human Rights Arguments in Non-Western Culture: *Shari'a* and the Citizenship Rights of Women in a Modern Islamic State', in Joanne R. Bauer and Daniel A. Bell (eds), *The East Asian Challenge for Human Rights* (Cambridge: Cambridge University Press, 1999), pp. 169–92: 170.

50 Othman, 'Grounding Human Rights Arguments', p. 173.

51 Pierre Bourdieu and Hans Haacke, *Free Exchange* (Cambridge, MA: Polity Press, 1995), p. 84.

52 Leon Golub, 'What Makes Art Political?', in Jeanne Siegel (ed.), *Art Talk: The Early '80s* (New York: Da Capo Press, 1988), pp. 53–62: 61–2.

53 In Christopher Lydon, 'Salima Hashmi: In the Worst of Times, the Alchemy of Art', *Arts, Ideas and Politics*, Radio Open Source (7 September 2011), http://radioopensource.org/salima-hashmi-in-the-worst-of-times-the-alchemy-of-art/, accessed 14 August 2014.

54 Hanif Kureishi, *Collected Essays* (London: Faber & Faber, 2011), p. 280.

55 Jen Webb, '"Exactly Like Where You Are Right Now … Only Much, Much Better": Art and Human Rights in Unaustralia', *Continuum* 21.4 (2007), pp. 541–53: 551.

56 Christine Chinkin, 'The Language of Human Rights Law', p. 14. See also Caroline Turner, 'Art and Images', in David P. Forsythe (ed.), *Encyclopedia of Human Rights*, Volume 1 (Oxford: Oxford University Press, 2009), pp. 104–13.

57 Jacques Rancière, *The Philosopher and his Poor*, trans. John Drury, Corinne Oster and Andrew Parker (Durham, NC: Duke University Press, 2004 [1983]).

58 Michael Godby (ed.), *William Kentridge: Drawings for Projection: Four Animated Films* (Sandton: Goodman Gallery, 1991).

59 Costas Douzinas, 'The Legality of the Image', *Modern Law Review*, 63:6 (2000), pp. 813–30: 813.

60 Mouffe, 'Every Form of Art', p. 100.

61 Bourdieu and Haacke, *Free Exchange*, p. 39.

62 Donald Preziosi, *Rethinking Art History: Meditations on a Coy Science* (New Haven and London: Yale University Press, 1989), p. 49.

63 'Indonesia, Timor-Leste & Australia: Collaborations & Partnerships, Arts & Culture, Human Rights & Reconciliation', ANU Roundtable in collaboration with the University of Melbourne (Canberra, 24 September 2014). Genocide scholar Ben Kiernan estimates a death toll of something like a fifth of the population of East Timor, or some 150,000 people, following the Indonesian invasion and subsequent occupation of that country (1975–99). See his 'War, Genocide, and Resistance in East Timor, 1975–99: Comparative Reflections on Cambodia', in Mark Selden and Alvin Y. So (eds), *War and State Terrorism: The United States, Japan, and the Asia-Pacific in the Long Twentieth Century* (Lanham, MD: Rowman and Littlefield, 2003), pp. 199–233: 200.

64 On contemporary art in Tibet, including the art of Tibetan exiles, see Clare E. Harris, *The Museum on the Roof of the World: Art, Politics and the Representation of Tibet* (Chicago and London: University of Chicago Press, 2012); Clare Harris, *In the Image of Tibet: Tibetan Painting after 1959* (London: Reaktion Books, 1999).

65 Ayesha Jatoi, 'Interview with Salima Hashmi', *Dawn* (2 February 2011), www.dawn. com/news/603300/herald-exclusive-ayesha-jatoi-in-conversation-with-salima-h ashmi, accessed 7 August 2014.

66 Ai Weiwei, 'My Life under House Arrest', *FP Magazine* (19 August 2014), http://foreignpolicy.com/2014/08/19/my-life-under-house-arrest/, accessed 18 September 2014. Ai was detained by authorities for eighty-one days, from 3 April to 22 June 2011. He has maintained public attention through social media such as Twitter and, for example, protesting against police surveillance of his home by streaming continuous live coverage of himself for twenty-four hours in July 2012 until the police intervened. Gloria Davis, 'Kultur Bytes', in Geremie R. Barmé and Jeremy Goldkorn (eds), *China Story Yearbook 2013* (Canberra: Australian Centre on China in the World, Australian National University, 2013), p. 399.

67 For further information on Ai's art, see essays by Mami Kataoka and Charles Merewether in Deborah E. Horowitz (ed.), *Ai Weiwei: According to What?* (Hong Kong: Hirshhorn Museum and Sculpture Garden, the Mori Art Museum, 2012); Charles Merewether, *Ai Weiwei: Under Construction* (Sydney: University of NSW Press and Sherman Contemporary Art Foundation, 2008). Ai's father, the celebrated modern poet Ai Qing, had been sent into exile in a remote area of China for twenty years in 1957 (although Ai Qing was exonerated after the reforms in 1978). Ai is in many ways a product of the tumultuous changes in China in his lifetime. Art after the Communist victory was to be art for the people, but the reality in times of extreme social and economic change was often very different from that depicted in propaganda art and especially for creative artists and intellectuals during the Cultural Revolution (1966–76), when they could be denounced as enemies of the people.

68 Exhibited Mary Boone Gallery, New York (2008), www.maryboonegallery.com/exhibitions/2012–2013/Ai-downtown/gfx/WEIWEI%20press%20release.pdf, accessed 28 November 2014.

69 Golub, 'What Makes Art Political?', p. 62.

70 George White, *Nation, State, and Territory: Origins, Evolutions, and Relationships*, vol. 1 (Lanham, MD: Rowman and Littlefield, 2004), p. 95.

71 Donald Horne, *Arts Funding and Public Culture: Cultural Policy Studies*, Occasional Paper No. 1 (Brisbane: Griffith University Press, 1988), p. 4.

72 Article 23 of Bangladesh's constitution reads: 'The State shall adopt measures to conserve the cultural traditions and heritage of the people, and so to foster and improve the national language, literature and the arts that all sections of the people are afforded the opportunity to contribute towards and to participate in the enrichment of the national culture'; see The Constitution of the People's Republic of Bangladesh, Legislative and Parliamentary Affairs Division, Ministry of Law, Justice and Parliamentary Affairs, http://bdlaws.minlaw.gov.bd/pdf_part.php?id=367, accessed 8 September 2010.

73 Commissioner for Cultural Affairs, 'Policy of Cultural Affairs in Japan' (2013), www.bunka.go.jp/english/pdf/2013_policy.pdf, accessed 12 September 2013, pp. 1, 2.

74 Government of India – Ministry of Culture, 'Mission Statement', www.indiaculture.nic.in/mission-statement, accessed 9 January 2015.

75 Ministry of Culture of the People's Republic of China, 'About the Ministry of Culture' (28 April 2009), www.ccnt.gov.cn/English/Introduction/200904/t20090428_62706.html, accessed 12 September 2013. This responsibility is no longer listed; see the contemporary website at www.chinaculture.org/2014-12/05/content_576202.htm, accessed 9 January 2015.

76 John Beynon and David Dunkerley (eds), *Globalization: The Reader* (Milton Park: Routledge, 2000), p. 3.

77 Zillah Eisenstein, 'Cyber Inequities', in Beynon and Dunkerley, *Globalization: The Reader*, pp. 212–13.

78 See Michel de Certeau, *The Practice of Everyday Life*, trans. S. Rendall (Berkeley: University of California Press, 1984), p. xiii.

79 Pierre Bourdieu, *Acts of Resistance: Against the New Myths of our Time*, trans. Richard Nice (London: Polity, 1998), p. 19.

80 Đặng Thị Khuê, 'Contemporary Vietnamese Art: A New Stage', in *Beyond the Future: The Third Asia-Pacific Triennial of Contemporary Art* (Brisbane: Queensland Art Gallery, 1999), p. 162.

81 Benjamin R. Barber, *Jihad vs McWorld: Terrorism's Challenge to Democracy* (London: Random House, 2003), p. 4.

82 David Held and Anthony McGrew (eds), *The Global Transformations Reader: An Introduction to the Globalization Debate* (Cambridge, MA: Polity Press, 2000), p. 16.

83 Hou Hanru, 'On the Midground: Chinese Artists, Diaspora and Global Art', *Beyond the Future*, p. 191.

84 Jill Bennett, *Empathic Vision: Affect, Trauma and Contemporary Art* (Stanford, CA: Stanford University Press, 2005), p. 27. Though her focus here was on AIDS, the concept applies equally to other traumatic moments and events.

85 Roland Barthes, *Camera Lucida: Reflections on Photography*, trans. Richard Howard (New York: Hill and Wang, 1981), pp. 26–7.

86 'Vann Nath', *The Economist* (17 September 2011), www.economist.com/node/21529005, accessed 14 September 2014.

87 Tom Fawthrop, 'Vann Nath Obituary', *The Guardian* (6 September 2011), www.the-guardian.com/world/2011/sep/05/vann-nath-obituary, accessed 14 September 2014.

88 Tony Stephens, 'Bun Heang Un [*sic*]: Artist Endured the Worst of Pol Pot', *Sydney Morning Herald* (15 February 2014), www.smh.com.au/comment/obituaries/bun-heang-un-artist-endured-the-worst-of-pol-pot-20140214-32r76.html, accessed 14 September 2014.

89 Hannah Arendt, *Eichmann in Jerusalem: A Report on the Banality of Evil* (London: Penguin, 1963).

90 Martin Stuart-Fox and Bunhaeng Ung, *The Murderous Revolution: Life & Death in Pol Pot's Kampuchea* (Chippendale, NSW: APCOL Press, 1985). These art works are now in the library of the Australian National University and can be viewed on line in digital format at https://anulib.anu.edu.au/using-the-library/collections/asia-pacific-digital-collections/drawings-of-bun-heang-ung/.

91 Pat Hoffie, 'Santiago Bose: Magic, Humour and Cultural Resistance', in Turner and Sever (eds), *Witnessing to Silence*, pp. 65–7.

92 Santiago Bose, 'A Savage Look at Indigenous Art: Notes in Transit', Gallery of Philippine Contemporary Art, www.kulay-diwa.com/santiago_bose, accessed 8 August 2012.

93 Turner and Williams, *Thresholds of Tolerance*.

94 Htein Lin, Myanmar (Burma), Painter and Performance Artist, www.hteinlin.com/, accessed 24 September 2014.

95 Chaitanya Sambrani, 'Printing across Borders: The Aar-Paar Project', *Fifth Australian Print Symposium* (Canberra: National Gallery of Australia, 2004), www.printsandprintmaking.gov.au/references/7372/, accessed 8 August 2012.

96 Mar Khin Mar Mar Kyi, 'In Pursuit of Power: Political Power and Gender Relations in New Order Burma/Myanmar' (PhD thesis, Australian National University, 2013).

On the basis of this work she was awarded the Daw Aung San Suu Kyi Gender Research Fellow in Burmese Studies at the University of Oxford; and the Excellence in Gender Research prize from the Australian National University Gender Institute in 2013.

97 Interview with the artist, 2013. Since the reforms, the film has been shown to government officials in Myanmar.

98 SAHMAT is an acronym standing for 'we are together' (Nalini Malani, conversation with authors, December 2014). See 'About SAHMAT', Safdar Hashmi Memorial Trust, www.sahmat.org/aboutsahmat.html, accessed 9 January 2015; see 'The Sahmat Collective: Art and Activism in India since 1989', Smart Museum of Art, http://smart-museum.uchicago.edu/exhibitions/the-sahmat-collective-art-and-activism-in-india-since-1989/, accessed 9 January 2015.

99 Geeta Kapur, 'Mortal Remains', in Charles Merewether and John Potts (eds), *After the Event: New Perspectives on Art History* (Manchester and New York: Manchester University Press, 2010), pp. 132–55.

2 The artist as cultural and political activist

Introduction

Art historian Terry Smith has argued that 'contemporary art is – perhaps for the first time in history – truly an art *of* the world'.[1] Rather than being defined by national or local concerns, his thesis suggests, contemporary art is informed by and responsive to the global context. But, he continues, for artists working in postcolonial nations, as for some artists working within globally dominant nations, the drive is to produce 'a content-driven art, aware of the influence of ideologies, and concerned above all with issues of nationality, identity, and rights. All of these are conceived as being in volatile states of transition, and requiring translation in order to be negotiated'.[2] This chapter discusses the ways in which artists may take up the challenge of producing content-driven art while negotiating the balance between local and global concerns, and translating 'issues of nationality, identity, and rights'. There is, of course, a long history of artists participating in political action, and of making art that forms an important element in such activity. While this is certainly not peculiar to artists in the Asian region, we contextualise the history of both cultural and political activism in this region specifically as it touches on the creative field. We approach the issue by presenting case studies of three artists – Wong Hoy Cheong from Malaysia, Dadang Christanto from Indonesia, and Vasan Sitthiket from Thailand – who can be designated activist artists.

Generally, scholars distinguish cultural from political activism; the former refers to the production of creative artefacts and events designed to mobilise affect; the latter refers to the processes by which citizens organise and participate in actions designed to achieve political change. Artists can work across both categories; as cultural activists they use their creative skills and vision in an effort to achieve political change and social justice by mobilising people through emotional engagement; those who engage more directly in politics also make use of political means, such as mounting political demonstrations, circulating petitions, campaigning, working for a political party, or actively organising community events to achieve legislative or policy changes.[3]

Whether activists work primarily through cultural or political modes, degrees of involvement differ: activism may take place anywhere on a continuum that extends from a willingness to participate in occasional actions at one end, through degrees of commitment, up to revolutionary action at the other end. Regardless of the mode of practice, or of where individuals may be found on this continuum, such involvement can be understood as being directed towards a fairer society and a more just polity.[4]

While we focus on just three artists, there is evidence of significant activism right across the communities and nations in Asia. Muthiah Alagappa traces the movements and moments associated with political activism, and identifies their origins before the second world war, both in demonstrations of resistance to colonial governments, and in organised efforts to claim civic and cultural autonomy. Though the colonial governments of the Netherlands, Spain, Britain, France, Portugal, Japan and the United States (despite the US claiming never to have had colonies) controlled the political frameworks, Alagappa writes:

> social, cultural, and certain avenues of economic life remained largely outside state control. In these relatively free areas, indigenous groups organized to regulate affairs, provide welfare, educational, religious, cultural and economic services, and, when possible, make representations on behalf of their groups to the colonial authority.[5]

These patterns of organisation and resistance intensified and extended during the mass movements after the second world war, and saw the departure of the colonial authorities and the inauguration of nationalist governments. The same energy mobilised subsequent activism against those governments that proved to be repressive or dictatorial.[6] Alagappa cites a number of organised movements, including the People Power revolution in the Philippines, the Reformasi movements in Malaysia and in Indonesia, and the democracy movement in China, but also names practically every nation in Asia (and, of course, in Europe and North America) as the site of more or less organised political activism, and of struggles to resist social, cultural and economic inequities. 'The key point is this', Alagappa writes: 'contentions over national belonging, identity, the socio-political order, and protection and expansion of rights and interests have made struggle a central feature of many Asian civil societies'.[7]

Political activism only works when activists can successfully convince the general population that their efforts are both legitimate and of value, and there is therefore always a need to mobilise the public as well as to convince the rulers of the importance of their cause. Cultural activism has real traction in this regard and, as the essays in Kuan-Hsing Chen's *Trajectories* (1998)[8] set out, there has been an extensive pattern of cultural activism throughout the region.

Artists have taken a significant role in these movements, with their involvement often more directed towards cultural activism than towards direct or revolutionary action (though there are examples of this too). Some artists have limited their involvement to that of a witness, using their art work to record what happened; others have used their art to remind audiences of prior and still unresolved human rights infringements, and both Wong and Christanto fit this category; and others again have engaged in revolutionary action as well as art, as is the case for Sitthiket. Those cultural activists who are not artists per se also typically make use of the tools and techniques of art, deploying such creative devices as dramaturgy, performance, visualisation and narrative, and mobilising events through the use of music, performance art or media productions. Where this works effectively, it is usually because the artefacts shown, or the events curated, work to capture affectual engagement,[9] mobilising individuals to their cause. In this way it is possible to garner wider community support for the work of raising consciousness about issues of race and class, nationalism and multiculturalism, gay rights and women's rights, and in response to nation-building and state-creating projects.

Whether the focus is political or cultural activism, and whether the activists are located at the far edges of the activism continuum, or somewhere along that scale of possibilities, artists are frequently, and often deeply, involved in activism. Activism is the dream that things can be different, and contemporary art is, generally, committed to offering alternative ways of seeing and knowing. There is a real alignment between art's investment in such alternatives and the activist belief that change begins with our being able to imagine change. Moreover, both artists and activists share a concern with moral language, social understandings, and the drive to 'create new moral possibilities',[10] and both have a history of critiquing social institutions, and finding ways to look anew at normative modes of social organisation; and this is critical for any movement seeking social change. Jacques Rancière writes:

> Within any given framework, artists are those whose strategies aim to change the frames, speeds and scales according to which we perceive the visible, and combine it with a specific invisible element and a specific meaning. Such strategies are intended to make the invisible visible or to question the self-evidence of the visible.[11]

Art is at the heart of such strategies because of its capacity to offer alternative ways of seeing and knowing and alternative hopes. The engine of activism is the dream that things can be different. The artists who are the focus of this chapter have been selected for the case studies because they share an attitude of concern for social and political wellbeing, and have produced bodies of work that perform a kind of activism. They are of course not alone in their performance; but we select them as representative of this mode of practice because each came early to the attention of audiences beyond Asia, presenting a dream of alterity that was not yet familiar to those audiences, and thus can stand as exemplars of an approach to art and human rights engagement. To use Jacques Rancière's terminology, their work seeks 'to make the invisible visible', and to change perception; to use Terry Smith's terminology, it is 'aware of the influence of ideologies', and it translates those volatile 'issues of nationality, identity, and rights' into forms that are intelligible to others. While their art, biographies and trajectories are very distinctive, they have a number of features in common. Each has located himself within a local context while receiving significant international recognition for his art; the work of each is deeply informed by local contexts, while being framed by international perspectives; and each has produced a body of work that can be viewed as both ideologically conscious, and concerned about social justice.

Their involvement with social justice issues is not surprising, given the dramatic political and social changes in the region that have affected peoples' lives in extraordinary and tumultuous ways, and the complexity of their own relationship to nationality and identity. Wong and Christanto are members of Chinese minorities in societies where there has been major discrimination against those minorities, societies where Chinese nevertheless play significant economic and social roles.[12] Vasan Sitthiket grew up in a Thailand that was marked by phenomenal political change and unrest, 'the zeitgeist of an era full of oppression, alienation, and angst',[13] and we suggest that he was politicised early in his life, growing up as part of an often-exploited peasant farmer class. Though his art is deeply informed by traditional cultural values including Buddhist beliefs, he remains a committed 'anarchist' involved in demonstrations and political protests whose wish is – as Sitthiket is reported as saying – to 'destroy the dinosaurs that rule the country'.[14]

Their involvement in activism – or their position on the activism continuum – is not identical. Dadang Christanto can be categorised first as a cultural activist rather than a political activist. Though he has never been formally involved in political party activity, his work has consistently challenged the orthodoxies of what he experienced as a dominant ideology and a repressive regime in Indonesia in the Suharto years; and it is inspired, not to say haunted, by themes of injustice. Wong Hoy Cheong has a history of political activism, having been directly involved in politics in Malaysia, but operates as a cultural activist in much of his work that explores such issues as ethnic and cultural identity, 'Asian values' and global human rights. For Sitthiket, cultural and political activism go hand in hand; he has entrenched in his art ideas and images unambiguously challenging to the establishment in Thai society and often meant as acts of provocation; but as Apinan Poshyananda writes, Sitthiket has always been concerned with the 'great issues of our day – poverty, social conflicts, alienation, the decay of cities, and the destruction of the natural environment'.[15]

Though their biographies, and their political, cultural and ethnic identities and experiences, are very different, they are connected by a shared concern about human rights and social equity, which can perhaps be located in what has been described as a 'new cosmopolitan identity'.[16] The word 'cosmopolitan' derives, as Pnina Werbner reminds readers, from the Greek *cosmos* and *polis*, producing the meaning 'citizen of the world'.[17] New cosmopolitans are distinguished from the nineteenth- or early twentieth-century versions of the subject by being individuals who are conscious of the world as a whole community, and able to think globally, but who remain connected to their local communities. These contemporary 'citizens of the world' differ from earlier iterations because they are not necessarily elites; women, minority groups and working class people are equally able, and likely, to share this identity. As Werbner explains, 'proletarian cosmopolitanism, rooted in Marx's exhortation to workers of the world to unite, was undermined by popular nationalism, but in the post-liberal postcolonies of today, worker cosmopolitan consciousness of rights is a growing reality'.[18] Consequently, cosmopolitanism can be understood as a quest for an answer to what Steven Vertovec and Robin Cohen identify as the two 'basic cosmopolitan questions': 'Can we ever live peacefully with one another? What do we share, collectively, as human beings?'[19] Thus, as Pheng Cheah states: 'Simply put, cosmopolitanism and human rights are the two primary ways of figuring the global as the human.'[20]

As cosmopolitans, Wong, Christanto and Sitthiket effectively engage local audiences and contexts as well as international audiences. Each is local *and* global; each has had considerable international experience, but because of their connectedness to the local, their art does not present a 'top down' or elitist model. Consequently, they are well positioned to address social concerns very directly in ways that are accessible within their communities as well as striking chords on the international stage. The brief case studies we present of each of these artists suggest that, in their particular ways, they create spaces for debate and, in contesting dominant and official orthodoxies, they seek to allow other voices to be heard.[21]

Wong Hoy Cheong: art, human rights and the public intellectual

Wong Hoy Cheong was born in 1960 in Malaysia, and received an international education: a BA in English Literature from Brandeis, an MA in Education from Harvard, and an MA in Fine Arts from the University of Massachusetts, Amherst. In 1987 he returned to Malaysia, where his art has been shown and collected by major institutions, including the National Gallery. It has also been shown internationally in major exhibitions such as the second Asia-Pacific Triennial (1996) and the 2003 Venice Biennale as well as in Guangzhou, Gwangju, Taipei, New York, Oxford, Vienna and Istanbul.

His art is engaged with social change and social justice within the contexts of Asia and also globally.

Art critic and scholar Krishen Jit describes him as 'the ideal public intellectual with an artistic bent';[22] and critic Ooi Kok Cheun describes him as 'an art revolutionary, a Che Guevara of art who delves into socio-political and historical issues like post-colonialism and migration, diaspora displacement and alienation, racism and injustice, identity and hybridity'.[23] There is a sound foundation for both of these descriptions, and certainly in many respects Wong fits the category of political activist as we have defined it above. He has been involved in both human rights activities and political activism, including working with detainees who were imprisoned without trial under the Malaysian Internal Security Act during the 'Lalang [Weeding] Operation' of October 1987.[24] But in the early 1990s Wong felt that his NGO work 'wasn't doing enough' so, as he has stated in an interview, he

> joined the socialist party, which later merged with another party to become the opposition People's Justice Party … I've been involved in party politics for the past 20 years. I've been a campaign manager during elections, done strategy and planning, fund-raising, written and designed campaign materials, briefed candidates for elections.[25]

In recent years he has held policy roles, including supporting Anwar Ibrahim for the elections in 2013, and working on campaign strategies. He is also a founder-director of the party think tank Institut Rakyat.[26]

But Wong is also a cultural activist, again as we have defined the term. His 1994 performance and installation work *Lalang* is both art and a direct reference to the human rights infringement that was 1987's Operation Lalang. Wong overplanted the lawns of the National Gallery of Malaysia with lalang (an indigenous weed), then killed off the weed and replanted the area with grass. Speaking to a reporter from the *New Straits Times*, he observed mildly that 'Lallang [*sic*] has lots of meaning in Malay culture'; and then, more pointedly, 'there's the political Operation Lallang (1987) which is about controlling something'.[27] Later works treat similar concerns: in *diPULAUkan/Exile Islands* (1998), for example, he created replicas of islands used first by the colonial powers and then by postcolonial regimes as prisons. A major work, *Tapestry of Justice* (1998–2004), again functions as a political intervention (see Plate 1). It consists of a thirty-metre-long compilation of individual sheets of tracing paper bearing copies of 15,000 thumbprints of people who, like himself, are opposed to the Internal Security Act. The thumbprints were collected in various locations, from streets and pubs to museums, and after being copied, were sent to the then Malaysian Prime Minister and the Minister for Home Affairs as a kind of petition. He used the prints, he said, because 'the act of thumb-printing is often associated with criminality, authoritarianism, a mark and image with DNA-like uniqueness; an action which activates a discomfort'.[28] Any discomfort is perhaps offset by the linking of the thumbprints with leaves from trees and petals from national flowers – as fragile and translucent as are human and civil rights. Not only did this work engender discussion on the streets; it also tested how far the National Art Gallery in Malaysia would go in allowing a thumbprint petition to be part of its exhibition.

What has most distinguished Wong's political and artistic endeavours over two decades is an absolutely consistent commitment to social justice and human rights. But he does not claim that art is necessarily politically efficacious. He insists that education is a more reliable path to empowerment, and rejects any easy parallel between art and political action, saying, 'For me ... a political act has an end and expresses a desire for a transformation.'[29] In these views he seems to be channelling Robert Putnam's thesis of political engagement,[30] that political participation is linked to the possession of social capital. This position is enlisted also by Pattie *et al.* (2003), who argue that citizens engage in political activism where there is a degree of trust in the system; where they possess sufficient resources to involve themselves in the process; where they are confident that there will be at least some effective outcome from their action; and where they have been mobilised to participate.[31]

Wong certainly possesses the intellectual capital required, and therefore the skills to participate in activism; he is clearly motivated to keep up the effort over many years and has been able to do so in Malaysia.[32] Indeed, Wong has stated that his art works have not been censored. However, it seems at least one work included in his 2004 retrospective exhibition at the National Gallery of Malaysia was not shown in Malaysia during the years (1991–2003) that Prime Minister Mahathir Mohamad was in that post.[33] This work, *Vitrine of contemporary events*, was created in 1999, the year Deputy Prime Minister Anwar Ibrahim was jailed for corruption. Jacqueline Lo has suggested that the Anwar case had a 'considerable impact' on politicising art in Malaysia.[34] Wong's *Vitrine* included judges' wigs, police batons, and a Malaysia constitution made of cow dung and embellished with vacuum cleaner rubbish. It is also an indication of the comparative political liberty in Malaysia that Wong has been able to engage in both art and politics: he has never had to try to hide the potential political implications of his art, he said in an interview, but has 'always tried to balance my time and energy between political and artistic work'.[35]

Wong Hoy Cheong's sophisticated and intellectual art is an important contribution to a Malaysian modern art tradition that, as artist Redza Piyadasa has noted, began post-1945 in British Malaya. After Independence in 1957 the new Malaysian Government actively encouraged cultural and artistic developments with scholarships, educational initiatives and the creation of a Malaysian National Gallery.[36] Many Malaysian artists, including Piyadasa, studied abroad, and subsequently sought to explore regional practices and materials as well as local themes in art, including Islamic abstractionism (pioneered by Sulaiman Esa), in ways that coalesced with international streams of art theory. Piyadasa and Esa helped define and introduce conceptual art in the 1970s, and Piyadasa and Singapore-based art historian T. K. Sabapathy were key figures in developing an intellectual narrative for Malaysian modern art, one that is both local and international in its theoretical focus.

A significant stream of Malaysian art that comments on social issues includes Nirmala Shanmughalingam's paintings on the Vietnam war, Bayu Utomo Radjikin's depictions of the culture of Borneo's Dayaks – whose way of life is threatened by modern development – and Zulkifli Yusoff's and Liew Kung Yu's very different explorations of Malaysian institutions. Wong Hoy Cheong's celebrated early painting *The nouveau riche, the elephant and the foreign maid, or the discreet charm of the bourgeoisie* (1991), a critique of middle-class materialism, fits into this stream of socially conscious art in Malaysia.[37]

This interest in social issues is hardly surprising, given Malaysia's modern history and the multicultural composition of its population. The Chinese in Malaysia comprise 26 per cent of the population (compared with only 3 per cent in Indonesia); Indians comprise approximately 7.3 per cent;[38] and multicultural issues have emerged as social problems from time to time. The race riots of 1969 between Malays and Chinese were a key watershed for the nation and for art in Malaysia. These resulted in over a hundred deaths, and led to new economic and cultural policies for the nation – effectively, affirmative action policies designed to address Malay discontent at lack of educational and economic opportunities. This led to the development of a strong Malay middle class, and an impetus for Malay intellectuals to explore Malay identity which, by the late 1970s, had become 'enmeshed in Islamic idealism'.[39] But the affirmative action policies also led to policies that have been seen by many commentators as potentially discriminatory to other races. Piyadasa notes that leaders in all the communities have done major work to combat racial tensions, but the issues of history, race and identity remain critical issues for artists in Malaysia.

They have also been key themes in Wong's art, and this fits the context of his identity as a Malaysian of Chinese descent. Wong's father was from a family of Chinese rubber tappers, while his mother was from an elite Peranakan Chinese family, 'Peranakan' being a hybridised Chinese/Malay community culture. His monumental project of large-scale drawings in the '*Migrants*' series, including *Of Migrants & Rubber Trees* (1994), encapsulates his own family's history in the Malayan peninsula, and his 1996 work, *In search of faraway places*, explores a new generation of migration, and cultural change within his own family, who are now spread over many countries. As Krishen Jit has observed in the Migrant series, 'the artist's own family history is the source of experiential data that coax ruminations about the global travail of migration and the discord and displacements resonant in tales of merging social classes.'[40] *Sook*

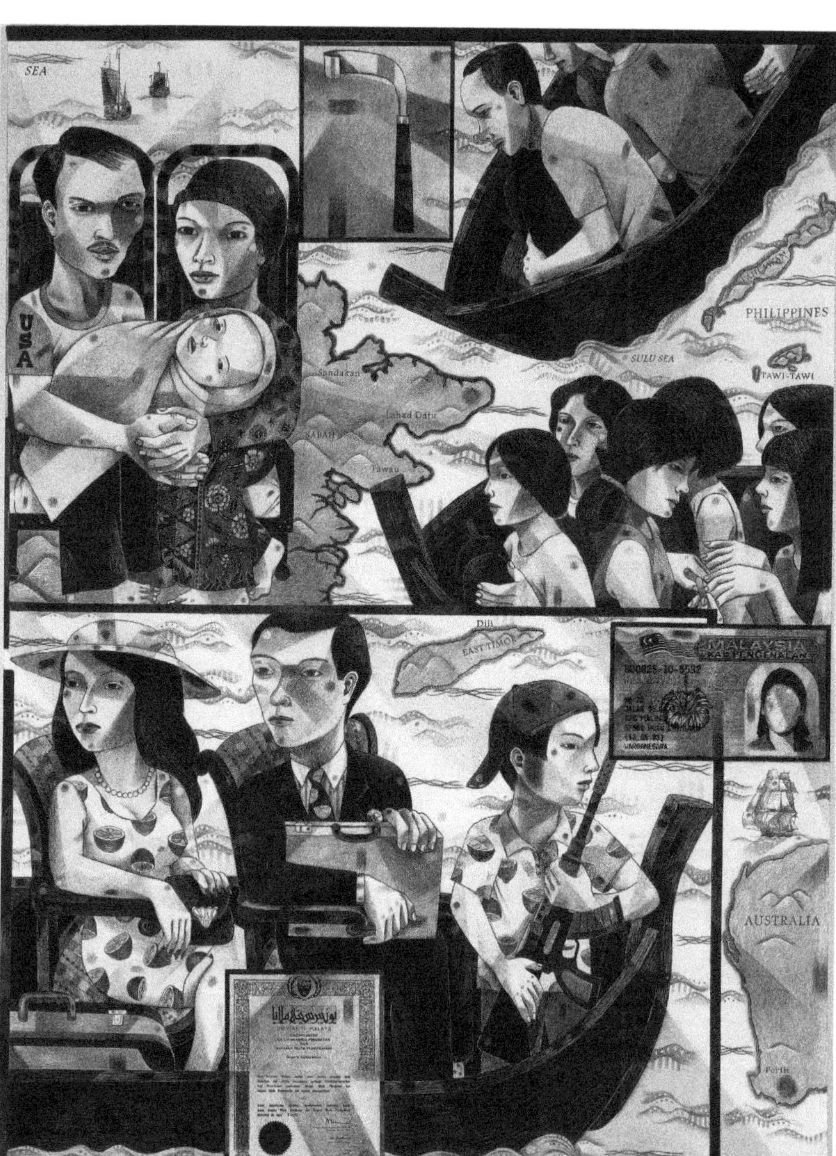

2.1 Wong Hoy Cheong, *In search of faraway places* (from *'Migrants'* series), 1996. Detail. Collection: Queensland Art Gallery. The Kenneth and Yasuko Myer Collection of Contemporary Asian Art. Purchased 1996 with funds from Michael Sidney Myer through and with the assistance of the Queensland Art Gallery Foundation.

Ching (*the Purge*) of 1990 and *Doghole* (2010), the latter a film about incarceration and torture, were both based on the Japanese occupation of Malaya and were also a memorial to Wong's father, who had endured imprisonment by the Japanese during the war.

Wong continued to treat the contentious issues of race and identity in Malaysia: in *Indigenous and Non-Indigenous Skins* (1998–2000) he used masks created from a variety of plant materials and modelled from faces of mixed races, Chinese, Indians, Malays, people who have changed religions or migrated from their birth place to deconstruct racial classifications. As Wong himself has noted, his works have always been about examining the slipperiness of race/ethnicity and problematising it.[41]

More recently he has produced art that addresses immigrant populations and transcultural interactions. In *Minaret* (2005), prepared for the Guangzhou Triennial in China, he used bamboo and construction netting to erect, on the tower of the Museum of Contemporary Art,[42] a work resembling an Islamic mosque. The Museum is located close to the site of a Tang Dynasty mosque, and hence *Minaret* commemorates the Chinese city's long links with Islam. It also elaborates Wong's own cultural identity: he is a Chinese non-Muslim living in a Muslim nation, and this work offers an interesting treatise on ethnic relationships and the position of minority groups. As Rugg notes, '*Minaret* was a reminder of the historical and contingent cultural configurations that have excluded Chinese Muslims, raising issues about the representation of Islam in a post-9/11 world … and the ideological fragility of concepts of the other.'[43]

In subsequent works he has developed this concern. His 2008 *Maid in Malaysia* is a series of photographs of Malaysian maids who, like their Filipina and Indonesian counterparts, are often denied basic rights by employers in the foreign countries in which they work. He filmed them posing in the homes of their affluent employers, in the characters of iconic female figures such as Florence Nightingale or Lara Croft. *Days of Our Lives* (2009) again took up themes of global immigration and postcoloniality; for this work, Wong produced a series of six photographs based on historical French paintings in the Museum of Fine Arts, Lyon. Wong substituted the European protagonists in the original images with members of immigrant populations, such as Muslim Nigerians, Iranians, Burmese and Turks, in order, as the Guggenheim Museum text notes, to trace 'the changing face of ordinary life in Europe while excavating the obscured cultural histories of marginalized communities elsewhere in the world … [It] thus deconstructs the systems of power that underwrite historical narrative.'[44]

Such critiques of the system of power and the problem of representation across cultures are also seen in earlier works. *Text Tiles* (2000), first shown in the South Korean Gwangju Biennale, is an example of this (see Figure 2.2). To

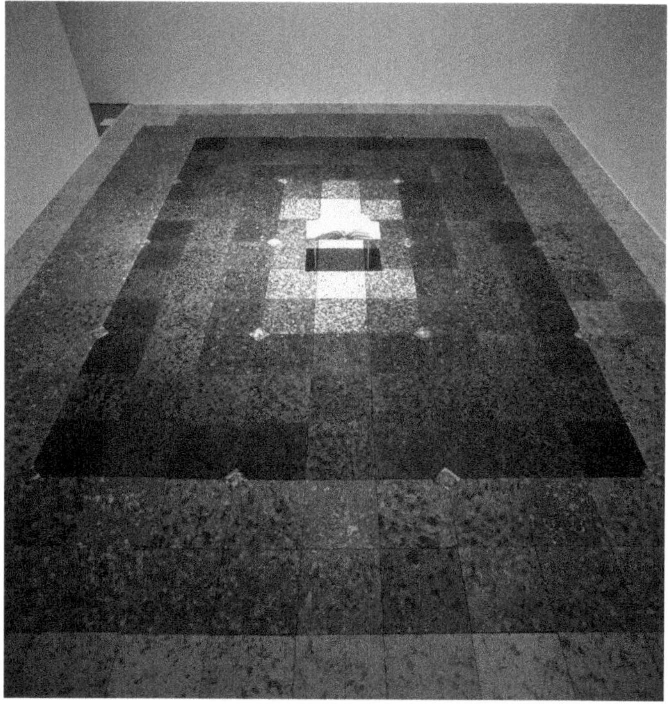

2.2   Wong Hoy Cheong, *Text Tiles*, 2000. Installation view.

make this work, Wong pulped textbooks, historical studies, books of Asian history, and biographies and autobiographies of European and Asian dictators, and then formed the pulp into 250 floor tiles, which were exhibited along with another 20 tiles that bore images of dictators. A related work is his pair of handmade books, *The Definitive ABC of Government* and *The Definitive ABC of Ethnography*. He created the first by pulping copies of Hitler's *Mein Kampf* (1925–26) and Mahathir's *Malay Dilemma* (1970), while the second book uses Margaret Mead's *Coming of Age in Samoa* (1928) and V. S. Naipaul's *Among the Believers: An Islamic Journey* (1981).

These works can be read as reminders of the need to sustain an attitude of resistance to colonialism in its contemporary forms, and of the problem of communication between and within cultures. Sumit Mandal observes that his pulping of published books for both these works is a gesture that tends 'to undo the authority of the text by rendering it meaningless. Text fragments are discernible in the works but they defy reading and logic, thereby subverting the commonplace notion of the certainty of knowledge and language.'[45] For an educator and scholar like Wong, the destruction of books is a profound act, and an act of resistance to conventional meanings and politics, including both 'colonial-era racialisation' and Asia's own histories.

Wong develops his views on this issue, explaining the problematics of representation associated with the fact that his Malaysia-specific works are likely to be (mis)read outside the context of their emergence:

> *Lalang* for example, strikes a deep emotional chord when shown in the local playing field. Supposing that this work was repeated/re-enacted in let's say Japan or Sydney or London, I would be gazed at quite differently. Not the provocateur, the 'subversive' gnawing at the State, but as the pitiful 'other' from the third/developing world where human rights abuses are a constant.[46]

To interrupt this western gaze on 'the other', he deliberately includes images more familiar to audiences in Japan, or Sydney, or London: 'That's why in *Text Tiles* Hirohito's and Kim Il Sung's and Thatcher's image are there, as much as Suharto's and Pol Pot's. It is important that "they" get to walk over their own leaders, and not merely tread over third world dictators.'[47]

But though Wong makes it clear that these works specifically relate to debates about universal values and human rights, they are not designed merely to tackle neocolonialism. Wong specifically points to his intention 'to provoke a more self-conscious look at Asian histories and the fashionable stance of Asian "values" and "democracy" as espoused by many Asian leaders', including, as we have noted, the then prime minister of Malaysia, Mahathir Mohamad.[48] What his works demonstrate is his sustained argument that the concept of Asian values is neither as unitary nor as stable as might be assumed – a position shared by a number of experts in the field.[49]

His challenge to the simplistic concept of 'Asian' values does not, however, negate his commitment to a local polity and set of principles. He does not hesitate to criticise the frequent expressions of hypocrisy over human rights abuses in Asian countries that come from western commentators (as indeed Prime Minister Mahathir has done), and has always been forthright in opposing colonial perspectives. Wong's 'mockumentary' *RE:Looking* (2002), shown at the 2003 Venice Biennale, is an example of his providing a counter-narrative to the continued colonialist impulses seen in western engagements with Asian nations. This work posits a mythical Malaysian/*Melakan* empire and the impact of decolonisation on some of its former European (Austrian) subjects. It is a brilliant intervention in a complex psychological framing of the question of colonialism and its victims.[50]

The simple message is that anyone can be colonised, and anyone can be a coloniser, but the immediate inspiration of *RE:Looking* was more subtle than merely reversed colonisation. In conversation with curator Hou Hanru, Wong explained that the concept was 'partly influenced by the aftermath of 9/11. I think around that period there was a lot of manipulated

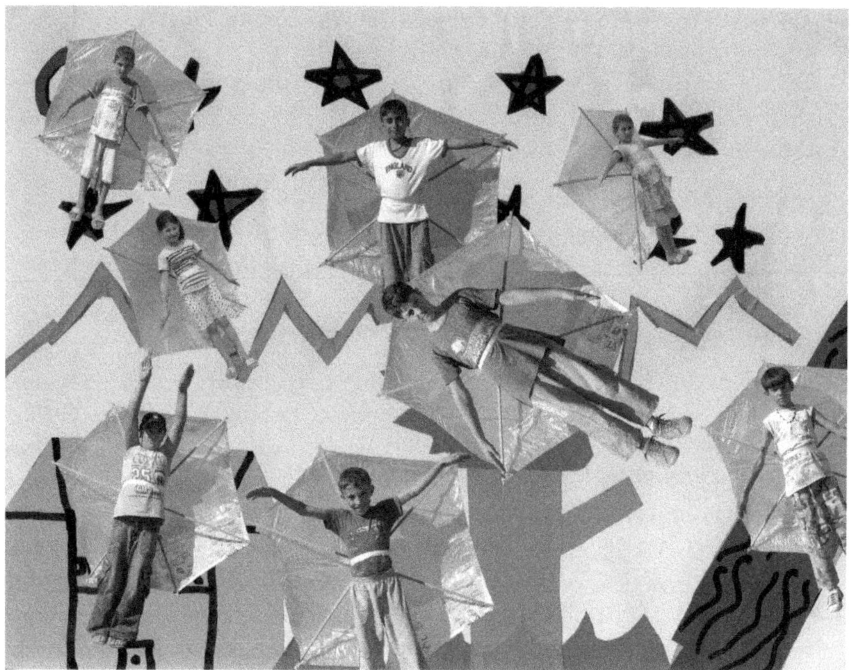

2.3 Wong Hoy Cheong, *Aman Sulukule Canim Sulukule (Oh Sulukule Darling Sulukule)*, 2007. Video still.

and faked information … I wanted to create that slipperiness between fact and fiction … And when you start doing that, you end up not knowing what is real anymore.'[51] The space between actuality and story, or between representation and propaganda, is one he has raised as being important to his work. Describing a project he conducted in the late 1990s, in response to the Reformasi movements, he explains that he produced postcards to be sent to government officials as a kind of provocation. People picked up and mailed these postcards – some 30,000 to 40,000 were sent to senior members of the government. He says, 'The agenda was to inform people of the lack of rule of law and let them know that they could be empowered to make a political act by simply picking up a postcard and mailing it.' Now, he says, 'I do question how effective the project was as art or even as propaganda … The political act took precedence over the aesthetic part of the project.'[52] Wong's essential conviction was, and remains, simply 'I think provocations of the senses are needed',[53] rather than didactic engagements. In addition, he is increasingly alert to the need to consider the impact of activist interventions. In correspondence with the authors, he said:

> artists must recognise and engage with their own complicity within the system. The interventions and activist actions, like pages of a book, are folded unto themselves

and unto others. The recognition of this 'foldedness' allows for a more reflexive and dialogical engagement with both the community and dominant powers.[54]

Perhaps in response to his concern about a more effective engagement and a less didactic approach, he has begun to involve himself more intensively in grassroots activism, and social justice issues focused on such pragmatic concerns as affordable housing. This was a theme he developed in his art work for the Istanbul Biennale 2007, *Oh Sulukule, Darling Sulukule,* where he worked with a Roma community in Sulukule who were facing eviction by the Turkish authorities.[55] Hou observes in this same conversation that his work 'is become less and less didactic, and more open to the actual context'. This represents a very interesting stage in his career: one in which his political activism is moving to more pragmatic grounds, while his cultural activism is perhaps even more capable of crossing communities, and producing effects. He says:

> I am beginning to realise that art or cultural activism need to be more sustainable. Often, these actions, interventions and projects, while allowing for momentary highs for both subjects and objects, are short term and because they are often personality/ies oriented, they have little lingering effect, little long-term empowerment for the community. The artist or cultural worker ends up benefiting more than the community (or subject) … So I guess, I am trying to understand and learn how such 'activism' can have a more sustainable effect.[56]

Dadang Christanto: artist as witness

Dadang Christanto was born in 1957 in Java to a Chinese Indonesian family, and into what became a legacy of violence that has deeply informed his art. His father was one of the suspected left-wing or communist sympathisers who were massacred in the 1965–66 killings that brought the late President Suharto to power.[57] Estimates of the numbers killed vary: Ariel Heryanto suggests that more than a million died, but other estimates are slightly lower. Though the Chinese – who constitute only 2 to 3 per cent of the population – were not necessarily the primary targets, many Chinese Indonesians died in the carnage.[58] Among them was Christanto's father, who ran a small business and who, Christanto believes, was not a member of the Communist Party, though he may have provided a venue for some of their events. He was taken away by local militias when Christanto was only eight years old, while he and his siblings were sleeping. His exact fate has never been discovered, but Christanto was left deeply affected by these events, and also by the difficult life his mother faced in supporting the family, running a small batik shop in a village where her neighbours may have been members of the militias that killed her husband.

Despite his family origin, and the tragic circumstances that have shaped his life, Christanto (like FX Harsono, discussed in Chapter 3) has always considered himself Indonesian. He never studied the Chinese language, he became a Christian – though as an adult he converted to Islam – and, as was required under Suharto's New Order, he adopted a non-Chinese name. He was enrolled as a student of painting at the Indonesia Institute of Art in Yogyakarta, despite a screening process that could deny university entrance to the families of the victims of 1965–66. There he became involved with activists associated with the iconic Indonesian poet and playwright W. S. Rendra. He was also engaged with a Catholic Education Foundation, which sought to use art as part of a campaign for social justice, working with Swiss human rights activist Jesuit Fr Ruedi Hoffman.[59] His art has been shown to acclaim in many international exhibitions, including the Asia-Pacific Triennial in Australia (1993, 1999), the Havana Biennale (1994), the Fukuoka Asian Art show in Japan (1995), *Traditions/Tensions* at the Asia Society in New York (1996), the São Paulo Biennale (1998), the Gwangju Biennale (2000) and the Indonesian pavilion of the Venice Biennale (2003).

In the first instance, Christanto seems to be an artist best categorised on the cultural, low-intensity end of the activism continuum. His commitment has been to bear witness to the 1965–66 killings, and to keep alive the memories of those events. But he is more than a witness; he is also an artist whose work is deeply marked by his strong commitment to ideas of justice and freedom, or *merdeka*, and who promulgates those ideas. Merdeka is associated with the struggle in the post-second world war era for independence from the Dutch. Indeed, Anthony Reid describes the end of the second world war as a moment when merdeka became 'not just a political program but a felt reality'.[60] By 1949 the colonial rulers, who had been in Indonesia for 350 years, were defeated, and Indonesia, a vast archipelago with a population then moving towards 100 million (and today 250 million), began the work of constructing itself as a nation.[61] Art played a part in this movement: key artists of that Independence period, such as Sudjojono (the 'father' of contemporary Indonesian art), Hendra Gunawan and Affandi, emphasised art that depicted ordinary people and reflected Indonesian values. This provided an important basis for an Indonesian art ideology that embraced a vision of freedom for all classes and individuals.[62]

The ideas mobilised by merdeka still have a major influence in contemporary Indonesian art, and Christanto's work exemplifies it, along with that of other key artists from the 1990s including FX Harsono and Heri Dono. Christanto's work both remembers the past, and calls out for freedom from oppression. This involves intervention in ways that remind people and the authorities of the values of merdeka; and his sustained work on the 1965–66 killings is a part of this intervention. He conceives of that traumatic period as 'The Unspeakable Horror',[63] and this is a critical reference to the determination of the Indonesian authorities until 1998 that the events should remain 'unspeakable', in the sense that they could never be spoken of and all records were suppressed.[64] This was an exercise in what Tessa Morris-Suzuki has described as 'a late twentieth-century "historiography of oblivion", whose purpose is not simply to "revise" understandings of the past, but specifically to *obliterate* the memory of certain events from public consciousness'.[65] In this context, art can perform a very powerful interrogation of government policy, as well as the preservation of history and memory.

Laine Berman notes, 'The Indonesian state under Suharto regarded culture as one of the areas requiring their direct and indirect guidance and took extensive measures to make sure anything cultural did not appear to be "political".'[66] Consequently, government policy during the New Order period of Suharto's regime (1965–98) had a demonstrable effect on arts practice, along two main trajectories. One trajectory drove artists to work in support of the government's view of the national identity, as Suharto's regime energetically co-opted art to its interests, using it to construct a vision of the nation where local differences were expressed as artistic traditions rather than political separatism.[67] The other trajectory placed artists in opposition to the regime, working instead in the interests of an autonomous art that remained committed to merdeka and to human rights.

Both came with a price, but activist or resistance art was heavily censored; Jörgen Hellman describes the production of performance art commemorating the murder of labour-activist Marsinah as having faced 'insurmountable difficulties'.[68] Art was, nonetheless, a key avenue for resistance in Indonesia under the New Order. Many Indonesian artists used hidden symbolism for political protest during the Suharto years,[69] but Christanto, who participated from the beginning in the second trajectory, made works whose critical content was easily understood by locals, and therefore usually could not be shown in Indonesia except to a select few, in underground exhibitions. Indeed, until the end of the Suharto regime it was not possible for Christanto to say openly that his art was about Indonesia. His 1991 work *Bureaucracy*, for example, was shown in the Fukuoka Asian Art exhibition rather than locally. It consisted of a row of two-dimensional heads, like a stand of Indonesian *wayang* puppets, each licking the back of the head in front, and with the foremost head wearing a soldier's helmet. This was obviously a challenge to the military-dominated government of Suharto; and for Rizki A. Zaelani, it 'points out the culture of corruption that had become acute within various layers of Indonesian society under the national leadership dominated by the military'.[70]

His 1993 work, *For those who have been killed, Who are poor, Who are suffering, Who are oppressed, Who are voiceless, Who are powerless, Who are burdened, Who are victims of violence, Who are victims of a dupe,* shown at the

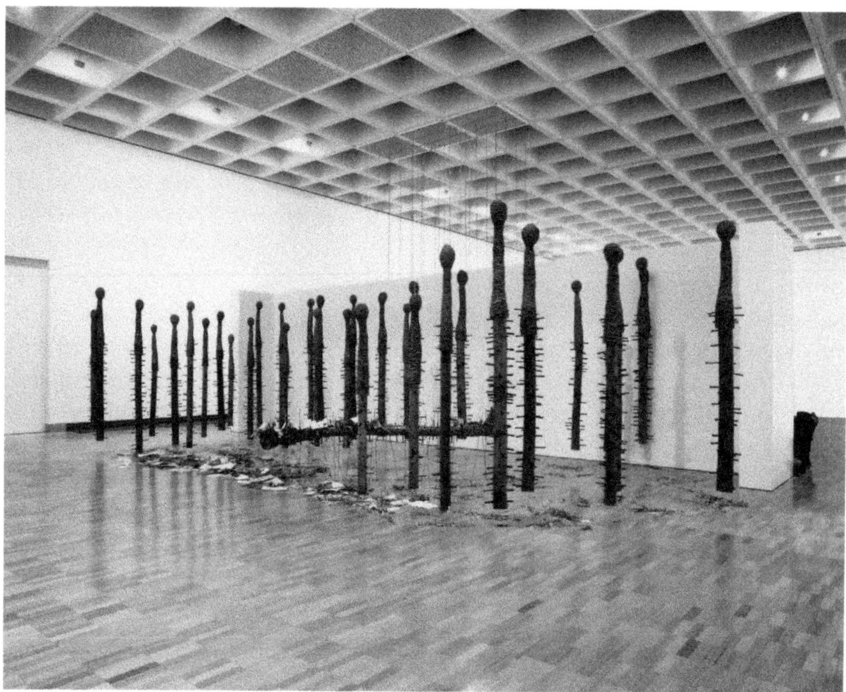

2.4 Dadang Christanto, *For those: Who are poor, Who are suffer(ing), Who are oppressed, Who are voiceless, Who are powerless, Who are burdened, Who are victims of violence, Who are victims of a dupe, Who are victims of injustice*, 1993. Collection: Queensland Art Gallery. The Kenneth and Yasuko Myer Collection of Contemporary Asian Art. Purchased 1993 with funds from The Myer Foundation and Michael Sidney Myer through the Queensland Art Gallery Foundation.

first Asia-Pacific Triennial in Australia in 1993, shows a different approach to this critical engagement. Audiences interpreted the work in terms of their personal grief and their personal responses to tragedies beyond those specific to Indonesia. During the Triennial, many left flowers and notes under the installation (a phenomenon which recurs whenever the work, which the Gallery purchased, is on display). However, there were almost no references to Indonesia in the hundreds of handwritten testimonials left by visitors in 1993. Most of the notes related to events then occurring in the former Yugoslavia, and to the treatment of Aboriginal people in Australia.[71]

Christanto was required to deny any reference to Indonesia in this installation of hanging bamboo sculptures, which was actually a memorial to the victims of 1965–66, and the victims of the Dili cemetery massacre of 1991 in East Timor, when Indonesian troops fired on demonstrators. Christanto had seen television footage of these events while in Australia but this information was censored in Indonesia. He certainly could not have stated publicly the direct connection to these events in Indonesia in the 1990s. But the effect of this censorship was that he was able to extend the focus of the suffering from the (Indonesian) particular to the universal, and the work thereby achieved a global resonance. It is the essence of Christanto's art that it is about violence in every time and place, and it can evoke emotional empathetic responses in viewers who might have no idea of its actual inspiration. His *Kekerasan/Violence 1* in *Traditions/Tensions*, shown at the Asia Society in New York in 1996, had a similar effect. The work consisted of piled terracotta heads, their mouths gaping wide, which suggested to North American audiences the piles of skulls from the Cambodian genocide. Another example is his *Heads from the North* (2004), which consisted of bronze heads in a pond, at the National Gallery of Australia. This work is specifically about 1965–66 in Indonesia but more than one viewer has associated it with refugees coming to Australia by boat.

Similarly, Japanese viewers of his sculptural installation *Mereka Memberi Kesaksian/They Give Evidence* (1996–97) identified tragedies including the dropping of the atomic bomb on Hiroshima, and one Japanese viewer appeared to apologise for the occupation of Java in the Pacific War.[72] In this work, Christanto's larger-than-life-sized and unclothed terracotta figures, male and female, hold in their outstretched arms bundles of clothing that suggest the bodies of children. They are silent witnesses who testify to injustice throughout history, but the work does not attempt to identify any specific victims or perpetrators of particular atrocities. Marsha Meskimmon has eloquently described this work in terms of its register of generosity: 'The figures neither raise their hands to threaten, avenge or admonish, nor fold their arms to protect or exclude. They offer, they *give*.'[73] (See Figure 2.5b.)

This work was created in Indonesia in the mid-1990s and shown in Tokyo and Hiroshima in 1997 but was not shown in Indonesia until after the fall of Suharto in 1998.[74] He brought the installation to Jakarta in 2003, and though government political censorship was not a problem at that stage, an Islamic group successfully protested against the display on the grounds that the sculptures, being nude, were necessarily pornographic. As he reflected later, 'When Suharto fell, it did not mean that everything would be solved. A change in power or leader does not have to be regarded as the end of a cultural resistance.'[75]

Despite the earlier censorship, one of his most influential works was shown in Suharto's Indonesia. *1001 Manusia Tanah/Earth People* (1996) was commissioned by a wealthy art patron, and displayed at the Ancol Marina Beach amusement park near Jakarta. The 1,000 life-sized fibreglass male and female sculptures (the artist himself was the thousand and first) stood in the sea, unclothed, arms dangling helplessly at their sides, confronting the beachgoers, visitors to the amusement park and fishermen, with the symbolism of human

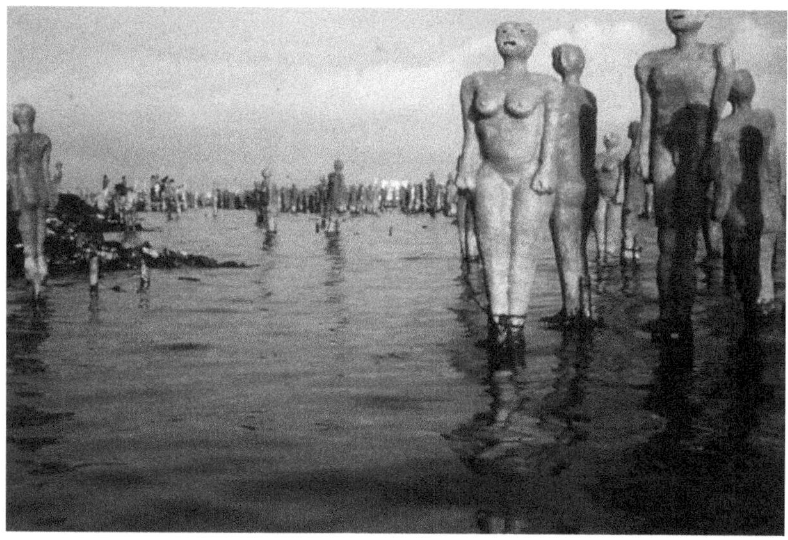

2.5a Dadang Christanto, *1001 Manusia Tanah/Earth People*, 1996. Ephemeral sculpture Ancol Marina Beach, Indonesia.

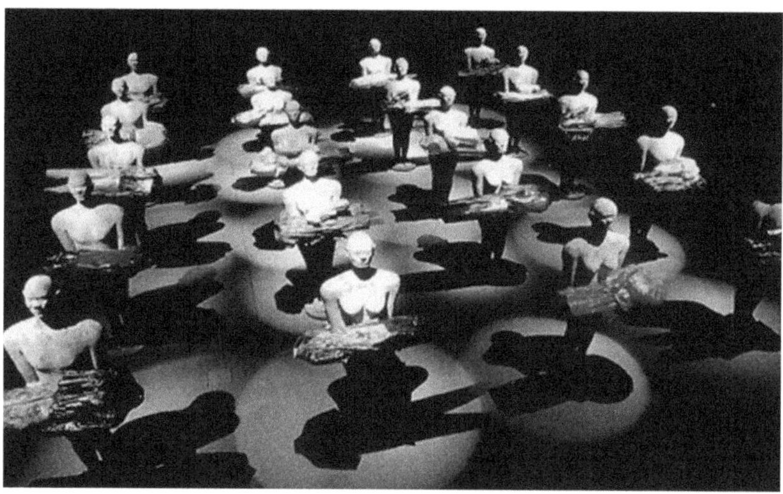

2.5b Dadang Christanto, *Mereka Memberi Kesaksian (They Give Evidence)*, 1996–97. Installation view.

beings displaced and the environment destroyed in the interests of globalisation. It was a commentary on villagers dispossessed by the construction of the Kedungombo Dam, though unstated. As Christanto explained, 'the military bureaucracy gives permission, because … they're not sophisticated enough to make sense of it'.[76] Indonesian intellectuals, however, have noted that the authorities were highly selective in responses to politically sensitive issues.[77] It may be that the private sponsorship not only made it possible for the artist to create this work, but also protected him from censorship or adverse reaction from the authorities.

We noted earlier that a key factor in cultural activism is the capacity of the activists to use creative actions and artefacts in order to capture emotional responses, and thereby mobilise action, in the community. Meskimmon has noted the affective capacity of contemporary art to allow empathetic and sensory connections between people across cultural, linguistic and social borders, 'transforming our relationship with/in the world',[78] and we suggest therefore that contemporary artists are particularly well suited to engage in cultural activism. Certainly Christanto's art has always elicited strong responses from audiences, and it has always focused its themes on ongoing human suffering, whether these were occasioned by human beings or by natural forces such as the Boxing Day tsunami of 2004. Though he has a significant international profile as an artist, much of his practice is devoted to working with ordinary people at community level. This is indicated in his use of 'humble' materials like bamboo, batik and even mud, and in his active community participation, such as the performance *Survivor* that he produced and curated in Jakarta in 2008. This work related to the ongoing disaster in Indonesia in 2006, when mudflows from a gas-drilling borehole in East Java displaced thousands of people. The artist and 600 participants caked in mud kept a silent vigil holding photographs of the victims of the disaster: an event that shows the permeable line between the artist and the activist.

Christanto moved to Australia in 1999. This, and the overthrow of Suharto, allowed him to be open about the sources of his work. At the 1999 performance in Brisbane of *Apu di bulan Mei /Fire in May*, for example, he declared that the performance was related to the 1998 violence in Jakarta when hundreds were killed and a large number of Chinese women raped, but that it also honoured all victims of the twentieth century. That atrocity was memorialised in the exquisite series of paintings *Behind the Veil* (2010), which treated violence and human rights abuses directed specifically against women and the brutal rapes that, Kathryn Robinson argues, were used as a deliberate policy by the regime, not only in 1998 against Chinese women but also earlier in Aceh and East Timor.[79]

His retrospective exhibition in Canberra in 2010, *Wounds in our heart*, reinforced the connection of his art to themes of human rights.[80] *I found your faces on the street* consisted of unidentified portraits of those who had disappeared; the 'River' series (see Plate 2) included paintings of abstracted bodies floating in water, the bodies referred to in many accounts floating down the Brantas River in the killing times in the 1960s.[81] Christanto's identification with

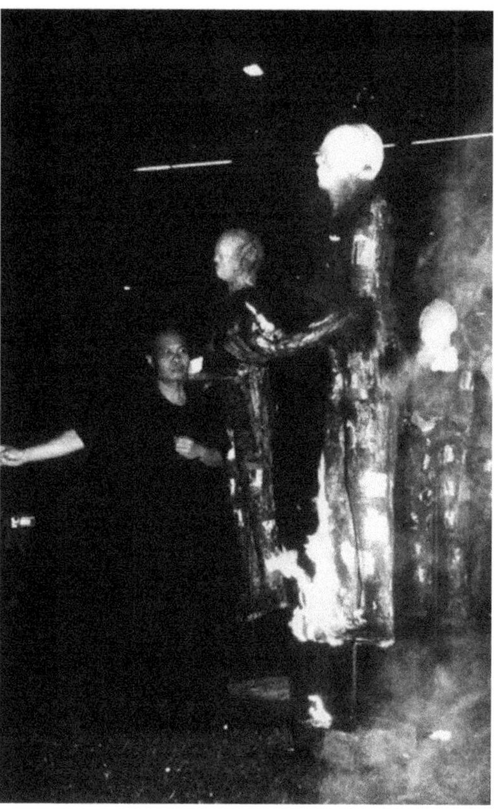

2.6 Dadang Christanto, *Apu di bulan Mei /Fire in May*, 1999. Installation and performance. Queensland Art Gallery, Third Asia-Pacific Triennial, 1999.

victims is apparent also in the performances he does to accompany many of his works. 'I'm concerned with suffering anywhere in the world', he declared; 'yesterday Kosovo, today East Timor.'[82]

This enduring concern was the genesis of his continuing 'Count project', a project intended to memorialise all victims of violence in the twentieth and twenty-first centuries. One major work from that project, *Hujan Merah/Red Rain* (2003), explores the loss of identity through violent death. This is an installation of 1,965 drawings of heads sealed in plastic in the manner of official identity cards and fixed to the ceiling. A line of red thread falls from each card to clotted balls on the floor, evoking the concept of a delicate mist of red rain. His point here is that 'we have always failed to stop violence'; and that crises such as the 11 September 2001 attacks, the war in Afghanistan, the Bali bombing and the war in Iraq are all 'actual global evidence that violence is becoming the solution to problems … these things are still hidden and people won't talk about it.' He concludes, 'And that is my project – still counting and still remembering.'[83]

Christanto's latest works are also testing the limits of official tolerance in the new Indonesia, and protesting against injustice, by seeking to revive the memory of communist intellectuals whose voices were suppressed during the Suharto regime.[84] A recent exhibition in Jakarta celebrates intellectuals such as the famous Indonesian writer Pramoedya Ananta Toer (who had been imprisoned first by the Dutch, and again by Suharto for nearly a decade from 1969),[85] and others of his intellectual heroes who were also jailed under Suharto. He also, in 2014, completed a new work on the 2006 mudslides, which is related to the *Survivor* performances; this is a memorial, based on the *They Give Evidence* figures, to those who lost so much.

Christanto provides an important example of activist art, because he does not precisely fit the expected criteria. One of the truisms of political and cultural activism is that political participation tends to be a middle-class or even elite movement, rather than something likely to involve people from across the social field.[86] Yun Fan's 'map' of social movement activists in Taiwan supports this, showing that half of the activist community are either members of the social elite or students; blue-collar workers comprise only 10.3 per cent of that cohort.[87] Christanto does not fit the mould because he does not hail from the elite sector of society. This is perhaps what allows him to use his 'voice' to plead effectively for change – a voice whose legitimacy is found in his membership of a minority group in the community, and as the child of a widowed mother struggling to cope.

He identifies with the oppressed and empathises directly and experientially with the victims of history but he has, in recent years, indicated that he is finding it 'very tiring to continue to speak of life with themes related to the wounds of a generation … I don't wish to reproduce violence.'[88] Nonetheless, his approach exemplifies the complexities of the context faced by many artists and activists in the region at the time, and the ways in which they were able to negotiate those complexities, and continue to make work that resonates with audiences in many contexts.

Vasan Sitthiket: anarchist of art

In the last decades of the twentieth century Southeast Asia produced a number of artists whose speciality was the production of what might be considered 'dangerous ideas' in terms of the relation of art to the structures of power. In various ways, and using various media, they interrogated the relation of art to the structures of power, exploring issues of identity, politics, and Thailand's recent history of coups and protests. Among them was Thai artist Vasan Sitthiket, named by Loredano Pazzini-Paracciani as one of a handful of pioneers of a socially engaged art in Thailand.[89] From the start he seems to have been committed to disturb normativities, and interrupt traditional practices, often by shocking his audiences. Along with a few other Thai artists, such as Sutee Kunavichayanont and Manit Sriwanichpoom, he has explored issues of history and memory, as well as consistently confronting the forces of power and oppression. His work also disrupts the widely held perception of Thai society as conformist, deeply conservative and committed to what distinguished Thai scholar and curator Apinan Poshyananda has called the 'king-country-religion triad' which results in the 'myth of homogeneity'.[90]

Sitthiket's consistent acts of resistance and protest have led to his being named an anarchist, and his own description of his work seems to support this classification. He has said, 'As an artist I use my art as my weapon, to crash the public, to change what I disagree with',[91] which is reminiscent of the great 'anarchist' poet Stéphane Mallarmé and his 'I know of no bomb other than a book'. Mallarmé, whose work and ideas influenced many early twentieth-century artists, belongs within a genealogy of anarchist avant garde artists. This genealogy dates from the late eighteenth century in Europe, with activists and artists reacting against the massive socioeconomic and political disruptions.[92] Michael Scrivener traces the line of thought and practice from that point, through the nineteenth-century Romantic movement, to the early twentieth century, when artists such as Picasso, Kandinsky and Rothko, and movements including post-impressionism, fluxus and punk, took the stage and shaped practice.[93] This activist, avant garde attitude is associated not only with radical changes to the form and content of art, but also with an ethical imperative, the search for 'the moral antidote to a violent and exploitative world'.[94]

Sitthiket fits well in this genealogy; like the Romantics and their attempt to align art and everyday life, he often uses the imagery of the streets, referencing billboards and posters. Like Mallarmé – to use Julia Kristeva's analysis of that poet's work – Sitthiket mounts 'a sort of anarchist assault that is followed through right to the end',[95] in his simultaneous lifetime commitment to art and to social change. His is not necessarily a subtle approach; he has proclaimed himself 'rude, crude and proud of it',[96] and deeply opposed to what he identifies as destructive social forces including consumerism and global capitalism. 'Capital is madly killing mother earth and human beings', he asserts and, in a reversal of the king-country-religion triad, lays the blame on politicians, bureaucrats and those monks who, he says, 'betray the Dhamma and their doctrine'. He concludes, bleakly, 'This world has no future, for sure.'[97]

The roots of his activism can be found in his family circumstances. Sitthiket was born in 1957 in Nakhon Sawan, 'the heavenly city', a small centre of some 93,000 people, about 238 kilometres north of Bangkok. Sitthiket, whose father was a peasant farmer, does not immediately fit the activist category. However,

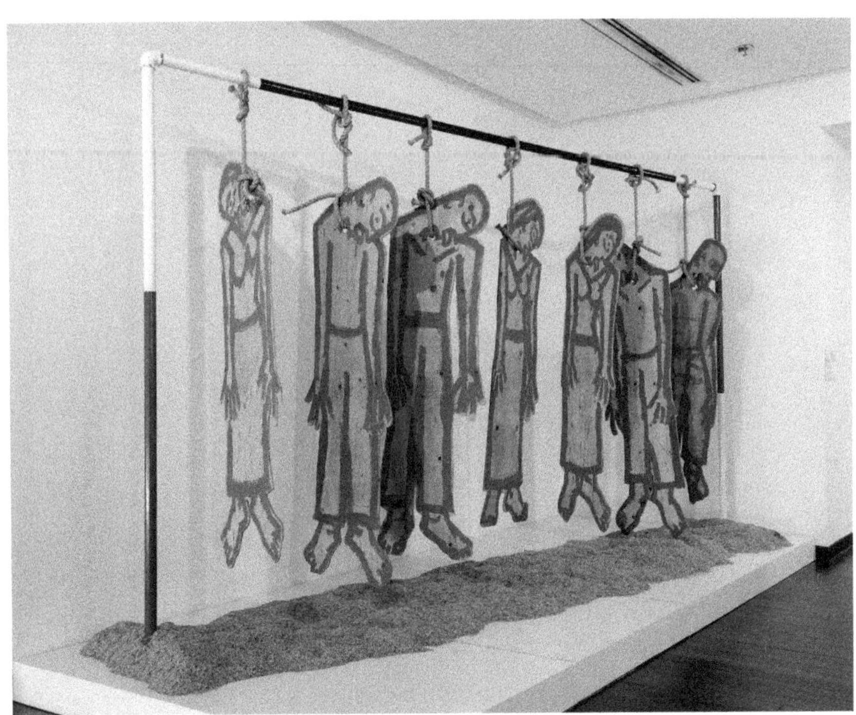

Vasan Sitthiket, *Committing Suicide Culture, The Only Way Thai Farmers Escape Debt*, 1995. Installation. Collection: Singapore Art Museum.   **2.7**

the family's fortunes changed when his father was conscripted to serve with the Royal Thai Army contingent in the Korean War, and was trained as a medical practitioner. His mother also changed from being a worker in the family's paddy fields to a trained nurse when, during his father's absence, a woman philanthropist intervened to support her education. Their improved financial status enabled Sitthiket to study at the College of Fine Art in the capital, which we can assume provided him the educational and social capital that is typically part of the activist experience.

The roots of his anarchism can be found in the nonconformist 1970s, when Sitthiket came of age. This was a highly volatile political moment, when Thailand was still establishing itself as a constitutional monarchy. The revolution of 1932 had brought about the overthrow of absolute rule, but it was followed by decades of turbulence, and many military coups.[98] Sitthiket grew up, therefore, and began his career as an artist and an activist, in what Poshyananda describes as 'an era full of oppression, alienation, and angst'.[99] He also experienced what Iola Lenzi describes as 'one of Thailand's most demented examples of state-sponsored butchery',[100] the Hok Tulaa massacre of 6 October 1976. On

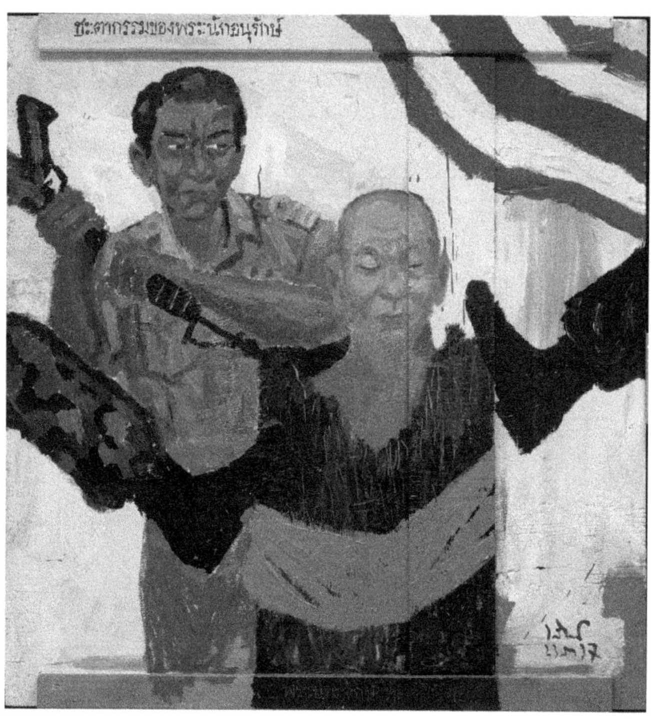

2.8 Vasan Sitthiket, *Fate of the Conservationist Monk* (from '*Nature is dying*' series), 1994. Collection: Queensland Art Gallery. The Kenneth and Yasuko Myer Collection of Contemporary Asian Art. Purchased 1994 with funds from The Myer Foundation and Michael Sidney Myer through the Queensland Art Gallery Foundation.

that day, thousands of students gathered at Thammasat University to protest against the return to Thailand of Thanon Kittikachorn, the military dictator ousted by student protests in 1973. The official forces – elements of the military and police, aided by right-wing militia – responded with extraordinary violence. The official death count is forty-six students, but the actual number of students killed, apart from those who were injured, sexually assaulted and humiliated, may be far higher.[101] Sitthiket later said this experience 'made me focus on politics. Previously, I was interested in Buddhism and believed that suffering was only in our mind. But the massacre made me understand that those who are in power are the ones who make us suffer.'[102]

As the 1970s drew to a close, Poshyananda writes, 'the political climate became calmer'. This heralded a change not only in violent street demonstrations, but also in art practice, he continues, noting that 'there was a shift in contemporary art in the late 1970s and early 1980s towards abstraction and traditional themes'.[103] Sitthiket, however, has remained committed to an art

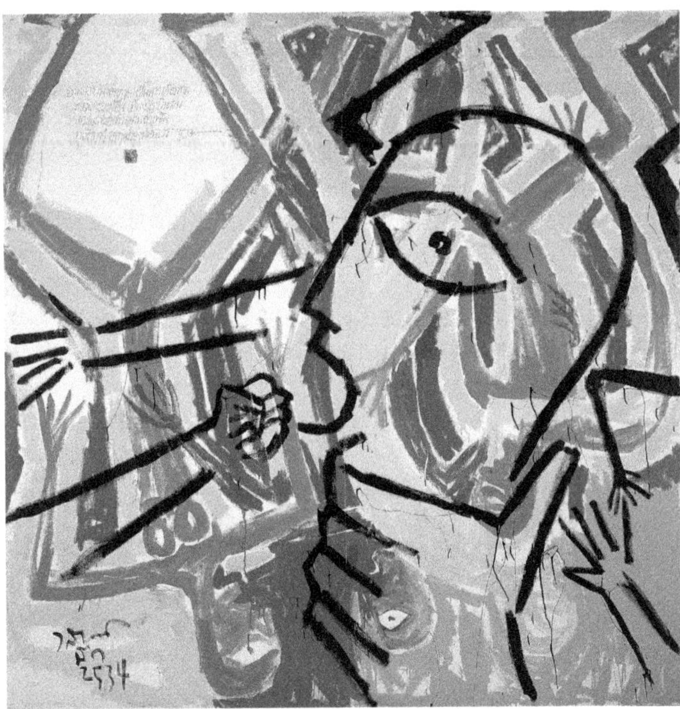

Vasan Sitthiket, *Sinners are weapon merchants; who profit from suffering and*   **2.9**
devastation. Their heads will be hanged down in cave of conflagration; hitting each
other to death (from *'Inferno'* series), 1991. Collection: Queensland Art Gallery. Gift
of Peera Ditbunjong through the Queensland Art Gallery Foundation 2005. Donated
through the Australian Government's Cultural Gifts Program.

which is polemic, anti-imperialist and on the side of the masses. He continues
to be involved in political demonstrations in Thailand, protesting against the
role of elites in Thai society, and – at the time of writing – opposing the return
of populist former Prime Minister Thaksin Shinawatra. But he also denounced
the military coup that toppled Thaksin in 2006. Jørn Middelborg, Director
of Thavibu Gallery in Bangkok, notes, 'It can be difficult to pin him down
since he turns against anyone in power and he loathes the hypocritical ways
of politicians and bureaucrats, as well as of business leaders and "capitalists".
He seems to be an anarchist at heart.'[104] With this comes a tendency to produce
what Lenzi describes as 'often bluntly wielded, bawdy sexual and scatological
iconography', although, she also insists, his 'pictorial language can be as meta-
phorically complex, lyrical and conceptually elegant as it can [be] literal …
Doubtless less discussed than its sometimes provocative thrust and shocking
imagery, is the visual splendour of Vasan's art, arguably beholden, at its core, to

classical South East Asian aesthetic tradition combined with a rigorous mastery of form.'[105] John Clark writes of Sitthiket's work that it is 'often crude and proclamatory in a way that has sometimes left little room to discern whether the artist was propagandising a cause or propagandising himself as the cause'. He does, however, point out that 'in the late 1990s, at no probable benefit to himself, he was willing to name political murders for what they were.'[106]

Certainly his work can at times seem closer to propaganda than to art. But, as Clark notes, Sitthiket has been unafraid to speak out against oppression and to remind viewers of that massacre; and he has continued to make and exhibit art despite the censorship he has faced. Curator Steven Pettifor notes, too, that Sitthiket's direct intervention in political matters is rare in Thailand, where 'domestic audiences are more used to seeing local practitioners deliver their art with a non-confronting sensibility and a certain degree of self-censorship. Therefore Vasan's accessible critical wit is considered appallingly close to the mark and unrivalled by other contemporary Thai artists.'[107]

Sitthiket had his first solo exhibition, *Time: Fate of the urbanite*, at the Ruang Puang Art Community Centre in Bangkok, in 1984. He has exhibited since then in many exhibitions, including internationally, and been collected by the National Art Gallery of Thailand, the Museum of Modern Art in New York, the Queensland Art Gallery and the Singapore Art Museum. He is also known as a poet. His oeuvre includes a remarkable variety of mediums: oil and acrylic painting, sculpture, ceramics, wood-cut, performance, staging three plays, video, installation, impassioned speeches, song, books of poetry, political polemics and – perhaps unexpectedly – children's books.[108] Sitthiket exhibited internationally first in Japan, but it was with his work in the ninth Biennale of Sydney 1992 and at the first Asia-Pacific Triennial of Contemporary Art (APT) in Brisbane in 1993 that he achieved major international attention. His contribution to the APT was two enormous paintings, *Resurrection* and *Buddha returns to Bangkok '92*.[109] The first depicted the resurrected Christ using his cross to smash symbols of global capitalism, like the World Bank, the Bank of Tokyo and the Bank of America. The second work, *Buddha returns to Bangkok '92*, a response to the Black May 1992 protests in which at least fifty-two demonstrators were killed by the military, was extremely confrontational. It depicts the Lord Buddha with one hand in the Bhumisparsa mudra, summoning the earth goddess Sthvara to bear witness to his awakening, and the other in the Abhaya mudra, conveying reassurance, blessing and the injunction 'Do not fear', all most appropriate to the setting which is crammed with images of decadence and disgrace, and the Chao Praya River, on which Bangkok is situated, choked with garbage and industrial waste. A green three-headed monitor lizard symbolising the bringers of misfortune bears the faces of Generals Suchinda Kraprayoon and Issarapong Noonpakdee and Air Chief Marshal Kaset Rojananin, the disgraced leaders of the coup in 1991 in which as many as 750 protestors were reported to have been killed. Other characters in the scene include politicians, a young woman dressed only in a traditional conical head-dress and, as the ultimate provocation, one monk raping a girl and another monk masturbating.

This is particularly shocking in the Thai context, where Buddhism infuses the work of contemporary art. One example is the contemplative and refined meditative installation of ceramic bells and a gold lotus bud created by Montien Boonma for the same exhibition – the first APT in 1993. Almost 95 per cent of Thais are officially Theravada Buddhist, and though there is no formal state religion, Buddhism pervades every aspect of Thai life. Some negative reaction to *Buddha returns to Bangkok '92* was thus inevitable in Thailand and no doubt expected, not least because, as Sasanka Perera observed, it was 'commenting in a very graphic and easily communicable manner [Sitthiket's] own thoughts on the events surrounding the 1992 coup in Thailand.'[110]

A Thai newspaper ensured that reaction to the work would be negative by publishing only a detail from the painting, showing the rape. 'Forty-three Buddhist organizations were so angry, and condemned me to death as a penalty,' Sitthiket recalled; 'Lucky for me, my friend went to meet their leader and showed them a full copy of my work, so they understood that I didn't attempt to destroy and insult Buddhism, but had tried to attack the fake monk.'[111] Though he insists that he respects religious freedom, Sitthiket insists on the right to call any oppressive or corrupt institution to account. But he acknowledges there are risks in challenging power: 'I am an artist who criticizes vulgar power. If I am in a Muslim system, maybe they will cut off my hands or head. But as an activist, I stand beside the poor.'[112]

His fury against those persons and institutions that he regards as violators of human rights has continued and even accelerated in recent years. *Buddha returns* was followed in 1994 by a solo exhibition, *Nature is Dying*, at the Bangkok Art Gallery, and in 1996 by *With Love and Hate* at the Art Forum Gallery, Bangkok. In the same year he showed the arresting *Blue October* series, which commemorates the Hok Tulaa massacre, in what Iola Lenzi describes as a 'frigid blue', 'numbing, terse and nearly detached vision' of that atrocity.[113] *Blue October* is clearly one of the artist's most important series, with none of the crudeness observed by some critics in others of his works. It shows a restrained aesthetic approach, offering perhaps a tiny aperture of hope of a reformed and more just society beyond the events it depicts (see Plate 3). As Lenzi eloquently puts it, the paintings in this series

> are also intensely beautiful in their icy execution and pathos for the victims, immortalized for ever. His formal treatment blurring to a certain extent the distinction between thug and victim (the latter adorned with small patches of gold leaf, badges of merit-cum-martyrdom), the artist eschews the polarization between good and evil habitually present in his work, so avoiding facilely righteous moral judgment.[114]

This is in direct contrast to many of his other works, which constitute a frontal assault on corruption and oppression. Sitthiket's exhibition *What's in our Head* (2000) included fifty paintings of Thai politicians and high-ranking military officers in sexually compromising poses, and the ritual lynching of forty-nine dummies of Prime Minister Chuan Leekpai and his cabinet. It was perhaps not surprisingly cancelled by the Chulalongkorn University Art Center five days before it was scheduled to open. Sitthiket was nonetheless chosen to represent Thailand at the Venice Biennale in 2003. His contribution there was a series of large-scale portraits of US President George W. Bush and other world leaders as a critical commentary on the Iraq War of April–May that year. In March he had visited Baghdad, and met with ordinary Iraqis as well as political leaders. He concluded that the invasion of Iraq was 'an atrocious act of American imperialism, never to be forgotten from the memory of humanity',[115] and responded with the impassioned works in *The Red Planet*, a series of paintings using blood red, including one of George Bush trampling on an Iraqi child, and showing the horrors of war and the violence of power. Art writer and curator Carla Bianpoen observes: 'He wants people to feel the horror in his canvases and feel the anger he feels … He is a master of simple images that render a sense of helpless desolation.'[116] He does not remain in helpless desolation though. Recently Sitthiket has opened a new space for political artists in Bangkok, Rebel Art Space, to nurture other rebellious artists.[117] He insists that '[a]n artist's duty is documenting today's society. We should record the suffering of unknown people', not least because: 'Reform might sound utopian, but it's better than doing nothing.'[118]

Conclusion

There is a significant history of artists, across the world, involving themselves in cultural activism. These three artists are among the trailblazers of activist art in the Asian region, and can count among their antecedents the members of the revolutionary avant garde – the Dadaists, the Surrealists and the Situationists. They, and many other artists in their region and beyond, subscribe to a view of art in contemporary society as a domain that is capable of challenging and changing perceptions of the world, and of producing a counter-narrative that interrupts the usual discourse, and offers an alternative point of view. The objective of all three artists is to use their art to call for the creation of a more just world and, to this extent, all are activists, bringing together activism and art in an effort to achieve both political change and social justice.

Activism is largely 'a struggle to convey dissident viewpoints, truth claims, and alternative significations to the public by making use of the means to which activists are able to gain access.'[119] Though none of these artists has substantial resources of economic capital, they are rich in the sort of resources that are particularly useful to capture attention, and engender in their audiences both the experience of agency and a sense of collective responsibility.[120] These resources include their capacity to shock and to charm; to use humour and anger; to encourage thought; and to mobilise others to action. Though art audiences can seem to engage only in spectatorship, Jacques Rancière argues convincingly that this is itself a mode of active engagement. It involves the work of translating what is being looked at, and is therefore capable of generating the sorts of personal change that may lead ultimately to social and political change. He urges that

> we dismiss the opposition between looking and acting and understand that the distribution of the visible itself is part of the configuration of domination and subjection. [Emancipation] starts when we realize that looking is also an action that confirms or modifies that distribution, and that 'interpreting the world' is already a means of transforming it.[121]

The artists we discuss in this chapter consistently capture their audiences through humour, empathy or shock, and through the beauty of the works they exhibit. They also consistently interpret the world, engaging not only with aesthetic traditions, media or imagery, but with ways of looking, and of reconfiguring the patterns of 'domination and subjection'. This is a significant part of the work of many Asian artists of the late twentieth century: a cohort of practitioners who, in their creative work and in their lives as citizens, 'reflect and express a resistant way of thinking, acting, and being. They are the Culture of a resistant culture.'[122]

Notes

1   Terry Smith, 'Contemporary Art in Transition: From Late Modern Art to Now', *Global Art and the Museum*, ZKM | Center for Art and Media Karlsruhe (December 2010), www.globalartmuseum.de/site/guest_author/298, accessed 12 March 2011.

2   Smith, 'Contemporary Art in Transition'.

3   Pippa Norris, 'Political Activism: New Challenges, New Opportunities', in Carles Boix and Susan Stokes (eds), *The Oxford Handbook of Comparative Politics* (Oxford: Oxford University Press, 2009), pp. 628–49: 629.

4   Begüm Özden Firat and Aylin Kuryel (eds), *Thamyris/Intersecting – Cultural Activism: Practices, Dilemmas and Possibilities* (Amsterdam: Rodopi, 2010), p. 11.

5   Muthiah Alagappa, 'The Nonstate Public Sphere in Asia: Dynamic Growth, Institutionalization Lag', in Muthiah Alagappa (ed.), *Civil Society and Political Change in Asia: Expanding and Contracting Democratic Space* (Stanford, CA: Stanford University Press, 2004), pp. 455–77: 459.

6 Dayana Parvanova and Melanie Pichler, 'Activism and Social Movements in South-East Asia', *Austrian Journal of South-East Asian Studies*, 6:1 (2013), pp. 1–6.

7 Alagappa, 'Nonstate Public Sphere', p. 467.

8 Kuan-Hsing Chen (ed.), *Trajectories: Inter-Asia Cultural Studies* (London: Routledge, 1998).

9 Gavin Grindon, 'The Notion of Irony in Cultural Activism', in Firat and Kuryel (eds), *Thamyris/Intersecting*, pp. 21–34.

10 James Jasper, *The Art of Moral Protest: Culture, Biography, and Creativity in Social Movements* (Chicago: University of Chicago Press, 1997), p. 97.

11 Jacques Rancière, *Dissensus: On Politics and Aesthetics*, trans. Steven Corcoran (London: Continuum, 2010), p. 141.

12 Benedict Anderson, *The Spectre of Comparisons: Nationalism, Southeast Asia, and the World* (New York: Verso, 1998).

13 Apinan Poshyananda, 'The Development of Contemporary Art in Thailand: Traditionalism in Reverse', in Turner (ed.), *Tradition and Change*, pp. 93–106: 99.

14 Lekha J. Shankar, 'An Artist at War', *Asiaweek* (20 October 2000), www-cgi.cnn.com/ASIANOW/asiaweek/magazine/2000/1020/as.art.html, accessed 21 August 2013.

15 Apinan Poshyananda, 'Thailand', *The First Asia-Pacific Triennial of Contemporary Art* (Brisbane: Queensland Art Gallery, 1993), pp. 46–52: 52.

16 Pheng Cheah, *Inhuman Conditions: On Cosmopolitanism and Human Rights* (Cambridge, MA: Harvard University Press, 2006).

17 Pnina Werbner, *Anthropology and the New Cosmopolitanism: Rooted, Feminist and Vernacular Perspectives* (London: Berg, 2008), p. 2.

18 Werbner, *Anthropology and the New Cosmopolitanism*, p. 12.

19 Steven Vertovec and Robin Cohen (eds), *Conceiving Cosmopolitanism: Theory, Context and Practice* (Oxford: Oxford University Press, 2002), p. 1.

20 Cheah, *Inhuman Conditions*, p. 3.

21 Anthony J. Langlois, *The Politics of Justice and Human Rights: Southeast Asia and Universalist Theory* (Cambridge: Cambridge University Press, 2001), p. 160.

22 Krishen Jit, *Krishen Jit: An Uncommon Position* (Singapore: Contemporary Asian Arts Centre, 2003).

23 Ooi Kok Chuen, 'Rebel with a Cause', *The Star Online* (24 September 2006), www.thestar.com.my/Story/?file=%2F2006%2F9%2F24%2Flifearts%2F15508106&sec=lifearts, accessed 12 February 2014.

24 Beverly Yong, *Wong Hoy Cheong: An OVA Touring Exhibition 2002–2003* (Kuala Lumpur: Valentine Willie Art and OVA Organisation for Visual Arts UK, 2002), p. 9.

25 Andrew Maerkle, 'Complicit Consciousness: Wong Hoy Cheong', *Art IT* (30 May 2011), www.art-it.asia/u/admin_ed_feature_e/o3xMiH2K1mrAIZ6l8oDO/, accessed 12 August 2012.

26 Wong Hoy Cheong, correspondence with the authors, 2014.

27 Ooi Kok Chuen, 'There's Art in Growing Lalang', *New Straits Times* (3 September 1994), p. 15.

28 Wong, correspondence with the authors, 2014.

29 Maerkle, 'Complicit Consciousness'.

30 Robert Putnam, *Bowling Alone: The Collapse and Revival of American Community* (New York: Simon & Schuster, 2000).

31 Pattie, Charles, Patrick Seyd and Paul Whiteley, 'Citizenship and Civic Engagement: Attitudes and Behaviour in Britain', *Political Studies*, 51:3 (2003), pp. 443–68: 445–6.

32 Malaysia has a federal system of democratic government and is a constitutional monarchy. It has not experienced the dictatorships of some other nations in the region. Nevertheless, most commentators note that Malaysia incorporates a mix of democratic and authoritarian characteristics; see Harold Crouch, *Government and Society in Malaysia* (Ithaca, NY: Cornell University Press, 1996). A number of high-profile cases, including the Anwar Ibrahim trial, have raised issues related to justice and even human rights.

33 Sonia Kolesnikov-Jessop (2004), 'Dissenters on Display', *Newsweek* (19 December 2004) http://www.newsweek.com/dissenters-display-123083 (accessed 8 June 2015).

34 Jacqueline Lo, *Staging Nation: English Language Theatre in Malaysia and Singapore* (Hong Kong: Hong Kong University Press, 2004), p. 174.

35 Maerkle, 'Complicit Consciousness'.

36 Redza Piyadasa, 'Modern Malaysian Art, 1945–1991: A Historical Overview', in Turner (ed.), *Tradition and Change*, pp. 58–71: 58.

37 Piyadasa, 'Modern Malaysian Art', p. 68.

38 Department of Statistics, Malaysia Official Website (2014), www.statistics.gov.my/portal/index.php?lang=en, accessed 13 January 2014.

39 Piyadasa, 'Modern Malaysian Art', p. 64.

40 Krishen Jit, 'Wong Hoy Cheong', *Second Asia-Pacific Triennial* (Brisbane: Queensland Art Gallery, 1996), p. 107.

41 Correspondence with the artist 3 April 2015. The artist has noted in this correspondence with the authors regarding the issues of race and ethnicity that in his discussion of his work *Doghole* at the Guggenheim, he especially highlighted both human resilience and the irrelevance of race in such circumstances as war. His father had been imprisoned by the Japanese but he had been arrested by 'two Chinese', saved from execution by a 'Japanese', fed by a 'Gurkha' and, despite his wartime experiences, he greatly appreciated Japanese culture.

42 Judith Rugg, *Exploring Site-Specific Art: Issues of Space and Internationalism* (London: I.B.Tauris, 2010), p. 94.

43 Rugg, *Exploring Site-Specific Art*, p. 92. On Wong's art see also Michelle Antoinette, 'The Art of Race: Rethinking Malaysian Identity Through the Art of Wong Hoy Cheong', in Daniel P. S. Goh, Matilda Gabrielpillai, Philip Holden and Gaik Cheng Khoo (eds), *Race and Multiculturalism in Malaysia and Singapore* (London: Routledge, 2009), pp. 200–12. See also Michelle Antoinette, *Reworlding*

Art History: Encounters with Contemporary Southeast Asian Art after 1990 (Amsterdam: Brill/Rodopi 2014), pp.136–55; pp. 330–41.

44 Guggenheim Collection Online, 'Wong Hoy Cheong' (2014), www.guggenheim.org/new-york/collections/collection-online/artists/bios/11634, accessed 2 January 2014.

45 Sumit Mandal, 'Valuing Asia: Wong Hoy Cheong's Quest for a Post-colonial Visual Vocabulary', *ArtAsiaPacific*, 29 (2000), pp. 73–77: 73.

46 Yong, *Wong Hoy Cheong*, p. 23.

47 Yong, *Wong Hoy Cheong*, p. 23.

48 Yong, *Wong Hoy Cheong*, p. 12.

49 See Michael Jacobsen and Ole Bruun (eds), *Human Rights and Asian Values: Contesting National Identities and Cultural Representations in Asia* (Richmond: Curzon, 2000).

50 For a discussion of victimhood in relation to colonialism and its continuing reverberations in Asia, see Manjari Chatterjee Miller, *Wronged by Empire: Colonial Memories and Victimhood in Indian and Chinese Foreign Policy* (Stanford: Stanford University Press, 2013).

51 Hou Hanru, 'Wrapping up History: Interview with Wong Hoy Cheong', *Flash Art*, 263 (November–December 2008), www.flashartonline.com/interno.php?pagina=articolo_det&id_art=275&det=ok&title=WONG-HOY-CHEONG, accessed 4 August 2011.

52 Maerkle, 'Complicit Consciousness'.

53 Hou Hanru, 'Wrapping up History'.

54 Wong Hoy Cheong, interview with authors, 2014.

55 Hou Hanru, 'Wrapping up History'.

56 Wong Hoy Cheong, interview with authors, 2014.

57 The Communist Party had been legal under President Sukarno, and was the largest in Asia after the CCP and third largest in the world.

58 Ariel Heryanto, *State Terrorism and Political Identity in Indonesia: Fatally Belonging* (London: Routledge, 2006), p. 9.

59 Dadang Christanto, conversation with Caroline Turner, 2002.

60 Anthony Reid, 'The Concept of Freedom in Indonesia', in David Kelly and Anthony Reid (eds), *Asian Freedoms: The Idea of Freedom in East and Southeast Asia* (Cambridge: Cambridge University Press, 1998), pp. 141–60: 155.

61 Indonesia today has the fourth largest population in the world. Over 85 per cent are Muslim, but 'traditional' belief-systems, Hinduism and Buddhism have influenced the nation culturally and Christianity is officially recognised. See Syed A. Hayat, 'Indonesian Global Expansion: A Case Study', *International Journal of Global Business*, 7:2 (December 2014), pp. 9–33.

62 Jim Supangkat, 'Art and Politics in Indonesia', and Caroline Turner, 'Indonesia: Art, Freedom, Human Rights and Engagement with the West', in Caroline Turner (ed.), *Art and Social Change: Contemporary Art in Asia and the Pacific* (Canberra: Pandanus Books, 2005), pp. 218–28; pp. 196–217; Astri Wright, *Soul, Spirit and Mountain: Preoccupations of Contemporary Indonesian Painters* (Kuala

Lumpur: Oxford University Press, 1994); and Cecelia Levin, 'Unity in Diversity: The Formation of Modern Indonesian Art', *ArtAsiaPacific*, 59 (July/August 2008).

63 See Dadang Christanto, Hendro Wiyanto and Bentara Budaya Jakarta, *Kengerian tak Terucapkan=The Unspeakable Horror* (Darwin, NT: Dadang Christanto, 2002).

64 Hermawan Sulistyo, 'The Forgotten Years: The Missing History of Indonesia's Mass Slaughter (Jombang-Kedin)' (PhD thesis, Arizona State University, 1997).

65 Tessa Morris-Suzuki, *The Past Within Us: Media, Memory, History* (New York: Verso, 2005), p. 8.

66 Laine Berman, 'The Art of Street Politics in Indonesia', in T. Lindsey and H. O'Neill (eds), *Awas! Recent Art from Indonesia* (Melbourne: Indonesian Arts Society, 1999), pp. 75–84.

67 Jörgen Hellman, *Performing the Nation: Cultural Politics in New Order Indonesia* (Copenhagen: Nordic Institute of Asian Studies, 2003), p. 29.

68 Hellman, *Performing the Nation*, p. 182, n. 7. The visual artist Moelyono also did an installation work about this case: see M. Taufiqurrahman, 'Moelyono: The Arts and Social responsibility', *Jakarta Post* (3 February 2006), www.thejakartapost. com/news/2006/02/03/moelyono-arts-and-social-responsibility.html, accessed 24 September 2014.

69 Helena Spanjaard, 'Reformasi Indonesia! Protest Art, 1995–2000', *IIAS Newsletter*, 20, (1999), www.iias.nl/iiasn/23/asianart/23ART2.html, accessed 27 August 2011.

70 Rizki A. Zaelani, 'The Change Interpreted: Dadang Christanto' *CP Biennale* (2003), http://biennale.cp-foundation.org/2003/bio_dadang_christanto.html, accessed 12 February 2012.

71 In particular the notes referred to the death in police custody a few weeks before the exhibition opened of a young Aboriginal dancer, Daniel Yok. The discussion of Christanto's art that follows is based on extensive interviews 1992–2015 by Caroline Turner, who selected Christanto's work for the 1993 and 1999 Asia-Pacific Triennial exhibitions and curated his 2010 retrospective. The revelation of his own family's history was made by the artist to Christine Clark in 2003: Christine Clark, 'Keeper of Memories', in Caroline Turner and Nancy Sever (eds), *Witnessing to Silence: Art and Human Rights* (Canberra: Drill Hall Gallery and School of Art Gallery, Australian National University, 2003), pp. 52–5.

72 Dadang Christanto, conversation with Caroline Turner, 2005.

73 Marsha Meskimmon, 'Response and Responsibility: On the Cosmo-politics of Generosity in Contemporary Asian Art', in Michelle Antoinette and Caroline Turner (eds), *Contemporary Asian Art and Exhibitions: Connectivities and World-Making* (Canberra: ANU Press, 2015), pp. 143–58.

74 Dadang Christanto, conversation with Caroline Turner, 2011.

75 Rosalie Higson, 'Interview with Dadang Christanto', *The Australian* (17 October 2003), p. 15.

76 Dadang Christanto, cited in Mireille Vignol, 'Asia-Pacific Triennial 3: Multimedia Arts Asia Pacific', *ABC Arts: Postcards* (1999), www.abc.net.au/arts/headspace/ postcards/vignol/vig_day.5.htm, accessed 18 May 2005.

77 Conversation with Caroline Turner, 10 November 2009.

78 Marsha Meskimmon, *Contemporary Art and the Cosmopolitan Imagination* (London: Routledge, 2010), p. 8.

79 Kathryn Robinson, *Gender, Islam and Democracy in Indonesia* (London: Routledge, 2009), p. 3.

80 Caroline Turner and Nancy Sever (eds), *Dadang Christanto: Wounds in our Heart* (Canberra: Drill Hall Gallery, ANU, 2010).

81 Anderson, *The Spectre of Comparisons*, p. 294.

82 Caroline Turner, 'Wounds in Our Heart: Identity and Social Justice in the Art of Dadang Christanto', in Kathryn Robinson (ed.), *Asian and Pacific Cosmopolitans: Self and Subject in Motion* (New York: Palgrave Macmillan, 2007), pp. 77–99.

83 Higson, 'Interview with Dadang Christanto'.

84 Dadang Christanto, conversation with Caroline Turner, 2011.

85 Originally on Buru island, a prison camp treated by Wong Hoy Cheong in an art work.

86 See Garry Rodan (ed.), *Political Oppositions in Industrialising Asia* (London: Routledge, 1996); Garry Rodan and Caroline Hughes, *The Politics of Accountability in Southeast Asia: The Dominance of Moral Ideologies* (Oxford: Oxford University Press, 2014).

87 Yun Fan, 'Taiwan: No Civil Society, No Democracy', in Muthiah Alagappa (ed.), *Civil Society and Political Change in Asia*, pp. 164–90: 168.

88 Dadang Christanto, 'Interview with *Suara Merdeka*', trans. Angie Bexley, *Suara Merdeka* (10 July 2005), p. 23.

89 Loredano Pazzini-Paracciani, 'Twenty-First Century Thai Art Practices: Common Themes and Methodologies', *Working Paper Series #181* (Singapore: Asia Research Institute, National University of Singapore, 2012), p. 3.

90 Apinan Poshyananda, 'The Development of Contemporary Art of Thailand: Traditionalism in Reverse', in Caroline Turner (ed.), *Tradition and Change: Contemporary Art of Asia and the Pacific* (St Lucia: University of Queensland Press, 1993), pp. 93–106: 102, 100.

91 Richard S. Ehrlich, 'Vasan Sitthiket, Thailand's "anarchist" artist', *CNN Travel* (28 January 2010), http://travel.cnn.com/bangkok/none/vasan-sitthiket-thailands-anarchist-artist-019899, accessed 20 August 2011.

92 See David Goodway, *Anarchist Seeds Beneath the Snow: Left-Libertarian Thought and British Writers from William Morris to Colin Ward* (Liverpool: Liverpool University Press, 2006); Allan Antliff, *Anarchy and Art: From the Paris Commune to the Fall of the Berlin Wall* (Vancouver: Arsenal Pulp Press, 2007); Josh MacPhee and Erik Reuland (eds), *Realizing the Impossible: Art Against Authority* (Oakland, CA: AK Press, 2007).

93 Michael Scrivener, 'The Anarchist Aesthetic', *Black Rose*, 1:1 (1979), pp. 7–21.

94 Richard Sonn, *Sex, Violence, and the Avant-garde: Anarchism in Interwar France* (University Park: Pennsylvania State University Press, 2010), p. 8.

95 Julia Kristeva, 'The Revolt of Mallarmé', in Robert Greer Cohn and Gerald Gillespie (eds), *Mallarmé in the Twentieth Century* (Cranbury, NJ and London: Associated University Presses, 1998), pp. 31–53: 48.

96 Shankar, 'An Artist at War'.

97 Vasan Sitthiket, 'No Future', *Rama IX Art Museum: The Website of Thai Modern and Contemporary Art* (2012), www.rama9art.org/vasan/, accessed 8 September 2014.

98 Nicholas Farrelly, 'Counting Thailand's Coups', *New Mandala* (8 March 2011), http://asiapacific.anu.edu.au/newmandala/2011/03/08/counting-thailands-coups/, accessed 20 August 2011.

99 Poshyananda, 'The Development of Contemporary Art of Thailand: Traditionalism in Reverse', p. 98.

100 Iola Lenzi, 'Art Warfare: Vasan Sitthiket's Red Planet', *Offsite*, Valentine Willie Fine Art (2008), www.vwfa.net/sg/offsiteDetail.php?oid=46, accessed 20 August 2011.

101 Bryce Beemer, 'Bangkok Postcard: Forgetting and Remembering "Hok Tulaa". The October 6 Massacre', *Explorations in Southeast Asian Studies*, 1:1 (Spring 1997), pp. 1–12.

102 Monruedee Jansuttipan, 'Artist and Activist Vasan Sitthiket on Reforming Thailand', *BK: Bangkok Online* (16 January 2014), http://bk.asia-city.com/city-living/article/vasan-sitthiket-thai-artist-real-democracy, accessed 20 January 2014.

103 Poshyananda, 'The Development of Contemporary Art', p. 99.

104 Jørn Middelborg, 'Foreword', in *Vasan Sitthiket: Hypocrisy* (Bangkok: Thavibu Gallery, 2012), p. 5.

105 Lenzi, 'Art Warfare'.

106 John Clark, *Asian Modernities: Chinese and Thai Art Compared 1980 to 1999* (Sydney: Power Publications, 2010), p. 148.

107 Steven Pettifor, *Vasan Sitthiket: Capitalism is Dying!* (Bangkok: Thavibu Gallery, 2009), p. 3.

108 Clark, *Asian Modernities*, p. 182.

109 Anne Kirker notes these works were in the collection of Chulalongkorn University, Bangkok, but were not able to be displayed there because of their contentious nature. See Marjorie Anne Kirker, 'Printmaking as an Expanding Field in Contemporary Art Practice: A Case Study of Japan, Australia and Thailand' (PhD thesis, Queensland University of Technology, Brisbane, 2009), p. 219, n. 494.

110 Sasanka Perera, *Artists Remember; Artists Narrate: Memory and Representation in Contemporary Sri Lankan Visual Arts* (Colombo: Colombo Institute for the Advanced Study of Society and Culture, 2012), p. 15.

111 Ehrlich, 'Vasan Sitthiket'.

112 Ehrlich, 'Vasan Sitthiket'.

113 Lenzi, 'Art Warfare'.

114 Iola Lenzi, 'History and Memory in Thai Contemporary Art', *C-Arts* (November–December 2009), www.mutualart.com/OpenArticle/History-and-Memory-in-Thai-Contemporary-/5646BD3688C41A93, accessed 20 August 2011.

115 *Asian Tribune*, 'George W. Bush and Vasan Sitthiket – The One-Man Army', *Asian Tribune* (3 November 2003), www.asiantribune.com/news/2003/11/03/george-w-bush-and-vasan-sitthiket-%E2%80%93-one-man-army, accessed 4 August 2011.

116 Carla Bianpoen, 'Vasan Sitthiket: Expressing anger through "Red Planet"', *Jakarta Post* (15 March 2008), www.thejakartapost.com/news/2008/03/15/vasan-sitthiket-expressing-anger-through-039red-planet039.html, accessed 4 August 2011.

117 Jansuttipan, 'Artist and Activist Vasan Sitthiket'.

118 Jansuttipan, 'Artist and Activist Vasan Sitthiket'.

119 Emrah Irzik, 'A Proposal for Grounded Cultural Activism: Communication Strategies, Adbusters and Social Change', in Firat and Kuryel (eds), *Thamyris/Intersecting*, pp. 137–56: 137.

120 Claire Bishop (ed.), *Participation* (Cambridge, MA: MIT Press, 2006), p. 12.

121 Jacques Rancière, 'The Emancipated Spectator', *Artforum* (March 2007), http://members.efn.org/~heroux/The-Emancipated-Spectator-.pdf, pp. 271–80: 277.

122 Stephen Duncombe, '(From) Cultural Resistance to Community Development', *Community Development Journal*, 42:4 (2007), pp. 490–500: 491.

Introduction

War, violence and conflict necessarily provide the most extreme occasions for violations of human rights. The world wars of the twentieth century were the most destructive of human life and, in the case of the second world war, of human property, in recorded history. In Asia, the end of that war is also associated with struggles to achieve independence after what had been, in some cases, several centuries of colonial control. Though in most cases this was achieved fairly rapidly, that was not the end of the struggle. The effects of colonialism continued to be felt: in the need to construct a sense of national identity out of what was often a collection of communities arbitrarily combined by colonial governments; in the need to heal the wounds of conflict; and in the need to establish sustained economic and political infrastructure. In the decades following the end of the second world war and, with it, the effective end of colonial rule, several of the nations in this region experienced internal conflict and/or wars with neighbours or with western nations. Korea, Vietnam, Cambodia and Sri Lanka were racked by civil wars; China and Taiwan, India and Pakistan, Cambodia and Vietnam, Indonesia and Malaysia, Indonesia and East Timor, and Thailand and Laos were all involved in border clashes or other conflicts.

Those postcolonial struggles have been extensively treated by writers including Homi Bhabha, Gayatri Spivak, Arjun Appadurai, Kwame Anthony Appiah and Trinh T. Minh-ha, and we will not rehearse them here. What we do pursue in this chapter are the effects of the postcolonial moment on artists in the region. Those effects include the imperative for newly independent nations to find shared language, shared culture, and shared traditions sufficient to form a national community, while addressing the impacts of modernity, postmodernity, and both economic and cultural globalisation.

The first decade of the twenty-first century has been characterised, in Asia and further afield, by a state of constant, if fluctuating, conflict, war and violence. These have, in their turn, produced a continuing flight of refugees, the treatment of whom, according to Costas Douzinas, represents 'the greatest human catastrophe of the twentieth century outside war'.[1] Artists have taken on the challenge to use art as a way to draw attention to the ethical dilemmas involved, and the historiography of war now includes many more analyses of cultural and visual images. The realities of contemporary war worldwide are brought home to more people today through photography, television and the internet; consequently, as Susan Sontag suggests in her analysis of the effect of images of pain and violence, war has become terrifyingly 'normal'.[2]

In Asia such conflicts have arisen mainly from dissensions within societies that have emerged from what Ronald H. Spector has termed 'the ruins of empire':[3] British, French, Belgian, Dutch, Portuguese, Japanese and latterly Soviet. This chapter explores how four artists in Asia – Yoshiko Shimada from Japan, Sri Lankan artist Jagath Weerasinghe, Indonesian artist FX Harsono, and Vietnamese artist Dinh Q. Lê – have engaged with such issues in their art.

The work of these artists follows a long tradition of art about war and conflict over the centuries. One early example among many in Asia can be found in the superb reliefs and decorations of the temple complexes at Angkor Wat and Angkor Thom. Dating from the ancient Khmer Empire of the twelfth and thirteen centuries, these include elements that depict the many wars against the Cham peoples. Images of war and conflict, including art that opposes conflict, or depicts wars against former colonial rulers, also appear consistently during the twentieth and twenty-first centuries.[4] This has earlier precedents; for example, in the 1850s, Indonesian aristocrat Raden Saleh, a painter trained in Europe in the styles of Romanticism, depicted the capture by the Dutch, by trickery, of Prince Diponegoro, an event which brought to an end the Java wars of 1825–30. Scholars now agree that his famous painting showed his sympathy for the prince, who is today remembered as an Indonesian anti-colonial and national hero.[5]

More recent wars, such as in Vietnam, have inspired responses from artists in Asia. In Korea the war of 1950–53 has never formally ended despite the cessation of armed conflict in 1953. One harrowing treatment of this topic is Young-Hae Chang Heavy Industries' computer-generated vision of the effects of a nuclear holocaust in a potential new war between the two Koreas.[6] In the Indian subcontinent artists have confronted civil and religious violence and potential conflict, including nuclear conflict, between India and Pakistan, an example being the works of Salima Hashmi and Nalini Malani, discussed in Chapter 5. Japanese artists have been in the forefront of those who have produced images about war and conflict. An example is Yoko Ono, who experienced the firebombing of Tokyo and was deeply affected by the dropping of the atomic bombs on Hiroshima and Nagasaki, and who has been a long-term global peace advocate and activist. Another example of anti-war art from Japan is the *Hiroshima Panels* (1950–82), fifteen folding panels on Japanese rice paper, painted over a period of thirty years by Iri and Toshi Maruki, who were similarly affected by the dropping of the atomic bombs. Nowhere have memories of war been more troubled than in Japan, as we discuss in this chapter, in relation to the art of Yoshiko Shimada.

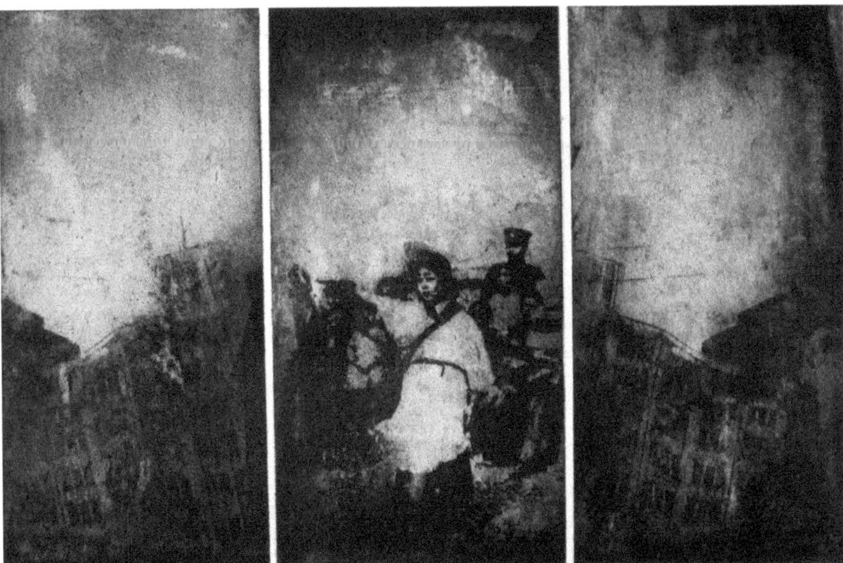

Yoshiko Shimada, *A Woman Shooting*, 1992.   **3.1**

Yoshiko Shimada: recovering history

Yoshiko Shimada is another transnational artist, who has lived and worked not only in her native Tokyo, but also in the US, Germany and Denmark. Born in 1959, she initially completed a BA in Fine Arts at Scripps College in California, and then returned to Tokyo where she studied etching under Katsuro Yoshida. She has since included installation, video and performance in her art practice, and exhibited internationally, including right across Southeast Asia. Her works deal extensively with the wartime history of Japan, its colonial relationship to Korea, and gendered histories of violence.[7] Though she challenges the treatment and the representations of women, she also reflects on women's own investment in the military-nationalist machine of second world war Japan, and states, 'I realised that Japanese women were not entirely voiceless victims of the male-dominated militarism. Many of them were enthusiastic fascists and willing to sacrifice themselves and to victimise others in the name of the Emperor.'[8] Core to her art practice is the work of determining identity, responsibility, and relationship to history. She says, 'For me, art is a tool of self-examination and communication. In order to know who I am (an Asian, a Japanese, a woman), examining the recent past history of Japan and the role of women and what we have done to the people of Asia is unavoidable.'[9]

Shimada challenges what she perceives as the myths and silences around Japanese identity. In a note for a 2000 exhibition she curated at Ota Fine Arts Gallery, *How to Use Women's Body* – an exhibition that Monty DiPietro says contains most of the items that would appear on a list of things taboo in Japan[10] – she acknowledges that 'sexual, national, racial, cultural or whatever' identity has ceased to attract the attention of artists; and that this gives greater weight to the imperative to interrogate historical foundations for identity, and especially to challenge the 'us/them' dichotomy that she observes in Japanese society. 'In this era of globalization,' she writes, 'one's identity is a multi-faced and hybrid one ... Rather than conform to black or white, one can swim through this grey zone, putting on layers of identities.'[11]

But she does not spend much time on personal identity or the 'inner life', reflecting more clearly on national politics and its role in confirming or denying both its recent history and the effects on members of the contemporary community. She has explored this in various ways, perhaps most starkly in *Family Photographs* (2002), a work she produced for the 2002 Gwangju Biennale. This work, made in collaboration with Korean women, was a collection of photographs and personal narratives, the centrepiece of which was a portrait of a Japanese man in military uniform. This, the text revealed, was Shimada's grandfather; she describes how, following the great Kanto earthquake of 1923, he was required to kill a number of Koreans in Tokyo. Her grandfather suffered a breakdown after this, quit the police force and became a farmer. This work, then, exposes a terrible family secret both to bring back into history the treatment of Koreans by Japanese, and to reveal the conscience of Japanese in relation to such actions. Shimada does acknowledge, though, that she has had difficulty in showing this work in Japan.[12] (See Figure 3.2.)

In this and many other exhibitions, her work constitutes what some have seen as a direct assault on conventions, practices, and modes of representation, especially in relation to the role of women and sexuality in society – given her coruscating critiques of the sexual enslavement of comfort women – and in her challenge to history as defended by ultranationalist ideologies. Nowhere in Asia has the memory of war and conflict been so potentially divisive, but in essence largely erased, as it has been in Japan. In the mid-1990s, fifty years after the conclusion of the Pacific War, the Yokohama Museum of Art mounted *Photography in the 1940s*, the only exhibition directly commemorating that decade. Curator Julia Thomas writes that, though it was a courageous act to install this exhibition, the photographs selected did little to revise history or restore memory. Thomas asks:

> Where were the pictures of Koreans, South Asians, Okinawans, Nazis, Jews, Russians, Chinese, and many others who might have complicated the neat oppositions on which this bifurcated tale rested? Where were Japan's leaders, Japan's soldiers, and the occupying Americans? These invisible images crowded the blank spaces on the museum walls.[13]

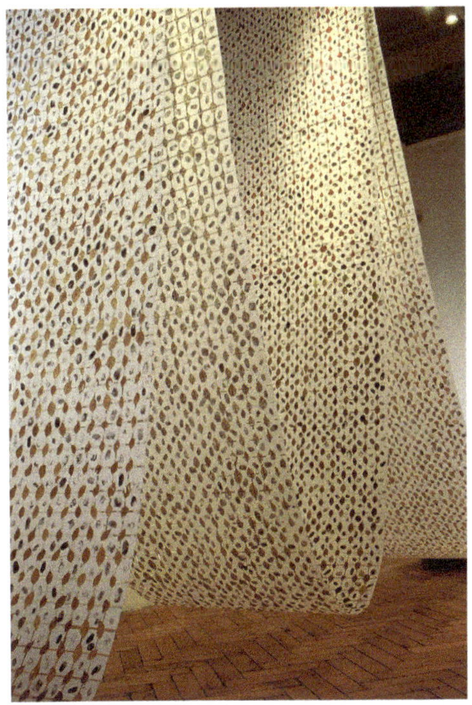

Plate 1 Wong Hoy Cheong, *Tapestry of Justice*, 1998.

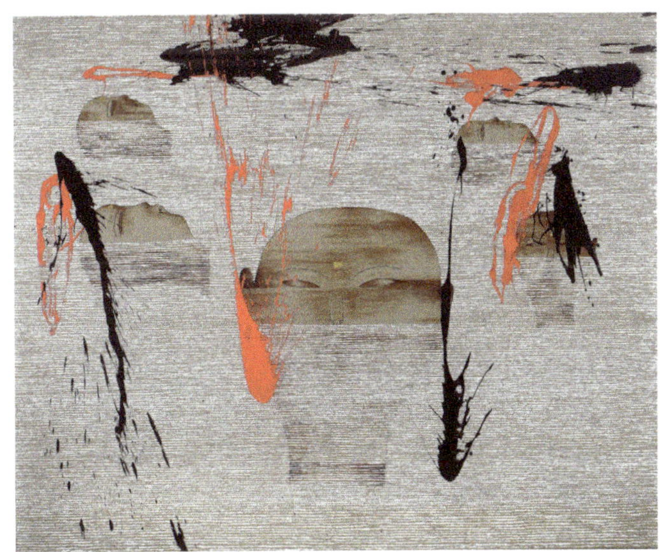

Plate 2 Dadang Christanto, *The water flows far away* ('River' series), 2009.

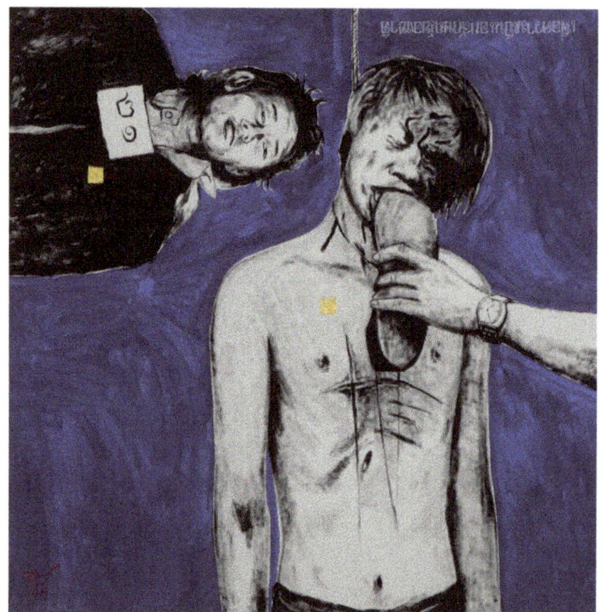

Plate 3 Vasan Sitthiket, *For the Nation's Identity* (from the '*Blue October*' series), 1996.

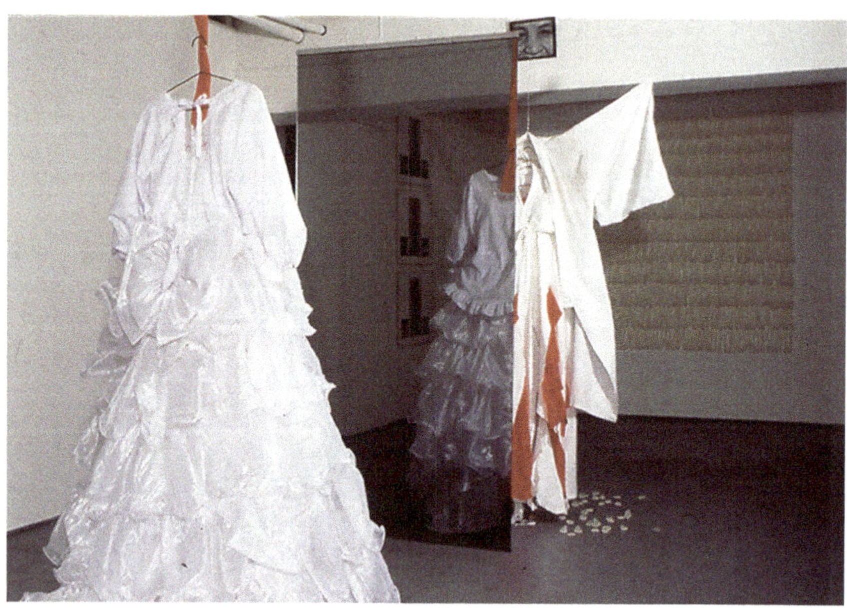

Plate 4 Yoshiko Shimada, *Look at Me/Look at You*, 1995. Exhibition view: Ota Fine Arts, Tokyo, 1995.

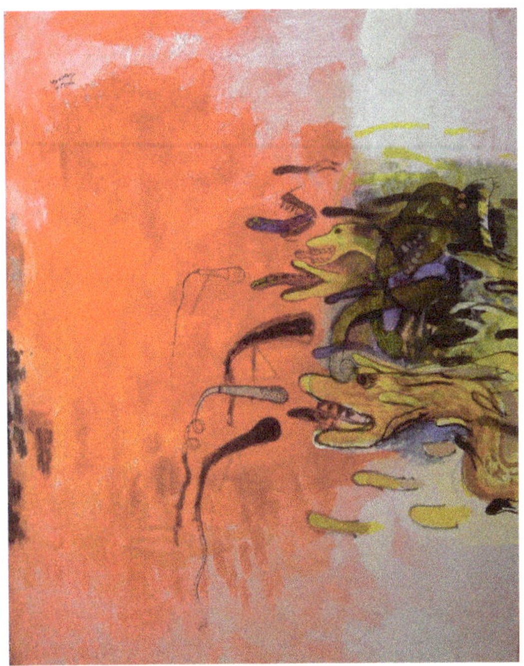

Plate 5 Jagath Weerasinghe, *Snakes and Mikes*, 2005.

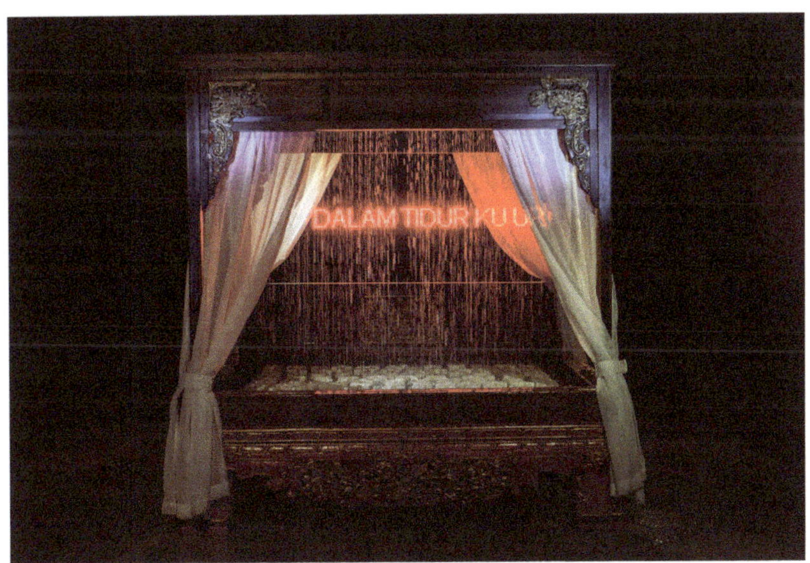

Plate 6 FX Harsono, *The Raining Bed (Ranjang Hujan)*, 2013.

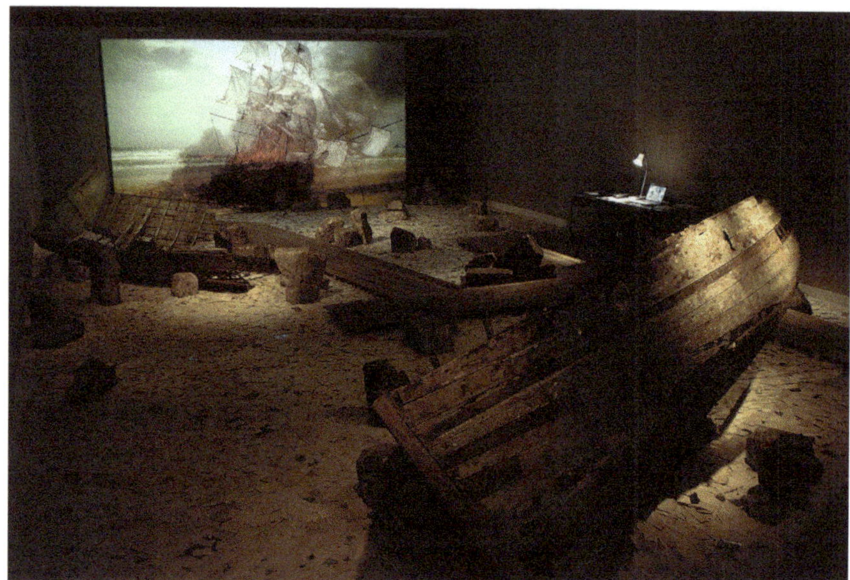

Plate 7 Dinh Q. Lê, *Erasure*, 2011. Installation view. Single-channel video, found photographs, wooden boat, sandstone, computer, online archive. Commissioned by Sherman Contemporary Art Foundation, Sydney. Supported by Nicholas and Angela Curtis.

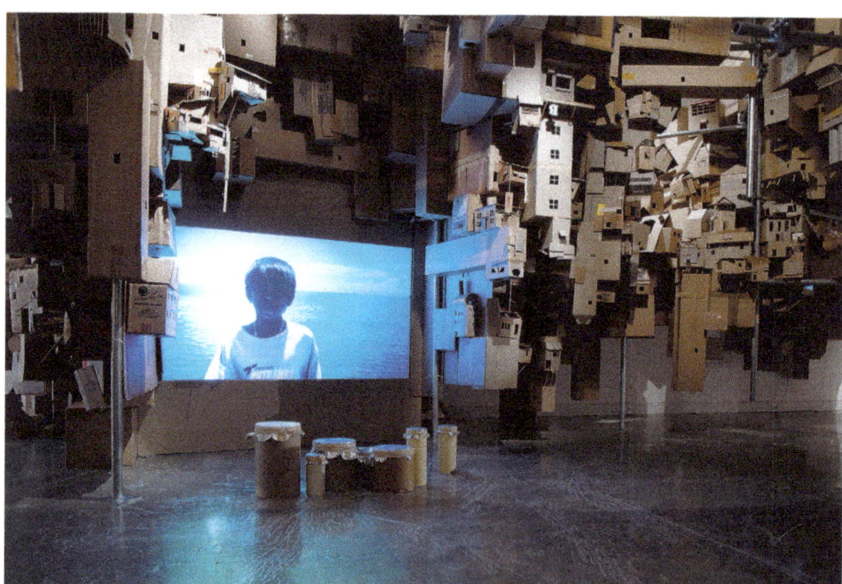

Plate 8 Alfredo Aquilizan & Isabel Gaudinez-Aquilizan, *In-Habit: Project Another Country*, 2012. Installation view. Commissioned by Sherman Contemporary Art Foundation, Sydney.

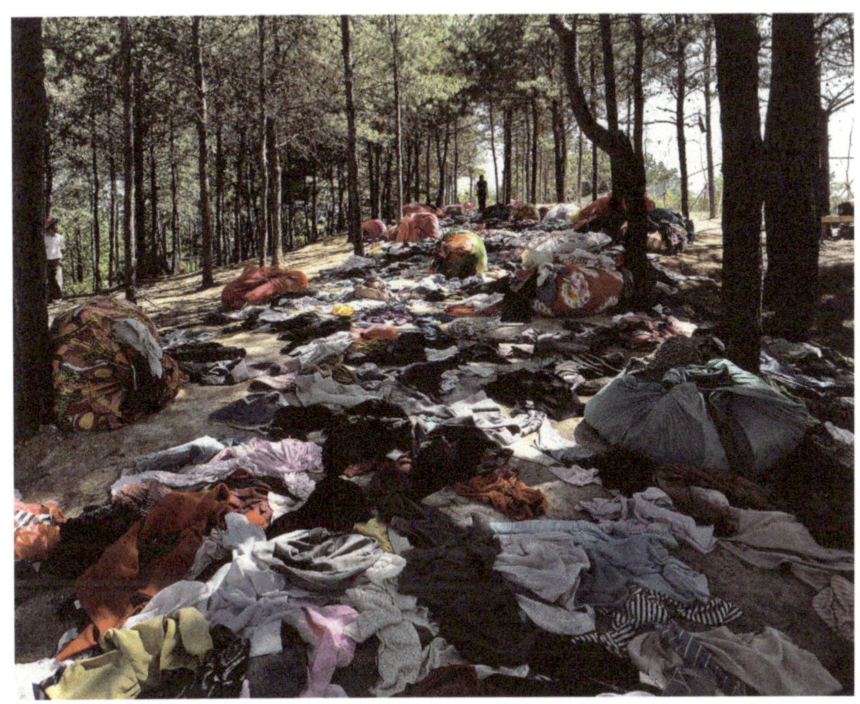

Plate 9 Kimsooja, *Sewing Into Walking – Dedicated to the Victims of Kwangju*, 1995. Installation at the 1st KwangJu Biennale, South Korea.

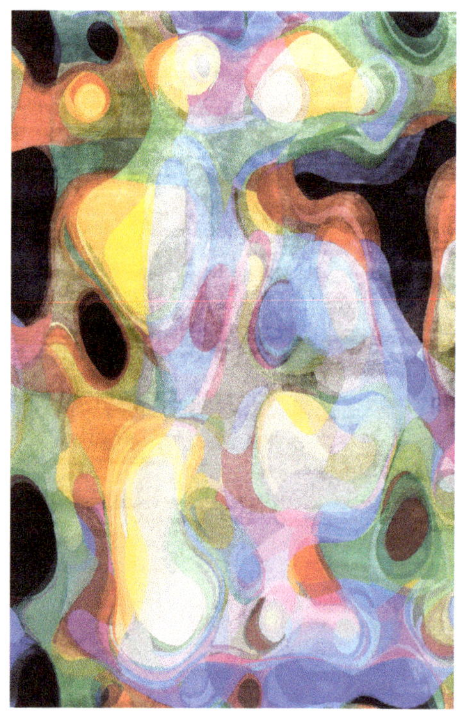

Plate 10 John Young, *Bonhoeffer in Harlem* (Tapestry, Chinese silk), 2009.

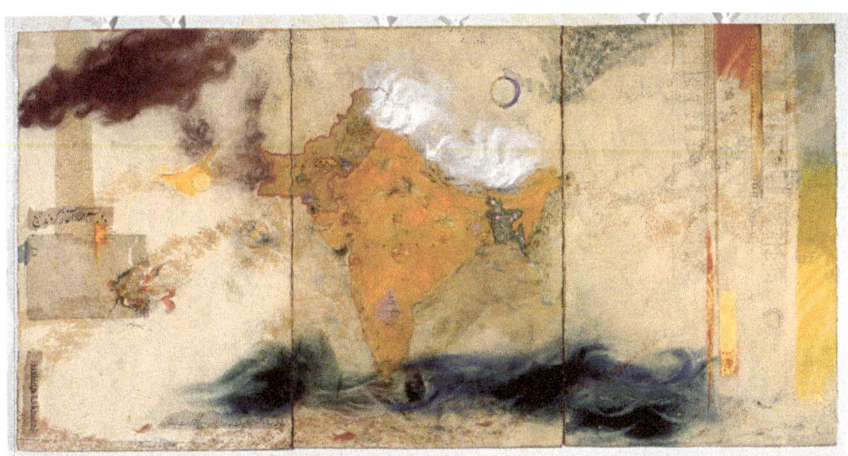

Plate 11 Salima Hashmi, *Zones of Dreams*, 1996. Painting (triptych). Collection: Bradford Museums and Art Galleries UK.

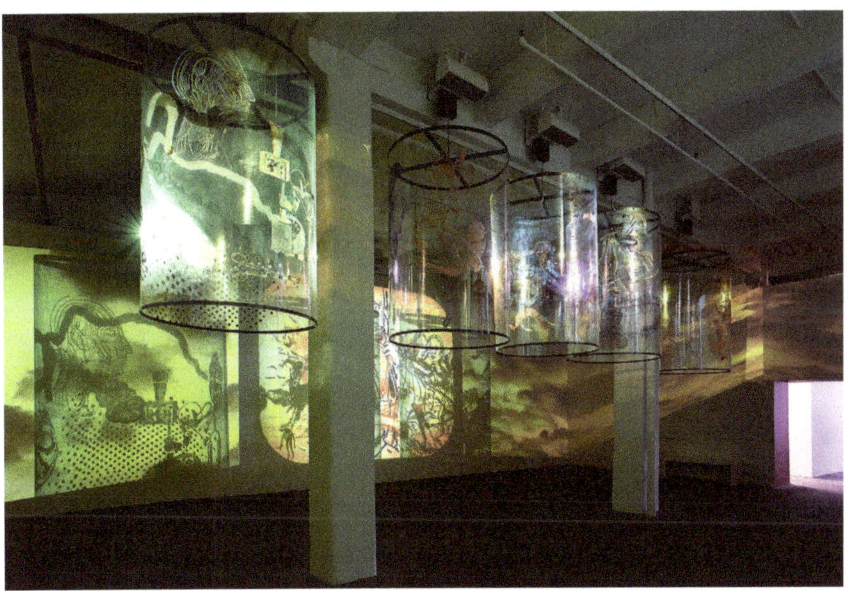

Plate 12 Nalini Malani, *In Search of Vanished Blood*, 2012. Six-channel video/shadow play. Installation view Galerie Lelong, New York.

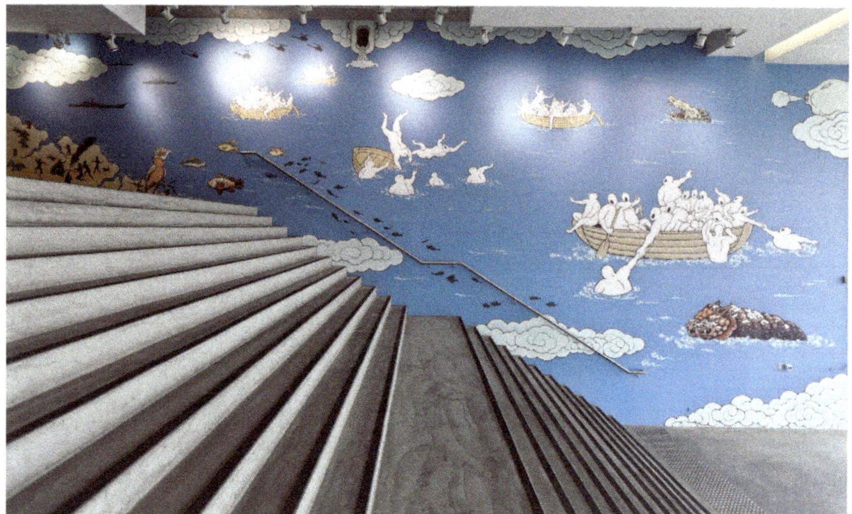

Plate 13 Guan Wei, *The Journey to Australia*, 2013. Installation view. Commissioned by the Museum of Contemporary Art, Sydney.

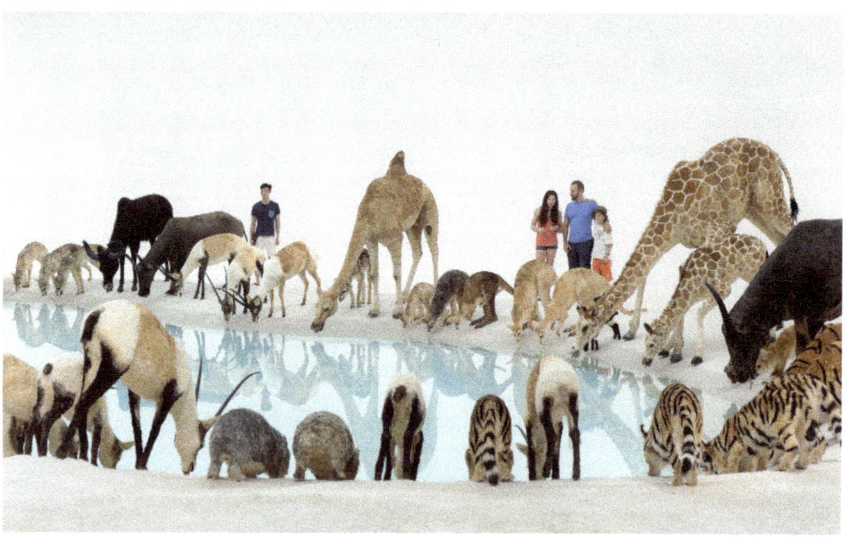

Plate 14 Cai Guo-Qiang, *Heritage*, 2013. Installation view. Collection: Queensland Art Gallery. Purchased 2013 with funds from the Josephine Ulrick and Win Schubert Diversity Foundation through and with the assistance of the Queensland Art Gallery | Gallery of Modern Art Foundation.

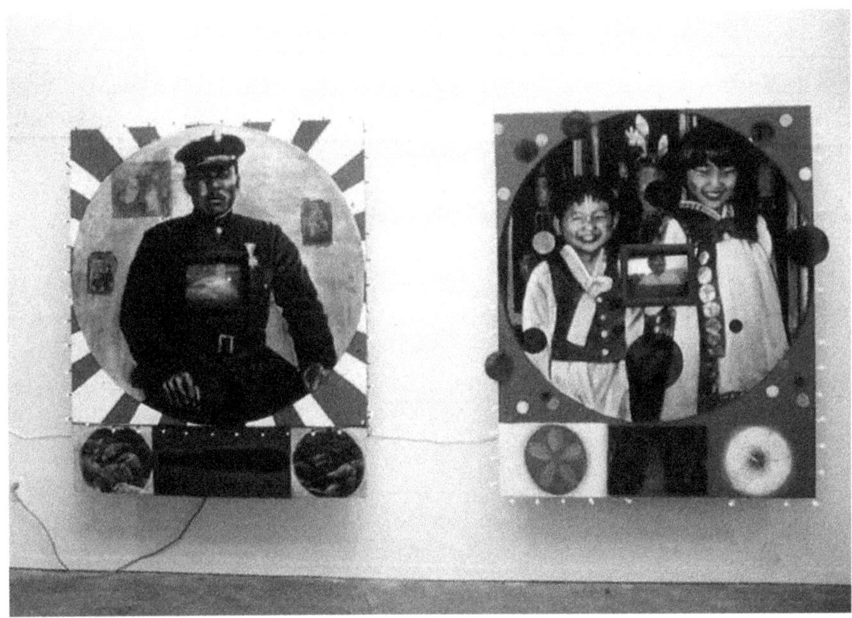

Yoshiko Shimada, *There: Sites of Korean Diaspora*, Gwangju Biennale project   **3.2**
2. Gwangju, Korea 2002.

However, as she continues, it was simply not safe to include such images, given the success of the ultranationalists in controlling the view of history: 'Art is destroyed, artists threatened, museums harassed, the police visit at midnight, and exhibitions are closed.'[14] She reports that Shimada was the only artist to challenge the ultranationalist attacks on another institution, the Toyama Museum of Modern Art, which acquired a series of images of the Emperor by Oura Nobuyuki and then was forced to give in to their demands.

Shimada did not merely protest against the censorship of others' work: she produced her own highly controversial interventions on the Emperor system. A famous example is her etching *A Picture to be Burnt* (1993), which uses a photograph of the (recently deceased) Emperor Hirohito, his face burned out, and the whole work 'tainted with rusty red, which is reminiscent of blood'.[15] This was published as the cover image of the 1994 issue of the Hong Kong *Asian Art News*, an issue featuring a review of the work and of local censorship written by Nancy Shalala.[16] This, Hiroko Hagiwara insists, is something no Japanese publication would have dared do 'for fear of ultranationalist attack'.[17] Curator Anne Kirker, describing this work, writes that '[t]his defacement is the only image that Shimada has produced that is overtly slanderous towards Hirohito',[18] but notes that though it could not have been circulated as it was in the Hong Kong journal, by 1996 it was exhibited at Keio University, Tokyo. Given this degree of censorship and control, and the fact that Shimada is routinely described as a 'controversial' or even 'offensive' artist,[19] and that her work 'was not tolerated' locally,[20] it is not surprising that in 1993 she decided to leave Japan, moving to Germany for the next three years.

The issue of this silencing of history is complex. Japan is a country with deep spiritual beliefs embedded in Shinto and Buddhist religions, a view of the world profoundly influenced by respect for nature and traditional ways of life. But the legacy of defeat in the Pacific War – the occupation and the effects of the atomic bomb blasts at Hiroshima and Nagasaki on the Japanese postwar psyche – has combined with the societal pressures caused by an amazingly rapid reconstruction after the war. Culturally Japan has, since the 1970s, significantly influenced world culture, with its architecture, art, cinema, animation, photography, consumer electronics, food, film, fashion, popular music all having high penetration in western societies. The significance of Japan's postwar avant garde art along with movements such as *gutai* and *mono-ha*, both locally and in western countries, has been documented by Alexandra Munroe in *Japanese Art after 1945: Scream against the Sky*.[21] But, at the same time, Japan is often seen as a conformist society. Despite the fact that the new constitution imposed on Japan after the war retained the Emperor as head of state while removing his status as a deity, respect for the Emperor remains a cornerstone of Japanese life. Criticism of the Imperial system takes on a much more radical note than similar treatment of royalty in western nations; and visits by some Japanese leaders to the Yasukuni shrine of the war dead (a shrine that includes convicted war criminals) are performed to appease right-wing elements in Japanese society.

Shimada has consistently challenged conservative dogma, and though she is unusual in this regard, she is not alone. Katsushige Nakahashi, too, has directly engaged the silence around Japan's part in the Pacific War in his series of installations that reference the lives of the soldiers, sailors and aviators who died in that conflict.[22] He has been seen as deliberately exposing and reconstructing painful memories, and though his work has been received enthusiastically in countries such as the United States and Australia, he is less well received in Japan.[23] Shimada, too, has experienced resistance to her work locally. In what could be seen as a rebuke for her work on Korean comfort women, for example, Bunkacho (the Japanese Cultural Ministry Fund) provided only half the funding she had requested to mount an exhibition of Korean and Japanese women artists, *Borderline Cases*, during the Korea–Japan Friendship Year in 2005; and other funding applications were rejected. She points to the context for this rejection: the 'very negative attitude toward comfort women', the 'more nationalistic mass media', that 'young people don't known history and say it's nothing to do with us' and 'a new nationalist attitude among young women',

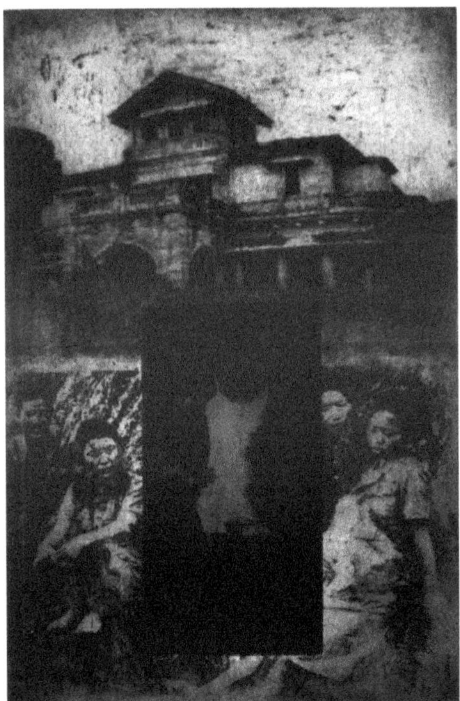

Yoshiko Shimada, *A House of Comfort*, 1993.   **3.3**

all of which makes it 'difficult to work on Korean women'.[24] She was not alone in her disappointment about the 'friendship' year: the Korean media reported the Korea–Japan Friendship Year as marked by 'ugly diplomacy, raging nationalism and the opening of old wounds',[25] which suggests that there is still considerable scope for Shimada's work on national identity.[26] It is worth noting, though, that a work by Shimada about Japanese colonisation in Korea was shown in Japan at Art Tower Mito, in the 1997 exhibition *Flexible Co-existence* curated by Eriko Osaka.

Her work on the Korean comfort women issue is often read as a focus on Japanese colonisation of the region, and to some extent this is valid. Certainly the treatment of Koreans in general, and of Korean women in particular, has been a special focus of her work. But she says, of this: 'I did not intend to make artwork about the comfort women. It was about us, the Japanese women who turned a blind eye to the issue for a half a century after the war.'[27] This attitude was evident in an exhibition she held at the Tokyo Metropolitan Museum of Photography in 1996, an installation titled *Black Boxes + Voice Recorder*. It featured chained wooden boxes containing photographs of the comfort women, the photos submerged in water, and accompanied by recordings of the women telling their stories. This demanded of viewers that they pay attention, recognise what had happened to these women, and acknowledge the impact not only on the Korean women, but also on the integrity and hence identity of Japanese women and men who had been complicit with this abuse. Another work addressing the same issue is her *Look at Me/Look at You* (1995) (see Plate 4), a hauntingly beautiful installation of two dresses: one is an apron covering a wedding dress – referencing the modern, westernised Japanese woman; the second a Japanese cotton kimono covering a Korean *chima-chigori* (traditional dress) – referencing the Japanese military preference for Korean women. Between the garments is a mirror, hung so that from the 'Japanese' side, the Korean side is obscured: it reflects the Japanese back onto itself, and the Korean is forgotten.

Much of Shimada's work therefore deals with particularly grim material, but she handles it with a fine aesthetic judgement and, often, with touches of humour. This is seen most often in the collaborative pieces she produced with the artist-prostitute Bubu.[28] The works deal with serious issues: the abuse of women, the treatment of prostitutes or transsexual people, the Emperor system, the US's occupation of Japan – all are handled with a mix of serious commentary and wit, designed to capture the attention of viewers, and offer them an alternative way of understanding difference. *A Month's Work* (1995), a wall displaying 600 unrolled condoms, references the number of men a Korean comfort woman was required to service in a month, while also raising questions about the role of sex work in contemporary society. *Made in Occupied Japan* (1998) is a series of photographs where Shimada and Bubu dress up, usually as men. We see them as MacArthur and the Emperor, for example; or as a US soldier and a Japanese prostitute. In each case they cross gender, culture and norms to tease viewers, and to provide commentary on ways of seeing, ways of being.

These works have not been very well received in Japan; Shimada points out that local audiences 'don't want to think about these issues in art; they just want feel-good factors'.[29] She has, more recently, departed from the 'big questions' of Japanese public discourse, and turned her attention to the personal and the private, seeking 'to grab people in a more personal way, a more approachable way'.[30] Her observation was that young people especially do not know about history, or the left/right debate in society, but they do know their family histories and their private stories. To engage them, she set up an installation that invited viewers to write down their secrets, and leave them in a locked box in the installation. Shimada later removed them from the box, and transformed them into collated works of art that she placed in the drawers of a *tansu*, or chest of drawers, where other viewers could read them. In late 2005, she had already collected over 1,000 secrets from only one exhibition site, the Metropolitan Museum of Art in Tokyo:[31] evidence that this work was as popular with young people as she had anticipated. The secrets included a surprising number of confessions about sexuality (with the confession from many that they had not been able to come out to their families), and a disturbing number of stories of family violence. She has extended this work, *Family Secrets: Bones in a Tansu* (2004), from its initial installation in the Museum of Contemporary Art in Tokyo, and toured it internationally, to Seoul, Chiang Mai, Manila and Yogyakarta, and also to Copenhagen, Shanghai and London. With each new location, Shimada creates new collages from the newly collected secrets, and this work has illuminated how each community's audience responds to the concept, and what acts as the important secret/s in each site. She does not see these viewer-participants as objects of research; her intention is to provide them with a voice. An outcome though is, arguably, that it assures viewers that they are not alone in their experience, and it may also engender deeper empathy among the participants.[32] Shimada says she still has hope for positive change in Japanese society: 'But something new has to happen, and not from mass movements – it has to come from an awareness growing inside the individual.'[33]

Jagath Weerasinghe: humanity, religion and civil war

One of the most remarkable anomalies about war is the passion with which it has been conducted by members of religions, the founders of which have consistently invited their followers to practise love and tolerance. Sri Lankan artist Jagath Weerasinghe has been deeply concerned in his art with this anomaly and the moral and ethical dilemmas it poses. His art has explored the horrific results of religious and ethnic conflict and civil war in his country.

Jagath Weerasinghe was born in 1954. His father was the Interpreter Mudliyar of the Supreme Court in Colombo – a role that required him to bridge the gaps in understanding between the Sinhala-speaking locals and the anglophone judges.[34] Weerasinghe studied for a BFA in aesthetic studies at the University of Kelaniya, one of the oldest universities in Sri Lanka and a centre for Buddhist studies, graduating in 1981. He was eventually to become Professor of Sri Lankan Art History and Archaeology at his alma mater. He also obtained qualifications in archaeology and conservation, studying in Rome, and at the Getty Conservation Institute in the US; he graduated as well with an MFA from the American University in Washington, DC. Weerasinghe is perhaps Sri Lanka's best-known contemporary artist internationally. His work has been shown in the United States, the Netherlands, Sweden, Germany and the UK, and was selected for the Fukuoka Asian Art exhibition in Japan (1994), the Asia-Pacific Triennial in Australia (1999) and the Singapore Biennale (2006). For nearly three decades, he has publicly challenged the moral grounds for the dominant narrative put forward during the Sri Lankan civil war, and explored

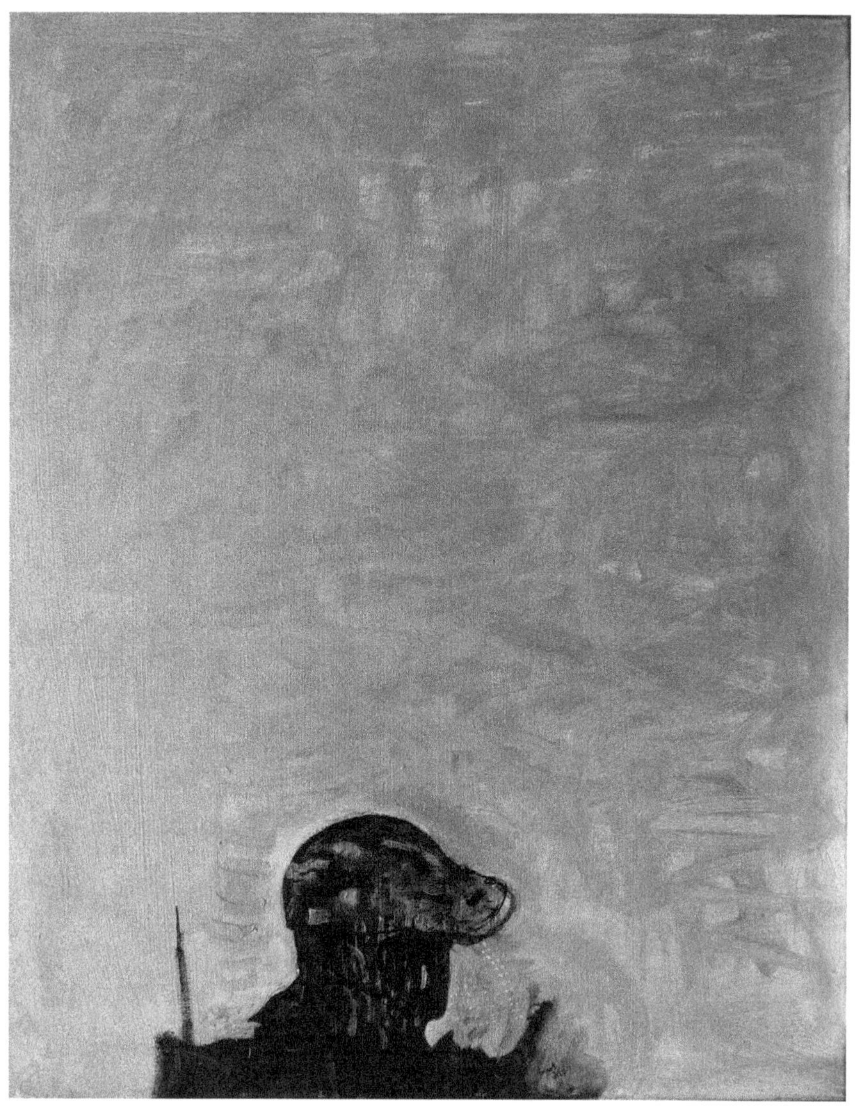

3.4 Jagath Weerasinghe, *Who Are You, Soldier?* 2007.

its ethical contradictions. He is convinced that the most unbearable truth he has had to confront in the contemporary world is that 'most of the now established religions and humanitarian traditions are incapable of helping, healing or saving the people caught in this tragic situation [of the Sri Lankan civil war]. These religious traditions have now become so institutionalised and they function as part of the establishment that justifies human rights violations.'[35] Sasanka Perera considers Weerasinghe's contribution is 'as an artist who used his works as a repository of violent memory and pain, and also as the trail-blazer who indicated the vast possibilities of politico-artistic narratives.'[36] In confronting the effects of civil war on his nation, Weerasinghe is also confronting the realities of a breakdown in normative moral and ethical standards that leads people to mob violence and terrorism in the name of a cause.

Sri Lanka is a country divided, not to say fractured, along the critical lines of ethnicity, religion and class. At the latest count, 73.8 per cent of the population are Sinhalese and 8.5 per cent Tamil; and the population is divided by religious adherence, too, with 69.1 per cent being Buddhist, and 7.1 per cent Hindu.[37] The great majority of Sinhalese are Buddhist and the great majority of Tamils are Hindu. Tamils had long protested against laws that effectively discriminated against them in respect of entry to higher education and the public service; while Sinhalese had earlier resented what they saw as British favouritism to Tamils under colonial rule. In 1983, thirteen Sri Lankan soldiers were ambushed and killed by the Liberation Tigers of Tamil Elam, described as 'undoubtedly one of the most organized, effective and brutal terrorist groups in the world'.[38] The immediate unofficial Sinhalese response to the events in 1983 was a series of violent episodes directed against the Tamil population.

The issue of violence was very real for Weerasinghe even prior to this. In 1978, when still a student, he was abducted in the street and beaten by thugs of Prime Minister Junius Jayewardene's pro-market United National Party. He later described the episode as a 'life-changing experience' in that it taught him that he was essentially mistaken in his assumption that there were certain human rights that no one could violate. Events at the beginning of the civil war in 1983 provided another extreme personal crisis in terms of violations of basic human rights, which have haunted his imagery ever since. In this year he personally witnessed a young Tamil man stripped naked and murdered by a Sinhalese mob. It was the start of a civil war, ferocious even by the customary standards of civil wars, that lasted twenty-six years until 2009, and caused an estimated 100,000 deaths, many of whom were civilians.[39] Most of the fighting was in the Tamil areas of the north, but in the 1990s the Tamil Tigers undertook assassinations, and launched many suicide bombings, including some by women suicide bombers, in the capital Colombo, in places such as transport hubs, public buildings and temples. A UN report published in 2011 said both sides in the conflict had committed war crimes against civilians.[40] The legacy, in the words of Chandraguptha Thenuwara, was that 'after 1983, what we Sri Lankans have gained was international contempt and hatred amongst us'.[41]

Despite the civil war raging for a number of decades in Sri Lanka, the Sinhalese at least have been able to sustain a highly dynamic and innovative art scene since the early 1990s. This has allowed space for works that are critical of the violence, such as Weerasinghe's, to be shown, and for reviews to be published that are forthright about the issues he treats. Weerasinghe has been a crucial actor in a number of significant developments in Sri Lankan art during the 1990s, and has had a major influence as an artist and as a teacher. His exhibition in 1992, titled *Anxiety* – his first in Sri Lanka after returning from his graduate studies in the United States – had a major impact. Two years later, in 1994, Weerasinghe and Chandraguptha Thenuwara (an artist who had returned to Sri Lanka after studying in Russia) both began to teach art at the Institute of Aesthetic Studies (IAS). They were able to influence a new generation of young artists and thus, as Weerasinghe notes, to contribute to new artistic directions in Sri Lankan art and to connect with 'artist-led international art workshops in the South Asian region, such as "KHOJ" in India and "Vasl" in Pakistan'.[42] In 2000 Weerasinghe became the founding Chairman of Theertha, an artist-led non-profit initiative based in Colombo, which was committed to exploring 'the possibilities of exchanging ideas and knowledge across ethnic, regional and artistic borders, in the context of contemporary critical art practice in Sri Lanka'.[43]

The civil war determined Weerasinghe's future art direction. He could not help feeling complicit in the outrages as a Sinhalese and a Buddhist. Nor could he accept the notion of Buddhism being used to justify violence. Yet he believes that anger is not the way to deal with manifestations of anger.[44] Weerasinghe's art is more of a philosophical reflection upon tragedy than an agency of political action, and he chooses to eschew the relatively simplistic solutions of ideology. His mission has been to reveal and deplore the failure of himself and his fellow Sri Lankan Buddhists to practice the essential precepts of their own beliefs. Hence the majority of his works, as Sasanka Perera writes, 'bear a significant preoccupation with issues dealing with violence, not only as someone who personally experienced it, but also as someone who experienced it as a member of a society torn apart by violence'.[45] In this his art draws from his Buddhist beliefs. As Suhanya Raffel, writing on his installation *Yantra Gala and the Round Pilgrimage* (1998), suggests regarding the Buddhist elements in the work, 'guilt is embedded in a cultural familiarity'.[46]

One of his most significant early artistic responses was *Broken Stupa 1992*, part of his exhibition *Anxiety*. *Broken Stupa 1992*, is a representation in charcoal and pastel of a pile of shattered and jagged stones. Friends and critics alike protested at the notion of destroying a stupa, an object of veneration. The image had been inspired by the real collapse of an ancient stupa due to incompetent restoration techniques, but Weerasinghe argued that it appropriately symbolised the violation of the most sacred Buddhist principles by the ongoing civil violence. Weerasinghe has continued to develop symbols to express the sacrilege of violence he has witnessed and his own anguish at witnessing it. Other images include men with weapons, and the tortured male

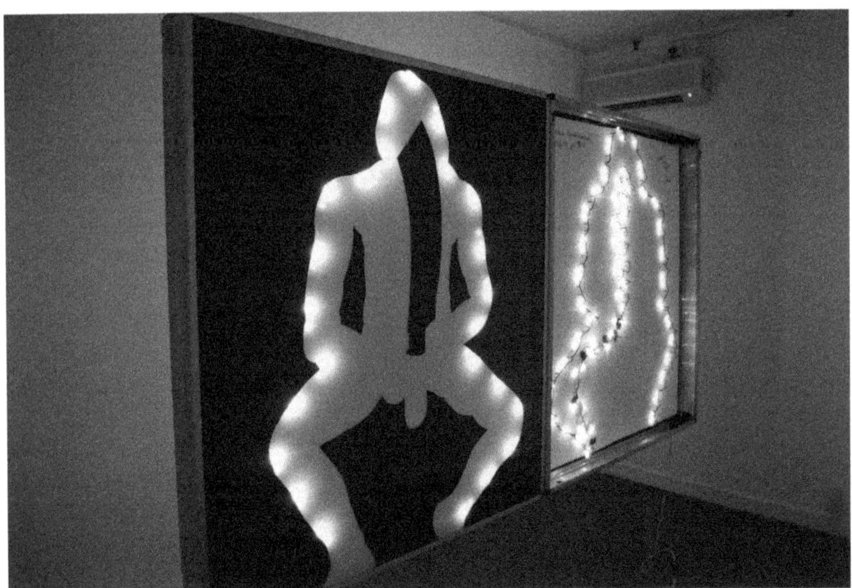

Jagath Weerasinghe, *Celestial Violence – Men with Arms*, 2009.   **3.5**

body, inspired by his experience of witnessing the young Tamil murdered; and the Long Necked Man, a figure that recurs in most of his paintings throughout the 1990s, as Anoli Perera describes it, 'in various contorted positions (in poses of pleading, defending, sprawled on the floor)'.[47]

Weerasinghe himself was unambiguous about his artistic intention. In a gesture of deep self-reflectivity, he states:

> the long-necked man was my attempt to portray myself as a Sinhalese Buddhist … Then I was working with an image of a head, probably a decapitated one, and I inscribed on my works the following line: 'I have enough guilt to start my own religion'. In a way, I was reacting or responding to 1983 communal fights in Sri Lanka. During these riots, thousands of Tamils lost their properties and hundreds of them were murdered in the Sinhala areas by the Sinhalese. I am Sinhalese and a Buddhist. I was fighting within me what I saw and felt during that time.[48]

There is irony in the fact that Weerasinghe was granted a commission by the government of Mrs Chandrika Bandaranaike Kumaranatun to design the *Monument for Democracy – Shrine for the Innocents*. This was completed in 1999, and dedicated to the innocent victims of political violence and human rights abuses in the southern part of the island in the 1980s and 1990s. This work might be read as expressing Weerasinghe's own feelings: it focused 'on the theme of human estrangement and spiritual malaise', in 'a world which is over saturated with … empty religious icons, that now serve no purpose, apart from as signs which refer to one another, contributing in reality to produce tensions and conflicts throughout the world'.[49] His intention had been to design the Shrine as an artwork made for the citizen, one that was not made by any political party, but he decided in retrospect that he had been mistaken; and he has also seen the eventual decay of the monument as symbolic of the situation in the country. He has, however, continued to resist conflict. In 2009, along with other artists from Sri Lanka and India who also treat the theme of peace, Weerasinghe travelled to India to participate in the 2009 KHOJ workshop *Imagine Peace*. In that same year he participated as co-founder and curator of the inaugural Colombo Biennale in 2009, which had been planned before the war ended, and had as its theme 'Imagining peace'.[50]

One of Weerasinghe's most original and poignant works is the series *Who Are You, Soldier?* (1996) (see Figure 3.4), which is concerned with an essential dilemma of human rights. 'I tried to capture our relationship with a soldier', Weerasinghe says:

> We see them everyday, guarding streets and checking people. For those Sinhala fundamentalists who think war is the answer to the problems in the north, a soldier is a war hero who sacrifices his life for the 'Motherland'. For some others, a soldier is a bastard, a rapist! Both of these extremes are deceiving us and deprive the soldier [of] his human rights as an individual … We have reduced him to someone who wears a uniform and carries weapons – we don't see his face. We don't think that he is an individual with his own personal pain and suffering; we have made him a victim as well.[51]

The concept of the soldier as victim as well as victimiser has become more reflective of the times with the continuing return of veterans, some of them mutilated physically or psychologically, from wars which significant elements of their relevant civilian populations might think should not have been fought in the first place.

Equally relevant to the times is the series *Snakes and Mikes* (2005) (see Plate 5) in which a mass of entwined snakes, coloured lurid yellow and black, writhe across a glaring red background, towards a battery of microphones – the most effective instruments, along with weapons, for manipulating public opinion. In a similar vein, his 2009 exhibition *Celestial Fervor* (see Figure 3.5),[52] with its weapon-bearing male figures framed with flickering lights, 'continuously nudges us to critically review our own anaesthetized, duped perceptions and unhesitant consumption of ideology and actions that are shrouded in over-used rhetoric linked to concepts such as nationalism, patriotism, authenticity, cultural purity and religiosity'.[53]

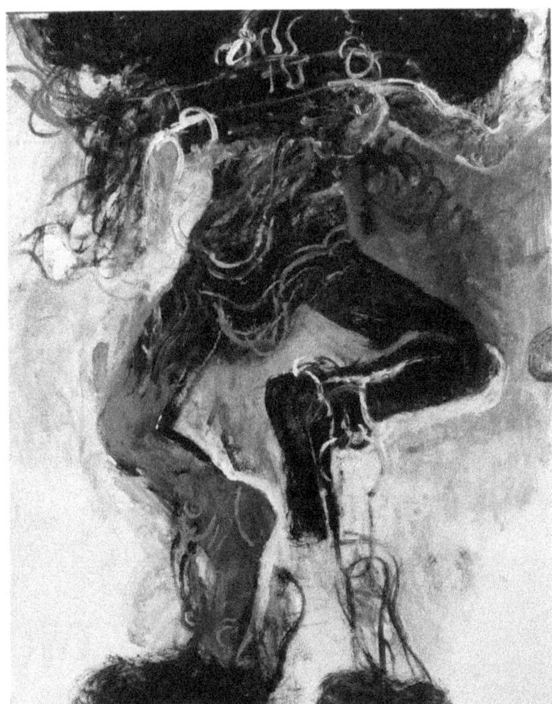

Jagath Weerasinghe, *Dancing Shiva*, 2009.   **3.6**

This series has led logically to Weerasinghe's continuing artistic investigations into the most fundamental question of human rights: the necessity or otherwise of the connection between violence and creation. His symbol for this dilemma is that of Shiva Nataraja, the Lord of the Dance (the Hindu deity central to the Chola Kingdom of the Tamils). It is a compelling image of the activity of God, beautiful, elegant, even joyful, which the artist represents in different versions with a riot of colour including red, gold and blue paint. But it is also, in Weerasinghe's view, a very disturbing image, depicting as it does the god dancing on the prostrate form of Apasmara Purusha, who is the personification of illusion and ignorance. Nothing can be more fundamental to any concept of human rights than deliverance from illusion and ignorance. But the image raises the most serious existential question of whether it is necessary to do violence in order to create peace; of whether it is necessary to destroy evil in order to do good.

FX Harsono: contesting history: confronting violence and injustice

FX Harsono's art and life has been a confrontation with violence and injustice in his home nation of Indonesia, and also a journey contesting the overarching official history related to the Suharto regime and to the Chinese minority in Indonesia. In the mid-1970s Harsono was one of the founding members of the New Art Movement, a movement opposed to injustices in the nation, and a critical intervention in Indonesian art and politics. He has exhibited in a number of important international exhibitions: Artists Regional Exchange ARX (1992) in Perth, and the 1993 Asia-Pacific Triennial in Brisbane, Australia; in Fukuoka, Japan in 1996; in *Traditions/Tensions*, Asia Society, New York in 1996; and in the third Gwangju (South Korea) Biennale in 2001. He was also included in the Japan Foundation's *Asian Modernism* exhibition in 1995. He had a major retrospective, *FX Harsono: Testimonies*, at the Singapore Art Museum in 2010, and again in 2011 was included in the Singapore Art Museum's *Negotiating Home, History and Nation: Two Decades of Contemporary Art in Southeast Asia*. In recent years he has exhibited in New York, Berlin, China, the Netherlands and the Moscow Biennale.

'Geographically I lived in Indonesia, but I was marginalised culturally and by laws', Harsono said in 2003. 'Have I not been displaced from the cultural roots of my forefathers? And is it not also true that my national identity as an Indonesian has no cultural meaning for me?'[54] In a conversation with art historian Farah Wardani he developed this sense of his identity, insisting that history matters more to him than the idea of homeland, because 'history is not fixed in only one culture, but instead a mix of cultures. Identity has no single meaning for me, but rather is created through diversity. All this makes me part of a hybrid identity.'[55] Hybrid identity with its inherent potential for conflict has to be a critical issue in a vast archipelago of over 17,000 islands; with a population of over 250 million people speaking some 700 languages or dialects; and with six officially recognised religions, including Islam, which accounts for about 86 per cent, and Christianity, which accounts for 8.7 per cent.[56]

Harsono certainly has a hybrid identity, being the descendant of Chinese immigrants but also having Javanese ancestors. He was born in the Chinese ghetto of Blitar, East Java, in 1948. His grandmother was a Catholic, a follower of Theosophy and a devotee of traditional Javanese shamanistic practices, who used to hang pictures of Sukarno, the communist leader D. N. Aidit and Jesus on the cross in the bedroom.[57] He was himself baptised as Catholic with the name of Fransiskus Xavierius, and went to a Catholic school. He thinks that he is probably sixth-generation Chinese (*Tiong-Hoa*) descent.[58]

His father was the town photographer with his own studio, whose role was to take passport photographs. He inadvertently provided the inspiration for a critical late development in his son's career by documenting with his camera the excavation of Tiong-hoa people killed in 1948–49 (discussed later in this chapter). In 1969 Harsono originally enrolled in higher education to become an engineer, but then dropped out of engineering and enrolled instead at the

Indonesian Academy of the Arts, STSRI 'ASRI',[59] Yogyakarta, where he studied painting from 1969 to 1974. He later enrolled at IKJ (Jakarta Art Institute) for further studies in painting (1987–91).[60] His initial venture in the struggle with the political dynamics in his country was in 1974–75, when with fellow students he signed a declaration entitled 'The Black December Statement'. He went on to help form the New Art Movement, *Gerakan Seni Rupa Baru*, in 1975. Indonesian art authority and one of the leaders of the movement, Jim Supangkat, notes that these protests were in part a rebellion against western art. The artists made works about social justice, and used performance and installation to make political comments on contemporary events, including exploitative capitalist programmes, the destruction of farming land, and situations such as minamata disease in children caused by industrial dumping.[61]

Harsono's art would remain essentially activist, protesting to the degree practicable at the time against the oppressive features of the New Order of General Suharto. In 1983 he produced *The Social Change*, an installation of fifty panels on the beach near Yogyakarta, which bore enlarged photographs of peasants, trees and factories and commentaries on the destruction of tropical forests as a protest against environmental degradation – a major concern in the 1980s. Wardani points to Harsono's work on the environment, noting his collaborations with environmental activists, including the Association of Indonesian Researchers, and the Vehicle for Living Environment Issues Indonesia (WALHI). She describes his work *Suara Dari Dasar Bendungan* (Voices from the Bottom of the Dam, 1994) as an example of his own artistic interventions. This work was based on an actual event in Sampang, Madura, when in 1992, 'three farmers were killed by the military for protesting over the government's plan to eradicate their paddy fields' in order to build a dam. She continues: 'Harsono went to the village and used objects he found there such as the farmers' clothes and water combining them with audio interviews with the villagers.'[62]

Harsono continued his explicit critique of human rights violations in the installation *Power and Oppression* (1992/1993), shown at the Artists Regional Exchange (ARX), Perth, 1992. This work consisted of small mounds of earth covered with cloths that appeared to be bloodstained, and small branches broken in two, facing a chair symbolising authority and ringed with coils of barbed wire representing the military. *Just the Rights* (1993), the work he exhibited at the first Asia-Pacific Triennial of Contemporary Art in Brisbane, Australia, consisted of boards with wood, cloth and rope attached to resemble bound figures. A copy of the Universal Declaration of Human Rights, printed on textile, lay on the floor as if discarded.[63]

Indonesia had poor infrastructure on a national and even local level for showing the work of artists during the Suharto years, and the National Gallery was only opened in 1999. Artists and writers had been imprisoned during

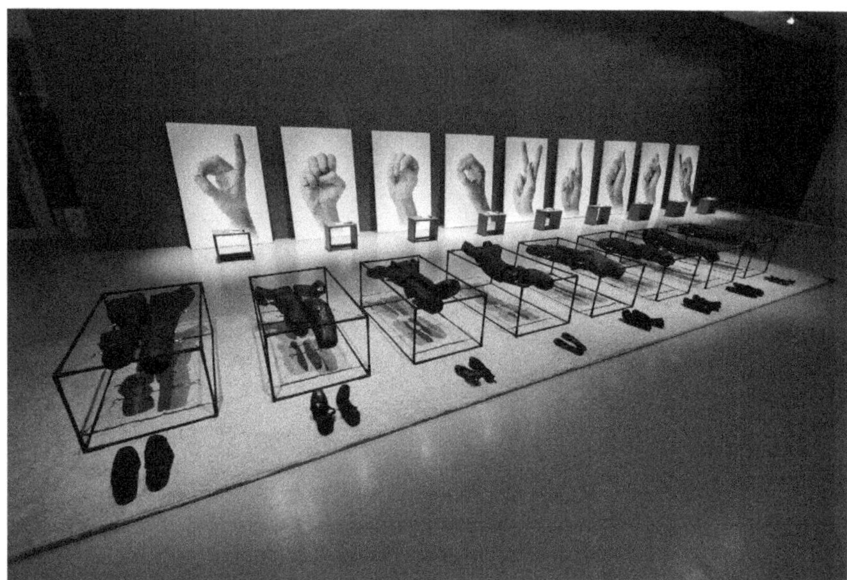

3.7 FX Harsono, *Demokrasi* (*Voice without Voice/Sign*), 1995. Installation view Singapore Art Museum. Foreground: *Burned Victims*, 1998. Collection: Singapore Art Museum. Installation and Performance.

the Suharto regime, especially immediately after 1965–66. By the 1980s and 1990s, however, as long as artists were not overly specific about targets and did not attack the regime itself, there was a selected response to such works, especially when exhibited in private galleries such as Cemeti (discussed in the Conclusion), or overseas. The only one of Harsono's works that seems to have attracted overt response from the regime was the installation *Demokrasi* (1993–94), which was later bought by both Fukuoka and the Queensland Art Gallery. This showed the word DEMOKRASI spelled out in international sign language, by hands bound with ropes. Apparently a 'government spy', as Harsono explains, came to view the work, but 'The military was fortunately not so clever at understanding the visual arts and interpreting the political connections … The person in the gallery lied and told him he didn't know the meaning of the work.'[64]

Another work from the early 1990s was a powerful denunciation of the banning of the journal *Tempo* after it had published an article exposing corruption in the Suharto regime dictatorship. This installation, *The Voices Controlled by the Powers* (1994), used wayang masks sawn off at the mouth to suggest the silencing of comment. His performance *Destruction* (Yogyakarta, 1997) was even more courageous and uncompromising. Harsono, wearing theatrical make-up as the demon king Ravana from the Ramayana epic and impeccably attired in a double-breasted suit, dress shoes, white shirt and tie, 'set fire to three wayang masks on chairs, which represented the only three political parties Suharto allowed to contest the elections'; then, wielding a chainsaw, 'Harsono destroyed the burnt chairs, as a metaphor for Suharto's brutal exercise of power over the electoral process.'[65] In an artist talk at the National Gallery of Australia (14 June 2014), Harsono said that although there had been a law in 1997 that there could be no political activity in public spaces, many people defied this to come to his performance.

In the following year, with the fall of Suharto, Harsono's artistic direction and his whole worldview experienced a fundamental change. The demise of the New Order had been provoked in part by the catastrophic impact on Indonesia of the Asian financial crisis in 1997. Many blamed the Chinese, who constitute less than 3 per cent of the population but are rumoured to control about 70 per cent of the nation's wealth.[66] Their position had always been equivocal, including under Dutch colonial rule. After the defeat of the Dutch in 1949 the motto of the new Republic was, most appropriately, 'Unity in Diversity', but its effect was limited to those ethnic groups with specific claims to territorial origin in the archipelago. The Chinese, as immigrants, had no such claims but, as Hendro Wiyanto points out:

> Indonesia does not consist only of indigenous ethnic groups: there are also those of Arab, Indian and Chinese descendants, some also from other Asian nations, and some of us are of European descendants. The fact is, it is only the Chinese descendants who have had to suffer the discriminatory treatment and been forced to become 'ostensibly' indigenous in order to be accepted as part of the Indonesian nation.[67]

Discrimination against the Chinese therefore persisted under Suharto who took power after the complex situation in 1965–66 described in the previous chapter, despite some of the dictator's closest supporters being enormously wealthy Chinese capitalists. The Chinese language could not be used, Chinese festivals and religious services could not be conducted publicly, and even Chinese names had to be Indonesianised. Harsono had already suggested in his art, by the use of Javanese symbols such as the wayang mask, the ambiguities of being an Indonesian of both Chinese and Javanese descent. But, he noted recently, 'During Suharto's era, we can say that democracy was non-existent. No one could talk freely, no one could criticise Suharto. People were oppressed and we depended on courageous people to voice criticism.'[68] The fall of Suharto heralded an era of greater political freedom, but Harsono sensed that the greater political freedom might in fact intensify the persisting social disadvantages of ethnic Chinese.

In a lecture in Australia in June 2014, Harsono explained the background and context for much of his recent work since 1998 in terms of the shifting political climate after the fall of Suharto. Initially, he said, there was 'euphoria', and everyone was speaking about 'Demokrasi'. Then in May 1998 the national economic crisis began in Jakarta, and with it the bankruptcy of his personal graphic design firm that had supported his artistic work and his family for many years.[69]

All this was made the more acute by the outrages of May 1998 when hundreds of people, mainly Chinese, were killed, some being incinerated in a Jakarta shopping centre when attacked by a mob. A large number of Chinese women were raped in succeeding attacks. The May 1998 riots, as Melani Budianta,[70] Kathryn Robinson[71] and Abidin Kusno[72] have suggested, proved a turning point both for Indonesians of Chinese descent and for activists seeking political change in Indonesia, particularly women who were horrified by the organised rapes of Chinese women associated with the riots. While the numbers killed and raped are not verifiable, a fact-finding mission established by the Indonesian Government reported over 1,000 dead, and the *Jakarta Post*, reporting on plans for a new monument in 2014, likewise gave a figure of at least 1,000.[73]

This violence, in the words of historian Jemma Purdey, 'was not normal or everyday. Unlike most anti-Chinese violence in Indonesia, it took place on a national scale, carried out by military agents with extreme brutality and purpose.'[74] As a result, she continues, it 'brought terror to the entire nation. Its victims were mainly women, urban poor and Chinese Indonesians, but the audacity and impunity assumed by its perpetrators shocked all of Indonesia and much of the international community.'[75] These instances of ethnic violence made Harsono feel personally betrayed, in the awareness that 'people of Chinese descent would always be victims during social change'.[76] For a time he considered leaving Indonesia, but instead he resolved to respond to the challenges of society, by joining a volunteer NGO to help victims of the violence, and also, as he had always done, through his art.

The immediate response was the installation *Burned Victims* (1998), comprising a row of torso-shaped sculptures which the artist drenched with petrol and proceeded to set alight with a blowtorch, as he had done in his previous performance *Destruction* (illustrated foreground of Figure 3.7). His work *May Bride* (1998) was about the rapes of the Chinese women. This was followed by the triptych *Displaced* (2003), shown at the National Gallery of Indonesia. *Displaced* presented three studies of a seated hooded figure holding a bouquet of white flowers, the studies becoming progressively more blurred and indistinct. These works certainly referred to his feelings of inhabiting an essentially marginalised position in a divided society, and he has stated that at the time he felt like a butterfly with needles pinning it – a visual image he used in some of his paintings at that time.[77]

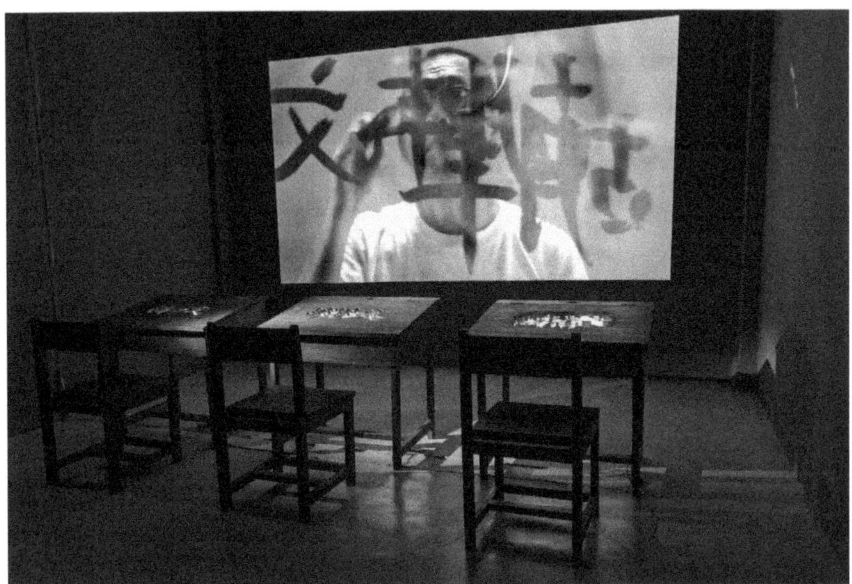

FX Harsono, *Writing in the Rain*, 2011. Single-channel video performance.   **3.8**

After 1998 there was a new freedom in Indonesia to talk about Chinese culture and to hold cultural activities – for example, the dragon dance and religious rituals that had not been practised for thirty-two years. The schools were now allowed to teach Mandarin, whereas before no one could even show Chinese calligraphy in public. Harsono has said he began to question now whether it was still necessary to highlight political and social issues related to government. So he decided to focus on tracing his roots both through a cultural history of the Chinese and through his own family history.[78]

His sense of estrangement from his roots had affected Harsono because, as he said to Hendro Wiyanto, 'I think I've never viewed myself only as my own self or as a lone individual. It is the awareness that I am part of the community that always encourages me to create works that have as their point of departure social issues, the things that are external to me'.[79] He tried writing his Chinese name, which he had had to change in 1966 to qualify as an Indonesian citizen, and presented a video performance, *Writing the Erased* (2009), in which he repeatedly tried to write that name. Equally poignant was the performance *Writing in the Rain* (2011), in which the artist repetitively writes his Chinese name on a glass wall while splashes of water wash the Chinese characters away. *The Raining Bed* (2013) (see Plate 6) used an LED display to present details of the history of the Chinese, and ceramic letters spelling out, on a traditional

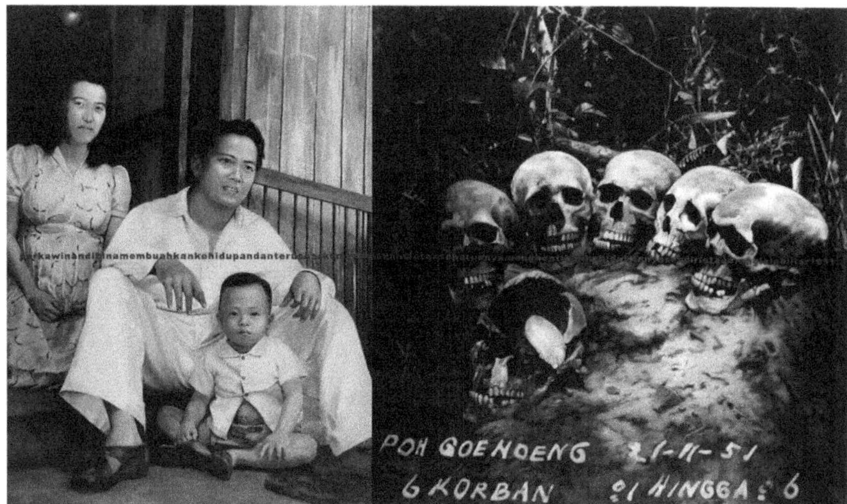

3.9 FX Harsono, *Preserving Life, Terminating Life #2*, 2009. Collection: Singapore Art Museum.

Chinese *peranakan* bed, the poem 'In my sleep I entangled the past, at the tip of the pen history is predicted, at the tip of the gun history is deceived, at the end of the fountain history is washed away'. Finally, *Journey to the Past/ Migration* (2013) consists of a boat filled with objects and with candles and thousands of terracotta letters, referencing the migration of the Chinese to Indonesia, to share their culture and make a hybrid culture.

The legacy of his father's profession as town photographer provided a profound inspiration for Harsono's heightened awareness both of his own Chinese identity, and of violence in his country. The Indonesian military had killed some 8,000 alleged Communists in Madiun, a town in East Java with a substantial Chinese population, after a failed uprising in September 1948. In 1951, Harsono's father was directed by a Chinese organisation, Chung Hua Tsung Hui, to document with his camera the process of tracing the identities of the Chinese buried in mass graves, including photographing the exhumations and reburials. Sixty of the photographs were preserved in a black album that 'was always placed in the sitting room', where, Harsono says, 'For years and years, it seems that everyone at his home had been afraid to touch it.'[80] His father had captioned all the photographs, recording the location of the shot, and how many bodies were found. Further research, Harsono says, produced a document titled *Memorandum: Outlining act of violence and humanity* [*sic*] *perpetrated by Indonesia band on innocent Chinese before and after the Dutch police action was enforced on July 21, 1947*: a document which he notes 'encouraged me to find other mass graves'.[81] In an ongoing research project he has found so far some 1,400 bodies buried in Chinese cemeteries, the graves surmounted by stone plinths that bear in Chinese characters the names of the victims. Harsono decided to photograph the cemeteries, and has created art works related to the project, including a filmed performance where he uses red crayon on white cloth to make rubbings from the monuments. Harsono's personal testimony to these killings was a diptych, *Preserving Life, Terminating Life 1*, and *Preserving Life, Terminating Life 2* (2009). He displayed two photographs from his father's album in association with portraits of a young married Chinese couple (his parents), who in the second work are shown with their child, Harsono, then aged three, and, on the adjacent panel, an array of skulls that were unearthed when the bodies were exhumed. A red thread was drawn across the two sets of photographs, a traditional Chinese charm to ward off bad luck but also to connect the images across the generations.

The importance of this investigation and retelling of history, for Harsono, is that history 'provides me with a new sense of awareness about how to serve fellow humans and the Indonesian nation'. His concern is for the nation to acknowledge the past, and learn from previous mistakes. 'At the very least', he continues, 'I will demonstrate to the public that there is another version of history that has truly taken place.'[82] This is a task he has described as a 'Pilgrimage to History' for the younger generation in Indonesia so that they will know the violence against human rights, and so that those dark events will not be repeated.

There are complexities in this. Under Sukarno, Indonesia had had a legal Communist Party, the third largest in the world. The Suharto government, in contrast, was opposed both to China as a nation and to Communism, and the influence of Chinese art and culture on Indonesia through the centuries was also not discussed during those years. The fall of Suharto coincided with the rise of China and the recovery of interest in many members of the Chinese diaspora in their Chinese identity.[83] Yet new tensions in the region over disputed territory may well see Chinese in countries such as Indonesia again facing questions about their loyalty where the legacy of hatred against the Chinese has a very long history.

The fall of Suharto revealed to all Indonesians, and to the world at large, the processes by which Indonesia's history over the previous decades had been manipulated, and the internal mechanisms of suppression utilised by the regime. But the destabilising of the state also led to religious and ethnic violence and a potential fracturing of the state in provinces such as East Timor, Aceh and Papua in the late 1990s and early 2000s.[84] The official Indonesian Human Rights Commission and many NGOs have put in place programmes related to trauma, human rights justice, and transitional justice and reconciliation. Truth and memory are critical to this process, but to date no formal truth and reconciliation legal process has been completed.[85] The fall of Suharto not only freed artists like Christanto and Harsono to address hidden histories, but also allowed responses such as Joshua Oppenheimer's enormously controversial Oscar-nominated documentary *The Act of Killing*, in which perpetrators appear to justify their actions in the 1965–66 killings.[86]

Harsono has fought for decades for a more just and a less divided society. He has done this at great personal cost and yet, like many activists, he found the fight was not over in 1998.

Dinh Q. Lê: Art and affirmation

Dinh Q. Lê's art and life need to be seen as transnational in focus. Like Shimada, Weerasinghe and Harsono, Dinh Q. Lê's art is related to collective memory and to history. Like Harsono he wishes to present a different view of history for the benefit of current and future generations but in a transnational context that includes US understandings of the Vietnam War.

Born in 1968 in Vietnam, Lê and his family went to the United States as refugees in 1979, escaping from the 1978 incursions of the Khmer Rouge into Vietnam. He graduated from the University of California, Santa Barbara, and then in 1992 was awarded a Masters of Photography from the School of Visual Arts, New York. Like many artists discussed in this book, his work has been shown in major international exhibitions. These include the Venice Biennale (2003), the Asia Society in New York (2005), the Asia-Pacific Triennial in Brisbane (2006), the Gwangju Biennale (2006), *Thermocline of Art* ZKM, Germany (2007), the Singapore Biennale (2008), the Museum of Modern Art in New York (2010), and Documenta 13 in Germany (2012). His art contains within it his own memories of being a ten-year-old boy in 1978, fleeing across the sand with his mother and siblings, gunfire behind them, desperately trying to escape to freedom. It includes the boat voyage, the refugee camp in Southern Thailand, and then the experience of arriving in Los Angeles as a refugee, still unable to speak English.[87]

Lê returned to Vietnam in 1993, shortly after graduating. He visited the family grave, and decided to settle in the country permanently in 1997, despite some reservations in Vietnam about those who had returned after being educated abroad, and despite the fact that his mother and siblings did not accompany him. His life experiences, including censorship in Vietnam, led him in 2007 to establish with other artists an independent artist-run exhibition space, Sàn Art, in Ho Chi Minh City, for the benefit of artists whose work had been overlooked by political and commercial systems in Vietnam. He also founded the Vietnamese Foundation for the Arts. Much funding for the space and the Foundation comes from the west. In 2010 Lê was awarded the Prince Claus Laureate Prize (from the Netherlands) for his work supporting the local community in Vietnam.

One critical impetus of his art for many years seems to have been his concern that American memories of the Vietnam War elided its effects on the Vietnamese. As he has stated, 'I wanted to give the Vietnamese the voices to speak.'[88] This was a feature of his first public art work. While still a student in the US, Lê took a course on the Vietnam War which was taught in a manner that stressed the sufferings of Americans and, he said, 'perpetuated the American point of view. I became frustrated. Their suffering during the War is incomparable to that of the Vietnamese people.'[89] His response was to produce the work *Accountability*, a series of posters he mounted on campus, setting American media images of the war alongside photographs of Vietnamese people, and captioned with narratives outlining the damage suffered by Vietnam. His teachers preserved these posters, which were later reproduced by the organisation *Creative Time*, and shown in 1992 in New York, Washington, DC, and Los Angeles. David Spalding concludes: 'The desire to intervene in dominant perceptions of the Vietnam War propelled Lê for much of his artistic career.'[90] Years later his series *From Vietnam to Hollywood* (2003–05) used Hollywood movies such as *Born on the Fourth of July* and *Apocalypse Now* combined with black-and-white footage from the Vietnam War showing other realities. He was concerned that the films presented a version in which the Vietnamese seemed absent: 'It seems as though the readers and the press only wanted the most violent and shocking of images of the war,' he says; 'But we had a life back then, even during the Vietnam war.'[91]

Much of his art is directly connected to human rights. Inspired by a visit to Tuol Sleng Genocide Museum in Phnom Penh in 1994, he produced art about the Khmer Rouge Cambodian genocide. These works include *Cambodia: Splendor and Darkness* (1994–99), in which he used photographs of prisoners – almost all of whom were later killed and whose only crime was usually ideological or class based – interwoven with images of the famous temple at Angkor Wat. Rebecca McGrew notes:

> Lê constructs his hauntingly beautiful woven photographs by cutting the original photographs into strips and weaving them together using a traditional Vietnamese method of grass-mat weaving he learned from an aunt. The subject matter of the photographs is also a weaving of the personal, historical, and mythological.[92]

Another work, *The Quality of Mercy* (1995), showed just the eyes of the victims. He explained that some of his relatives were born in Cambodia, and that the wider world at the time did nothing about the atrocities of the Khmer Rouge.[93] The visit to Angkor Wat in 1994 inspired a number of other art works. He had been moved, when there, by the sight of people worshipping headless Buddha statues – headless because tomb robbers had taken the heads. To Lê, the head

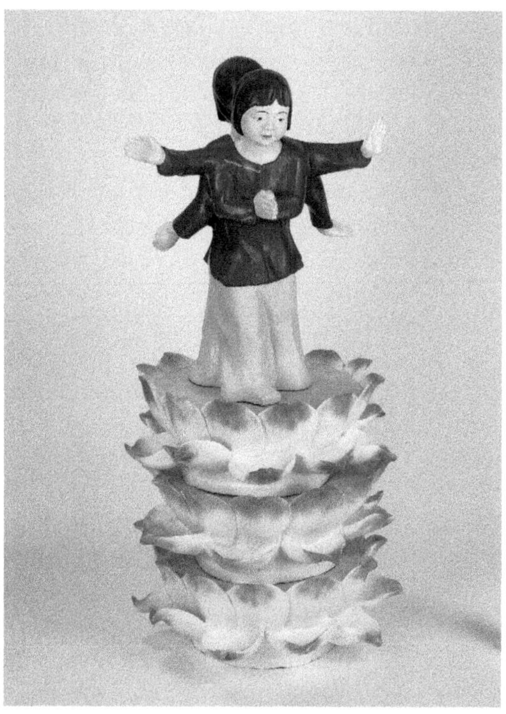

3.10 Dinh Q. Lê, *Lotusland*, 1999. Detail. Collection: Queensland Art Gallery. Purchased 2006. The Queensland Government's Gallery of Modern Art Acquisitions Fund.

separated from the body became a symbol of his own search for identity and also that of all people alienated from their culture.[94]

He has also maintained a project to collect Vietnamese antiques, historical material and photographic records of Vietnamese history to preserve that history. He bought boxes of family photographs of Vietnamese individuals and families, found while searching for the possibility he might find some photographs of his own extended family who been left behind when his immediate family fled.[95] He created a quilt from 1,500 of these photographs, *Mot Coi Di Ve* ('Spending One's Life Trying to Find One's Way Home', 1998). Inscribed on each photograph is a quote either from Nguyễn Du's nineteenth-century epic poem, *The Tale of Kiêue*,[96] or from interviews with Vietnamese-Americans about the war, or letters written by soldiers and their wives.[97]

Other powerful artworks are those about the effects of Agent Orange in Vietnam, which are surprisingly beautiful and poetic. They include *Damaged Gene* (1998), held in a market in Ho Chi Minh City where he displayed small statuettes, clothes for Siamese twins and T-shirts about the effects of Agent

Orange. *Lotusland* (1999), of course, references the lotus, which is a symbol of purity and also connects to Buddhist beliefs. Like *Damaged Gene*, it used small statues, this time statues of conjoined twins, beautifully crafted in fibreglass by Vietnamese craftsmen who make temple sculptures. These figures are essentially a memorial to children born with birth defects. There were many such children born as a result of the huge amounts of chemicals dumped on Vietnam by the US during the Vietnam War. The artist said he had seen deformed people begging in the streets, but no one wanted to talk about it. He says that the situation has improved since 1998, when the government in Vietnam started to take care of these people. A problem, though, is that Vietnam was already then the third largest exporter of rice in the world and the third or fourth largest exporter of coffee, and drawing attention to the continued impact of Agent Orange could affect agricultural exports. But also, he says, 'the urban myth was that by talking about it' you might give birth to a deformed child.[98]

The most poignant symbol of the Vietnam War was the helicopter swooping over fields to kill, and to poison the environment. Bitterness was, however, absent from his film *The Farmers and the Helicopters* (2006). It comprised a three-channel colour video, interlacing interviews with Vietnamese, including two who, in recent times, had decided to build a helicopter to help with agricultural work. Personal recollections of Vietnamese locals of what the helicopters were like during the war are combined with clips of Hollywood films. It has been shown in many countries, and in the US it was shown in the Museum of Modern Art, New York, along with the actual helicopter that had been handcrafted from spare parts by Lê Văn Danh, a farmer, and Trần Quốc Hải, a self-taught mechanic. 'Many of the people I interviewed', Lê has said, 'relayed childhood memories of the horrors associated with helicopters during the war and the priority for me was to let them speak.'[99] The farmer and mechanic explain that their vision of the machine was as a means of bringing strength to their community and a better life for the Vietnamese people. For most of those who view the film, it is a moving story of resilience.

The artist's impulse in these works, it can be suggested, was in part to mediate memories of the American war for the Vietnamese people, but more especially to present a different narrative for Americans. Lê said, 'People were surprised to find that in all my work, there is no anger, no accusation.' He suggested that it might be because of the influence of Buddhism where the 'belief in rebirth means that many people view their present life as a reflection of actions in a previous life'.[100] On that basis, his 3D animation *South China Sea Pishkun* (2009), depicting US helicopters crashing in the sea in vain efforts to reach their carrier after the fall of Saigon, might be regarded as an illustration of the principle of karma. Lê himself has compared it to a herd of bison

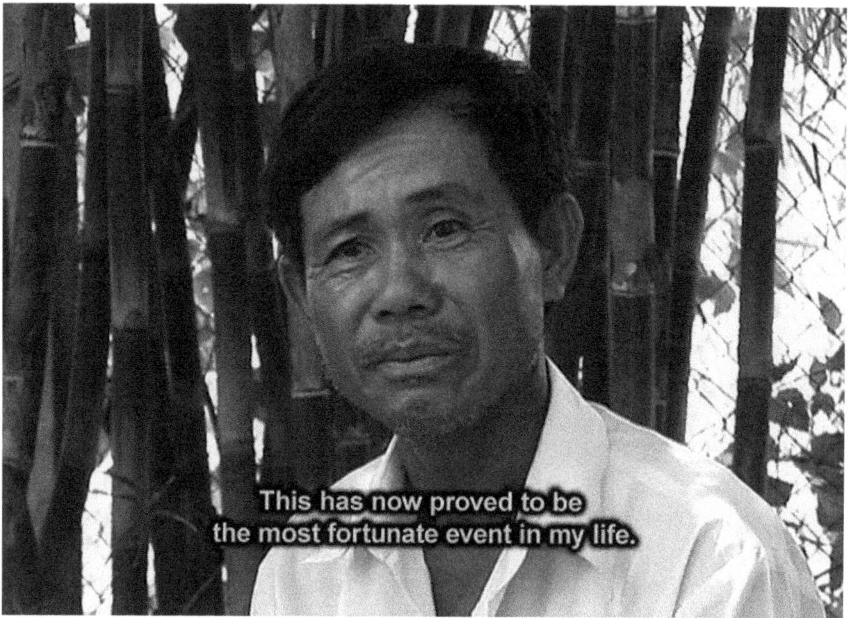

3.11 Dinh Q. Lê (with Tuấn Andrew Nguyễn and Thúc Phù Nam Hà), *The Farmers and the Helicopters*, 2006. Film still. Collection: Queensland Art Gallery. The Queensland Government's Gallery of Modern Art Acquisition Fund.

running off a cliff, and has stated that one of his purposes in these works is to 'take control of history'.[101]

The Vietnam War was not only an international war, but also a civil war fought on ideological grounds. This gives enormous complexity to the historical viewpoints, as many who fled the South after the war was lost maintain their original views. An article in the *Los Angeles Times* in 2008 discussed this issue in relation to the many Vietnamese living in California, stating that, while attitudes are changing, much bitterness remains: 'some … continue to mount street protests, fly the South Vietnamese flag from businesses and lampposts, and rail against communism on radio talk shows'.[102] Inevitably, these viewpoints also affect overall American memories of the conflict.

In a work first shown in Germany in Documenta 13 in 2012, Lê explored the Vietnam War in the installation *Light and Belief: Voices and Sketches of Life from the Vietnam War* (2012), working with Vietnamese artists Vũ Giáng Hương, Quang Thọ, Huỳnh Phương Đông, Nguyễn Thụ, Trương Hiếu, Phan Oánh, Nguyễn Toàn Thi, Dương Ánh, Minh Phương, Kim Tiến, Quách Phong, Lê Lam and Nguyễn Thanh Châu. They are some of the artists, women as well as men, who had been sent to the front both in the independence war against the French and in what is called in Vietnam the American war, fighting the South as well as the US and its allies. Their purpose was to document the fighting, producing posters and drawings of comrades and life in the camps; but they were regarded as soldiers and also required to participate in battles.[103] Nora Taylor, writing on Vietnamese artists from the colonial period to the present, notes that artists such as Tô Ngọc Vân were deeply concerned also with creating a new Vietnamese art, declaring in 1945 that 'tradition starts now'. This artist, educator and soldier was killed in battle against the French at Dien Bien Phu.[104] The defeat of first the French and then the Americans and their allies by the Vietnamese had an enormous impact on the postcolonial world, as historian Dipesh Chakrabarty has noted in relation to his own life, growing up in India where the defeat of the French at Dien Bien Phu was a mantra of anti-colonialism.[105]

For *Light and Belief: Sketches of Life from the Vietnam War* (2012), Lê produced a film featuring interviews with the artists from what then was called North Vietnam, and also exhibited their war drawings and watercolour sketches, showing how people sought normality in the midst of war. The now elderly artists speak, some with passion, others quietly; one describes hundreds, if not thousands, of years of war in Vietnam, of much sorrow in the land, and of a war where a mother could lose four children. Figure 3.12 is a portrait of a woman soldier by Vũ Giáng Hương, a woman artist who, after the war, had a prominent position in the arts in Vietnam. There is no real violence in the works, and Lê states that this was a decision of the artists. The drawings had been mostly done in camp in quiet moments. The images are all of young people, men and women. Very often the images of the soldiers were done as private mementos; they became the only record left for the families if they were killed, and were used for their funerals. The Carnegie Museum of Art in Pittsburgh, which also hosted the exhibition and has now purchased the installation, quotes artist-soldier Nguyễn Toàn Thi in the film as saying, 'The sketches are more precious than photographs, because they're drawn with our emotions.'[106] In this work the artist shows how history can be seen through a different lens at different times; its purchase by an art museum in the US, which was fighting these soldier/artists at the time when the works were made, is indicative of this. Dinh Q. Lê has stated, in relation to his approach to history: 'An individual with no knowledge of his or her history is an individual without an identity.'[107]

He also suggests that Vietnam needs to confront its own history in its entirety, and that the art organisation Sàn Art is central to his work. 'One cannot live responsibly in Vietnam, with all its problems and complexities, without engaging with society,' he says; 'Through Sàn Art, I hope some kind of transformation in the community can take place.'[108] It is clear that Lê exhibits more outside than within Vietnam, and these current issues may be part of the

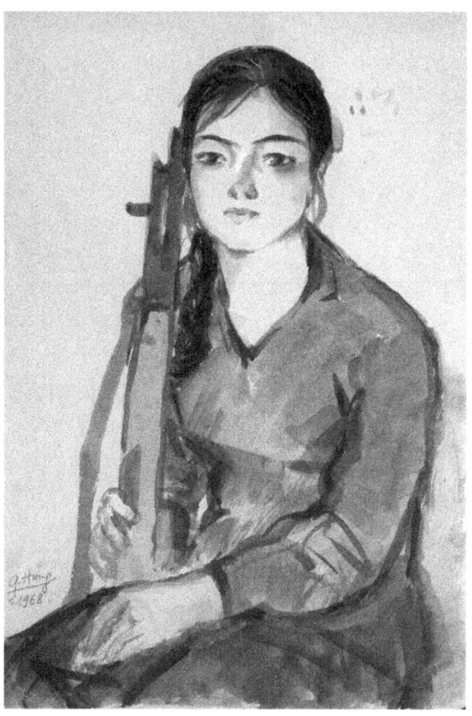

3.12 Dinh Q. Lê, *Light & Belief: Voices and Sketches of Life from the Vietnam War*, 2012–13. Detail: work by Vũ Giáng Hương, *Woman seated holding gun (Untitled)*, 1968. Complete installation: 101 drawings. Collection: Carnegie Museum of Art, Pittsburgh: The Henry L. Hillman Fund.

reasons. However, he has a critical role in the Vietnam art world, running Sàn Art and the Foundation, and being a mentor to younger Vietnamese artists.

Lê's concern is for the present, but for a present that has not erased the past from memory. This concern is manifested in his monumental installation *Erasure* (2011) at the Sherman Contemporary Art Foundation in Sydney (see Plate 7). *Erasure* was inspired by an horrific Australian event, the estimated loss of around fifty lives in the wreck of a refugee boat from Indonesia carrying mainly Iraqi and Iranian asylum-seekers, against the rocks of Christmas Island on 15 December 2010. Lê's hope in creating the installation was, he said, to enable audiences in Australia and in the world outside to remember that we are all immigrants – a reality that has been erased by bureaucratic procedures of crisis control and prevention – and to respond to the global phenomenon of boat people with some degree of compassion. The installation includes a projection of an eighteenth-century ship (presumably referring to Australia's founding in 1788), beached and burning in an endless cycle of self-combustion, while the floor is littered with thousands of family photographs of Vietnamese prior to the exodus of refugees, collected from antique shops in Ho Chi Minh City. Viewers were asked to scan these into a computer website to help those looking for images of their families to identify them. Australia has many immigrants who were refugees from South Vietnam, and these photographs would have had a special emotional significance to them. Lê has said, 'There is an urgent need for expressions of collective memory freed from restraint; many people are actively engaged in building these narratives – I chose to do so through art.'[109]

Conclusion

Divided societies and their communities and citizens who are attempting to deal with trauma through war or conflict need to find ways of healing, and of finding reconciliation with the past so that there is a possibility to build a future. There are three stages in this healing process, according to the literature of both the psychological and the political fields: first finding a place of safety; then dealing with remembrance and mourning; and finally seeking reconnection. The process requires a number of actions: the application of justice and the institution of good legislation, of course, but also, and importantly, actions that allow all those wounded by recent history to begin to heal. This involves the building of shared identities, often through symbols with which many people can connect.[110] This is where artists can play an important part in healing the wounds of the past, and beginning to suggest ways to find a future beyond conflict and trauma. Though the first step, a place of safety, is the task of legislators and government processes, artists are ideally equipped to support the acts of remembrance, to provide opportunities to mourn productively, and to help lay out paths towards reconciliation.[111] All four artists discussed in this chapter participate in such work through their concern with narrating violence, and with recalling collective memory and history. Shimada directly confronts the silences around history and Japan's colonial past; Weerasinghe and Harsono focus closely on their respective countries of Sri Lanka and Indonesia, while Lê pursues a more complex mediation between different histories in Cambodia, Vietnam and the US and between two sides in the Vietnam War. In each case, the imagery and narratives they produce, and the collaborations and performances that draw in their audiences, can contribute to the long and difficult work of recovering from war, and restoring divided societies.

Notes

1 Costas Douzinas, *The End of Human Rights: Critical Legal Thought at the Turn of the Century* (Oxford: Hart Publishing, 2000), p. 142.

2 Susan Sontag, *Regarding the Pain of Others* (New York: Farrar, Straus and Giroux, 2003), p. 105.

3 Ronald H. Spector, *In the Ruins of Empire: The Japanese Surrender and the Battle for Postwar Asia* (New York: Random House, 2007).

4 Caroline Turner and Glen St J. Barclay, 'Art against War', in Nigel Young (ed.), *Oxford Encyclopedia of Peace* (Oxford: Oxford University Press, 2010), pp. 132–7.

5 John Clark, *Modern Asian Art* (Sydney: Craftsman House, 1998), p. 241; Werner Kraus, 'Raden Saleh's Interpretation of the Arrest of Diponegoro: An Example of Indonesian "Proto-nationalist" Modernism', *Archipel*, 69 (2005), pp. 259–94.

6 The art work can be viewed on www.yhchang.com/OPERATION_NUKOREA.html.

7 Early this century she founded the Feminist Art Action Brigade; FAAB's manifesto is at http://home.interlink.or.jp/~reflect/GAAP/FAABe.html, accessed 15 September 2014.

8 Cited Diana Yeh, 'Past Imperfect, Present Tense', *The International Artist Database: Yoshiko Shimada* (2007), www.culturebase.net/artist.php?1516, accessed 12 July 2014.

9 Cited Yeh, 'Past Imperfect'.

10 Monty DiPietro, 'How to Use Women's Body at Ota Fine Arts', *Assembly Language Reviews* (2000), www.assemblylanguage.com/reviews/Shimada.html, accessed 12 August 2014.

11 Yoshiko Shimada, 'Grey Zone of Identity', *How to Use Women's Body: Transfiguration of Sex, Gender, Nationality* (Tokyo: Ota Fine Arts, 2000).

12 Shimada, interview with authors, 2002. See also Yoshiko Shimada, *Escape from Oneself* (Tokyo: Ota Fine Arts, 2002). The killings of Koreans after the earthquake in Tokyo because of fears there would be an uprising have been well documented by historians. For a discussion of nation and cultural identity, including minorities, in Japan see Tessa Morris-Suzuki, *Re-inventing Japan: Time, Space, Nation* (New York: ME Sharpe, 1998).

13 Julia Thomas, 'Photography, National Identity, and the "Cataract of Times": Wartime Images and the Case of Japan', *The American Historical Review*, 103:5 (December 1998), pp. 1475–501: 1485.

14 Thomas, 'Photography', p. 1489.

15 Hiroko Hagiwara, 'Comfort Women, Women of Conformity: The Work of Shimada Yoshiko', in Griselda Pollock (ed.), *Generations & Geographies in the Visual Arts: Feminist Readings* (London: Routledge, 1996), pp. 253–62: 253.

16 Nancy Shalala, 'Japan – Censorship Silences Japanese Artists', *Asian Arts News*, 4:5 (September/October 1994), pp. 62–7.

17 Hagiwara, 'Comfort Women, Women of Conformity'.

18 Marjorie Anne Kirker, 'Printmaking as an Expanding Field in Contemporary Art Practice: A Case Study of Japan, Australia and Thailand' (PhD thesis, Queensland University of Technology, 2009), p. 108.

19 Lisa Bloom, 'Gender, Race and Nation in Japanese Contemporary Art and Criticism', *N. Paradoxa* v (2000), pp. 35–43.

20 Kirker, 'Printmaking as an Expanding Field', p. 48.

21 Alexandra Munroe, *Japanese Art After 1945: Scream Against the Sky* (New York: Abrams, 1994). On new perspectives on Japan's postwar art, see Japan Foundation Symposium Report, *In Search of a New Narrative of Postwar Japanese Art: What becomes Visible through the Exhibitions at the Two Modern Art Museums in New York and Tokyo* (Tokyo: Japan Foundation 2014). See also on issues of history: Tessa Morris-Suzuki, 'Truth, Postmodernism and Historical Revisionism in Japan', *Inter-Asia Cultural Studies*, 2:2 (2001), pp. 297–305. See also references in Caroline Turner, 'The Enigma of Japanese Contemporary Art' in Turner (ed.), *Art and Social Change*, 2005, pp. 385–430. On issues of gender and human rights in Japan see Vera Mackie, *Feminism in Modern Japan: Citizenship, Embodiment and Sexuality* (Cambridge: Cambridge University Press, 2003); Anne-Marie Hilsdon, Martha Macintyre, Vera Mackie and Maila Stivens (eds), *Human Rights and Gender Politics: Asia-Pacific Perspectives* (London: Routledge, 2000).

22 Caroline Turner and Glen St J. Barclay, 'Recovering Lives Through Art: Hidden Histories and Commemoration in the Works of Katsushige Nakahashi and Dadang Christanto', in Paul Longley Arthur (ed.), *International Life Writing: Memory and Identity in Global Context* (London: Routledge, 2013), pp. 107–25.

23 Monty DiPietro, 'Artist Builds from Zero', *Japan Times* (11 August 2008), www.japantimes.co.jp/culture/2004/08/11/arts/artist-builds-from-zero/#.VB-coSuSxEA, accessed 12 July 2013.

24 Shimada, interview with authors, 2005. As a consequence of this, Shimada points out, the artists had to fund the money to support the exhibition themselves; the Korean artists compiled and sold portfolios of prints, but the Japanese artists were not able to do this because 'we knew collectors would not buy our works'.

25 James Card, 'A Chronicle of Korea-Japan "Friendship"', *Asia Times* (23 December 2005), www.atimes.com/atimes/Korea/GL23Dg02.html, accessed 12 July 2013.

26 Until the 1990s, the Japanese government still insisted that Japan was a monocultural country. Liberty Osaka: the Human Rights Museum challenged this with their permanent displays that treat Burakumin, Ainu and Okinawans as well as local Koreans, and the struggles for rights for other marginalised groups including women, the homeless, disabled people, gay people and others. Takahiro Takiguchi reports that both federal and city funding is to be withdrawn on the basis that these exhibitions do not provide children with hope for the future. See Takahiro Takiguchi, 'Japan's Only Human Rights Museum Strive to Survive, *Stripes Okinawa* (22 October 2013), http://okinawa.stripes.com/news/japans-only-human-rights-museum-strive-survive, accessed 12 July 2013.

27 Yoshiko Shimada, 'Art, Feminism and Activism', in Jennifer Chan (ed.), *Another Japan is Possible: New Social Movements and Global Citizenship Education* (Stanford: Stanford University Press, 2008), pp. 242–6: 245.

28 See, for example, *Bubu de la Madeleine: Art Works 1993–2005* (Tokyo: Ota Fine Arts, 2005).

29 Shimada, interview with authors, 2005.

30 Shimada, interview with authors, 2005.

31 Shimada, interview with authors, 2005.

32 Rebecca Jennison, 'Yoshiko Shimada: Silence, Secrets and Sex in the Gallery', *MutualArt News* (July/August 2009), www.mutualart.com/OpenArticle/Yoshiko-Shimada–Silence–Secrets-and-Se/E902A8BB9E13FF8F, accessed 15 August 2014.

33 Monty DiPietro, 'Skeletons Come out of the Closet', *Japan Times: Culture* (30 June 2004), www.japantimes.co.jp/culture/2004/06/30/arts/skeletons-come-out-of-the-closet/#.U8QzsbHb5Zg, accessed 15 August 2014.

34 Jagath Weerasinghe, communication with the authors, 2014. He recalls that his father also, on many occasions, performed as the Clerk of Assize to the Jaffna Supreme Court; on such occasions he would take his family to Jaffna, 'and would leave us with his Tamil friends in the circuit bungalow while he went on with his work in the court'.

35 Jagath Weerasinghe, 'Artist's statement', *Third Asia-Pacific Triennial* (Brisbane: Queensland Art Gallery, 1999). See also 'Art, War and Politics in Sri Lanka: An Interview with Jagath Weerasinghe' (video), www.youtube.com/watch?v=6CXioS8K37A, accessed 3 May 2014.

36 Sasanka Perera, *Artists Remember; Artists Narrate: Memory and Representation in Contemporary Sri Lankan Visual Arts* (Colombo: Colombo Institute for the Advanced Study of Society and Culture, 2012), pp. 33–4.

37 'Sri Lanka', *The World Factbook*, Central Intelligence Agency (23 June 2014), https://www.cia.gov/library/publications/the-world-factbook/geos/ce.html, accessed 5 August 2014.

38 Kate Pickert, 'A Brief History of the Tamil Tigers', *Time* magazine (4 January 2009), http://content.time.com/time/world/article/0,8599,1869501,00.html, accessed 20 July 2014. See also William Dalrymple, *The Age of Kali: Indian Travels and Encounters* (London: Penguin, 1998), pp. 237–62. For a review of methods used by the government see Visakesa Chandrasekaram, 'Do Tigers Confess: An Interdisciplinary Study of Confessionary Evidence in Counter-Terrorism Measures of Sri Lanka' (PhD thesis, Australian National University, 2012).

39 No accurate account of casualties has been determined, and figures are disputed. The UN Humanitarian Co-ordination Office considered, after the close of hostilities in 2009, that between 80,000 and 100,000 people had been killed; see the ABC News report (21 May 2009), www.abc.net.au/news/2009-05-20/up-to-100000-killed-in-sri-lankas-civil-war-un/1689524, accessed 22 July 2014. See also 'Shattered Lives: Sri Lanka's Bloody Civil War', *The Economist* (19 November 2012), www.economist.com/blogs/banyan/2012/11/sri-lankas-bloody-civil-war, accessed 5 August 2014.

40 United Nations, 'Report of the Secretary-General's Panel of Experts on Accountability in Sri Lanka' (31 March 2011), www.un.org/News/dh/infocus/Sri_Lanka/POE_Report_Full.pdf, accessed 14 September 2014.

41 Chandraguptha Thenuwara, *Artists for Peace 2005, 12th and 13th November* (Colombo: The National Art Gallery, 2005).

42 Jagath Weerasinghe, 'Contemporary Art in Sri Lanka', in Caroline Turner (ed.), *Art and Social Change: Contemporary Art in Asia and the Pacific* (Canberra: Pandanus Books, 2005), pp. 180–95: 187.

43 Theertha, Sri Lanka: Mission Statement, *Arts Collaboratory, Organisations* (2013), http://old.artscollaboratory.org/node/21, accessed 9 January 2015.

44 Jagath Weerasinghe, Artist's Talk, Queensland Art Gallery, Brisbane, 1999.

45 Sasanka Perera, *Artists Remember*, p. 29.

46 Suhanya Raffel, 'Jagath Weerasinghe: Embodied Terror – *Yantra Gala and the Round Pilgrimage*', *Beyond the Future: the Third Asia-Pacific Triennial of Contemporary Art* (Brisbane: Queensland Art Gallery, 1999), p. 144.

47 Anoli Perera, 'Jagath Weerasinghe: A Prelude to an Exhibition', *Raking Leaves: Artists* (n.d.), www.rakingleaves.org/artists/, accessed 22 July 2014.

48 R. J. Preece, 'Jagath Weerasinghe: Artist Voice from Sri Lanka', *artdesigncafe* (1997), www.artdesigncafe.com/Jagath-Weerasinghe-1997, accessed 14 July 2014.

49 Sharmini Pereira (curator), *New Approaches in Contemporary Sri Lankan Art*, Art Gallery of Colombo (17–23 May 1994).

50 Annoushka Hempel and Jagath Weerasinghe, *Colombo Art Biennale 2009: Imagining Peace* (Colombo: Colombo Art Biennale, 2009).

51 Preece, 'Jagath Weerasinghe'.

52 *Celestial Fervor: The Art of Jagath Weerasinghe* (Colombo: Red Dot Gallery / Theertha, 2009). Published to accompany the exhibition 'Celestial Fervor: The Art of Jagath Weerasinghe', Red Dot Gallery/Theertha, 2009.

53 Perera, 'Jagath Weerasinghe'.

54 FX Harsono, 'Invitation', for the exhibition *Displaced*, Cemeti Art House, Yogyakarta, 8 July 2003.

55 Farah Wardani, 'On FX Harsono', *Farah Wardani Archives* (25 July 2013), http://arsip-farahwardani.tumblr.com/post/56412030819/on-fx-harsono, accessed 20 June 2014.

56 See World Population Review: Indonesia Population (2014), http://worldpopula-tionreview.com/countries/indonesia-population/, accessed 5 August 2014.

57 Hendro Wiyanto, 'A Brief Biography from Tjoe Tien Alley', in Amanda Katherine Rath *et al.* (eds), *Re: Petition/ Position/ FX Harsono* (Yogyakarta: Langgeng Art Foundation, 2010), pp. 123–35.

58 Athina Ibrahim, 'Cultural identity and the Arts with FX Harsono', *Whiteboard Journal* (30 October 2013), www.whiteboardjournal.com/interview/12455/cultural-identity-and-the-arts-with-fx-harsono/, accessed 9 December 2014.

59 This acronym is an artefact of the original establishment of the Institute out of three independent schools of art.

60 See biographical details at 'FX Harsono', Arndt Gallery, Berlin (n.d.), www.arndt-berlin.com/website/artist_8554, accessed 4 August 2014.

61 Jim Supangkat, 'Indonesia', *First Asia-Pacific Triennial of Contemporary Art* (Brisbane: Queensland Art Gallery, 1993), pp. 12–20: 15.

62 Wardani, 'On FX Harsono'.

63 Author observations; and Harsono, conversation with Caroline Turner, 2014.

64 Sonia Kolesnikov-Jessop, 'FX Harsono's Rebellious, Critical Voice against "Big Power" in Indonesia', *New York Times* (11 March 2010), www.nytimes. com/2010/03/12/arts/12iht-Jessop.html?pagewanted=all&_r=0, accessed 20 June 2014.

65 Anita Hackethal, 'FX Harsono: Testimonies', *Designboom* (20 April 2010), www. designboom.com/art/fx-harsono-testimonies-part-01/, accessed 5 June 2014.

66 'The Happy Chinese', *The Economist* (2 February 2006), www.economist.com/ node/5476216, accessed 4 July 2014.

67 Hendro Wiyanto, *What We Have Here Perceived as Truth, We Shall Some Day Encounter as Beauty: A Solo Show by FX Harsono* (Jakarta: Indonesia Galeri Canna, 2013), p. 95.

68 FX Harsono, 'FX Harsono and the Art of Political Protest', Para Site Hong Kong artist talk (13 April 2013), podcast on Art Radar, http://artradarjournal.com/2013/04/23/ fx-harsono-and-the-art-of-political-protest-para-site-hong-kong-artist-talk/, accessed 5 June 2014.

69 Harsono, Talk at the National Gallery of Australia, 14 June 2014.

70 Melani Budianta, 'Discourse of Cultural Identity in Indonesia during the 1997–1998 Monetary Crisis', in Kuan-Hsing Chen and Chua Beng Huat (eds), *Inter-Asia Cultural Studies Reader* (Milton Park: Routledge, 2007), pp. 507–21.

71 Kathryn Robinson, 'Introduction', in K. Robinson (ed.), *Asian and Pacific Cosmopolitanisms: Self and Subject in Motion* (Basingstoke: Palgrave, 2007), pp. 1–15.

72 Abidin Kusno, 'Remembering / Forgetting the May Riots: Architecture, Violence and the Making of "Chinese Cultures" in Post-1998 Jakarta', *Public Culture*, 15:1 (2003), pp. 149–77.

73 Indah Setiawati and Corry Elyda, 'Dead of May 1998 to be Memorialised', *Jakarta Post* (3 April 2014), www.thejakartapost.com/news/2014/04/03/dead-may-1998-be-memorialized.html, accessed 7 August 2014.

74 Jemma Purdey, *Anti-Chinese Violence in Indonesia, 1996–1999* (Singapore: Asian Studies Association of Australia in association with Singapore University Press, 2006), p. 140.

75 Purdey, *Anti-Chinese Violence*. p. 143.

76 Prodita Sabarini, 'FX Harsono: Testimonies Through Art', *Jakarta Post* (27 April 2010), www.thejakartapost.com/news/2010/04/27/fx-harsono-testimonies-through-art. html, accessed 4 August 2014. FX Harsono was awarded the first Joseph Balestier Award for Freedom of Art in 2015. 'The prize … is to be awarded annually to an artist who exemplifies a commitment to art and to freedom of expression in art across ASEAN' and was awarded to him 'for his installation and performance work which is characterised by strong political messages promoting democracy and exploring the experiences of members of ethnic minorities'. See http://en.artmediaagency. com/100408/fx-harsono-wins-inaugral-joseph-balestier-award-for-freedom-of-art/, accessed 9 March 2015.

77 Harsono, Artist Talk at NGA, 2014.

78 Harsono, Artist Talk at NGA, 2014.

79 Wiyanto, *What We Have Here Perceived*, p. 87.

80 Wiyanto, *What We Have Here Perceived*, p. 15.

81 Wiyanto, *What We Have Here Perceived*, pp. 91–2.

82 H.G. Masters, 'FX Harsono', *ArtAsiaPacific*, 85 (September/October 2013), p. 132. The Chinese at the time had also been accused of collaborating with the Dutch who were trying to reassert their colonial authority, but Harsono told the audience at the National Gallery of Australia in 2014 that he believes the Dutch forced the Chinese who did so to collaborate.

83 Former President Corazon Aquino in the Philippines was one who recovered her Chinese ancestry. See Caroline Hau, *The Chinese Question: Ethnicity, Nation, and Region in and beyond the Philippines* (Quezon City: University of the Philippines Press, 2014).

84 John Braithwaite, Valerie Braithwaite, Michael Cookson and Leah Dunn, *Anomie and Violence: Non-truth and Reconciliation in Indonesian Peacebuilding* (Canberra: ANU Press, 2010).

85 'Indonesia', *International Center for Transitional Justice* (2014), www.ictj.org/our-work/regions-and-countries/indonesia, accessed 4 August 2014.

86 Mette Bjerregaard, 'What Indonesians Really Think about The Act of Killing', *Guardian* (6 March 2014), www.theguardian.com/film/2014/mar/05/act-of-killing-screening-in-indonesia, accessed 6 August 2014.

87 Zoe Butt, 'Archiving Fear in the Struggle against Forgetfulness', in *Dinh Q. Lê: Erasure* (Paddington, NSW: Sherman Contemporary Art Foundation, 2011), p. 53.

88 Dinh Q. Lê, video from Projects 93, MOMA (2010), www.moma.org/visit/calendar/exhibitions/1061, accessed 5 August 2011.

89 Zhuang Wubin, 'Dinh Lê: Engaging the Past', *Asian Art News* (November/December 2006), pp. 60–7: 63.

90 David Spalding, 'Dinh Q. Lê', MOMA: The Collection Online (2009), www.moma.org/collection/artist.php?artist_id=26740, accessed 7 August 2014. Another version of Accountability was published by Creative Time in 1992 when the US was seeking accountability from Vietnam about missing American soldiers. The question was raised in the work about US accountability for deaths and destruction in Vietnam, including the births of deformed children as a result of chemical pollution. (Correspondence with the authors, June 2015.)

91 Zhuang Wubin, 'Engaging the Past', p. 62.

92 Rebecca McGrew, 'Project Series 6: Dinh Q. Lê', Pomona College Museum of Art (4 March–9 April 2000), www.pomona.edu/museum/exhibitions/2000/project-series-6/, accessed 1 August 2014.

93 Zhuang Wubin, 'Engaging the Past', p. 64.

94 Claudine Ise, ' "Headless Buddha" Weaves History, Myth', *Los Angeles Times* (6 March 1998), http://articles.latimes.com/1998/mar/06/entertainment/ca-25909, accessed 7 August 2014.

95 Dolla S. Merrillees, 'An Interview with Dinh Q. Lê', *Dinh Q. Lê: Erasure* (Paddington, NSW: Sherman Contemporary Art Foundation, 2011), pp. 15, 20.

96 *The Tale of Kiêue* is about a heroine forced into prostitution and away from her country but eventually able to return, and symbolically is seen standing for Vietnam itself. See McGrew 'Project Series 6'.

97 Zhuang Wubin, 'Engaging the Past', p. 61.

98 Correspondence with authors, 2015.

99 Merrillees, 'An Interview', p. 17.

100 Merrillees, 'An Interview', p. 19.

101 Dinh Q. Lê, video from exhibition, MOMA (2010), www.moma.org/visit/calendar/exhibitions/, accessed 5 August 2011.

102 My-Thuan Tran, 'Lives Remembered, Lives Rebuilt, Attitudes Changing – 33 Years after South Vietnam Fell', *Los Angeles Times* (30 April 2008), www.latimes.com/world/asia/la-me-saigon30apr30-story.html#page=1, accessed 7 August 2014.

103 Dinh Q. Lê, 'Introduction: Carolyn Christov-Bakargiev in conversation with Dinh Q. Lê', *dOCUMENTA 13: 100 Notes – 100 Thoughts* (Berlin: Hatje Cantz, 2012).

104 Nora Taylor, *Painters in Hanoi: An Ethnography of Vietnamese Art* (Singapore: National University of Singapore Press, 2009), p. 43. For a discussion of the history of artists in the war against the French (the First Indochina War 1946–54), see Phoebe Scott, 'Forming and Reforming the Artist: Modernity, Agency and the Discourse of Art in North Vietnam 1925–1954' (PhD thesis, University of Sydney, 2012).

105 Dipesh Chakrabarty, author notes from seminar at Humanities Research Centre, Australian National University, 4 August 2014.

106 Julie Hannon, 'History Redux', Carnegie (Fall 2013), www.carnegiemuseums.org/cmag/feature.php?id=377, accessed 7 August 2014.

107 Dinh Q. Lê, 'In Conversation with Zoe Butt', Guggenheim Museum (22 January 2013), http://blogs.guggenheim.org/map/dinh-q-le-in-conversation-with-zoe-butt/, accessed 23 July 2014.

108 Dinh Q. Lê, 'In conversation with Zoe Butt'.

109 Dinh Q. Lê, 'In conversation with Zoe Butt'. See also: Zoe Butt 'Red Tape and Digital Talismans: Shaping Knowledge Beneath Surveillance', in Larissa Hjorth, Natalie King and Mami Kataoka (eds), *Art in the Asia-Pacific: Intimate Publics* (New York: Routledge, 2014), pp. 91–104.

110 See, for example, Erin Daly and Jeremy Sarkin, *Reconciliation in Divided Societies: Finding Common Ground* (Philadelphia: University of Pennsylvania Press, 2007); Judy Barsalou, 'Trauma and Transitional Justice in Divided Societies' (report for the United States Institute of Peace, Washington, 2005); Anthony Oberschall, *Conflict and Peace Building in Divided Societies: Responses to Ethnic Violence* (Milton Park: Routledge, 2007).

111 Marc Howard Ross (ed.), *Culture and Belonging in Divided Societies: Contestation and Symbolic Landscapes* (Philadelphia: University of Pennsylvania Press, 2009).

Introduction

In previous chapters we have referred to elements of the history of the various nations in the region, and the effect of local histories in shaping the possibilities of both art and civic practice. Our concern is with the question of whether art can provide new models for cultural, social and political understanding in a globalising world, or for understanding political and cultural identities. Historian Jörn Rüsen writes that 'aesthetics break [*sic*] through the practical constraints of historiography and liberates the audience in the way it related historical experience and its orientational potential in practical life … It introduces the chance of autonomy within the framework of historical determinism.'[1] His focus is on historians writing history, but it applies equally, we argue, to artists witnessing to and recording current events, or providing images and ideas about the past. Both modes of production provide ways of thinking about how the world is and how it might be, and both have the potential to be acts committed to human rights. As bell hooks observes, 'Our living depends on our ability to conceptualize alternatives … Theorizing about this experience aesthetically, critically is an agenda for radical cultural practice.'[2] It is the role of art in conceptualising alternatives, and theorising about community and culture, that is our focus in this chapter. To explore this, we present case studies of key artists in the region who have taken on this task. The artists selected are Kimsooja from South Korea; Alfredo and Isabel Aquilizan from the Philippines; and Oscar Ho and John Young, both from Hong Kong. All are articulate critics of, and contributors to, contemporary cultural and political practice; and all have engaged thoughtfully and critically, and developed a radical cultural practice that sheds light on their historical and contemporary contexts.

Singaporean academic Lily Kong commented in 2012: 'The reality is that our lives [today] are shaped by both the global and the local, the transnational and the nation';[3] and the artists in the group can be understood in these terms. All have travelled, studied and/or lived away from their countries of origin. Kimsooja retains a home and a practice in Korea, but also lives and works in

New York and Paris. Husband and wife team Alfredo and Isabel Aquilizan hail from the Philippines, and in 2006 emigrated with their children to Australia – a move that initiated a new installation, *Project Be-Longing: In Transit* (2006). Oscar Ho studied abroad, and for a while lived and worked in Shanghai, but remains a passionate advocate of Hong Kong culture; and John Young was born in Hong Kong but has pursued his vocation mainly in Australia. We follow Kong's lead in addressing their work and their contexts through the lens of 'the global and the local, the transnational and the nation': not only their national/cultural identity, but also how they find a place in the regional and the global contexts. Each artist exemplifies the complexities of political identity, and the accounts of their careers are reminders of the plurality of identity and its variability: that, to use Stuart Hall's term, it is never completed, but always in a process of becoming, and is something that 'belongs to the future as much as to the past'.[4]

Identity is even more complex when societies are in the process of significant change. The artists we discuss here have all experienced changing political situations in their countries of birth. Korea, an ancient civilisation known as the Hermit Kingdom, was occupied and colonised by Japan from 1910 to 1945. In 1948 the southern part of the country elected a national assembly and established the Republic of Korea, but the north rejected this option, and later in the same year established the Democratic People's Republic of Korea.[5] By the early 1950s North Korea had attempted a forcible unification, and the two halves of the country were at war: a war that is technically still in process. South Korea was at various times under martial law until the 1980s, when democratic reforms were instituted,[6] while North Korea has remained under a dictatorial communist regime. The Philippines has an equally difficult history: it was first colonised by Spain in the sixteenth century, and then ceded to the US in the late nineteenth century. The US maintained that it did not seek permanent colonial control over the Philippines, but US culture had a significant effect on the local culture and society.[7] In the twentieth century it was occupied by the Japanese, and during the Pacific War, Filipino resistance fighters engaged in struggle right across the archipelago. They finally achieved independence in 1946, but then between 1972 and 1981, under Marcos's regime, the country was placed under martial law.[8] Not until Marcos was overthrown by a peaceful revolution in 1986 did the nation begin to establish democratic government, but the years since have been marked by factionalism and violence.[9]

Japan has had a more stable history than either Korea or the Philippines since its defeat at the end of the Pacific War, and developed a highly advanced economy and democratic governmental structure during the second half of the twentieth century. However, it still has a complex relationship with its former colonies, and with neighbours such as China that were sites of occupation.[10] In addition, recent decades have been marked by political fragility and an economic downturn; and the social landscape is still marked by discrimination against, for example, the Ainu, or Koreans living in Japan. Hong Kong was colonised by Britain in 1842, and remained a colony until it was occupied by Japan in 1941; it remained under occupation until the end of the second world war, when Britain resumed control over the city state. In 1997, Hong Kong was returned to China as a Special Administrative Region, which permits it a degree of autonomy from Beijing. Since 1997, it has experienced the complexities of integration into the People's Republic of China.[11]

These four nations are not alone in their sometimes-tumultuous recent history. The latter part of the twentieth century and the early twenty-first century introduced greater complexities across the world, marked as the period is by a rapid increase in globalisation, travel and increasingly connected contacts between people to the point where new and extended global interactions have enormous impact on individual lives. Globalisation in particular has generated new debates about differences, similarities, parallel histories, art histories and art practices, and it is a key element in the experience and identity of many artists. Analyst Manuel Castells identifies globalisation as an effect of twentieth-century technology and the role it played in bringing about 'one of those rare intervals in history … the transformation of our material culture'.[12] We expand Castells's 'material culture' beyond the modes of digital technology to incorporate materials as fundamental as how we eat, how we dress, how we live, as well as artistic materials: media, production and exhibition processes, networks, and practices of communication between artists, galleries, publishers and agents. There is, however, little doubt that communication technology is central to globalisation, as Homi Bhabha, too, suggests: 'Wherever you live, whoever you may be, once the lights dim in a movie theatre, or the screen lights up on your TV or PC, you become, more or less, a part of the global world.'[13]

We agree that this may often be the case. Some of the effects – first of colonialism and then of globalisation – have undoubtedly been the vitiation of local and regional culture in favour of global culture, and the consequent loss of distinct local traditions.[14] Artists have responded in many different ways to this loss, with some of them taking up the challenge to explore, protect and preserve local values and identities, while still being able to engage in the larger, global debate, and in cross-cultural relations. Some artists have left their homes to become global travellers, immigrants or, at times, refugees. Others have remained connected to their home country, but focused on what artist Chen Zhen calls 'transexperience'. He has described transexperience as 'a kind of fusion-transcendence of experiences … which summarizes vividly and profoundly the complex life experiences of leaving one's native place and going from one place to another in one's life'.[15] This complex belonging and detachment can, Chen suggests, result in a type of 'cultural homelessness, namely, you do not belong to anybody, yet you are in possession of everything'.[16] Though there may be loss, the result may be an enriching change, with the transexperience providing a creative catalyst for art that bridges cultures.

Chen Zhen's comparatively positive view of the effects of globalisation is supported by contemporary analysis of this issue, which demonstrates that the networking of the globe does not necessarily mean the destruction of the local. Indeed, there are situations where global communication technologies actually help to retain or regenerate traditional practices, languages and art, enabling 'a denser, more intense interaction between members of communities who share common cultural characteristics', which can re-energise 'ethnic communities and their nationalisms'.[17] At the political level, Zygmunt Bauman insists, the nation state is by no means irrelevant, or disappearing, despite the sometimes radical changes brought about by globalisation.[18] Instead nation states are both actively organising their own internal processes, and seeking to develop transnational (especially regional) unions. These transnational relations, established for purposes of policy, trade and the management of crime, have also been leveraged by NGOs seeking improvements in the lives of everyday people,[19] and by activists seeking opportunities to collaborate in order to achieve sociopolitical changes.[20]

Michael Hardt and Antonio Negri take a less sanguine view of postcolonial globalisation, writing about the global-political patterns of market and media interventions across the globe as evidences of a 'transnational level of power' they call Empire.[21] Empire is this sense a grid of power whose 'task', they write, 'is to enlarge the realm of the consensuses that support its own power'.[22] As such, it is potentially a new form of colonialism, requiring 'a new type of resistance' – one that is as transnational as is the power being opposed. The epigraph to Hardt and Negri's book is from musician Ani DeFranco, and it reads: 'Every tool is a weapon if you hold it right'. This echoes the point made by Homi Bhabha that the process of being captured by what he calls 'the whirligig of our global age'[23] is interrupted by literary writers and other artists, who present an alternative because they are committed to the moment, and hence to the local. The artists we discuss in this chapter can be read in this light; they are transnational in terms of their own lives and careers – their capacity to cross borders, engage with other cultures and contexts, and both draw on different artistic traditions, and contribute their own aesthetic in that new context. They are not necessarily actively or deliberately engaged in transnational activism. But their own values, and the ways in which their work provides commentary on or a witness to events that we can term human rights issues, mean that they both enhance the local and transcend it.

The possibilities as well as the threats offered by globalisation have long been a point of discussion in art circles in the region. Finding ways to engage with it demands a genuine interrelationship among cultures around the world; it cannot be the effect of the global dominating the local, or the west dominating Asia, but is rather what Hou Hanru describes as the 'glocal'.[24] He takes this term from the writings of sociologist Roland Robertson, who introduced the term to describe social and economic flows between regions.[25] Robertson's point is that unless a new product or process resonates in a local culture, it will not be adopted; and that when a global process or product is adopted, it is typically also adapted, and takes on a local flavour. What this means for artists, Hou Hanru notes, is the possibility of producing art in a dynamic tension between global and local tastes and traditions.

This tension has been evident from at least the later part of the twentieth century, a time of great mobility, when artists travelled extensively within and beyond Asia. Artists, curators and scholars from outside Asia began to travel there frequently also, so that the global creative community began to network, collaborate, exchange ideas and practices, and form attachments. Culturally distinct art modes, movements, and approaches entered one another, informing and inflecting local practitioners, local audiences, and local understandings of what art might be and do. There is of course a history of this occurring much earlier, but the mood was, we suggest, different in the second half of the twentieth century – was more about genuine exchange, and less about appropriation on the part of the western travellers, or becoming imbued with dominant western approaches on the part of Asian artists. It also marked the beginnings of a troubling of the unproblematic binary of East/West or Asia/Europe. Catherine Diamond describes an extended theatre project that attempted 'to find common aesthetic roots' and in that way 'to "represent" Asia to Asians and non-Asians'.[26] For Sumit Mandal, who was an observer on the project, a key issue was to find ways to recognise differences, rather than attempting to impose a notion of 'Asia'; and of trying to find and adopt 'a credible transnational self'.[27] Catherine Diamond concludes with the observation that artists are exploring ways of being that allow them to relate to both the nation and the region, 'making it difficult to imagine that they will readily submit to traditional communalizing or nationalistic ideologies'.[28]

Kimsooja: walking and sewing

Kimsooja, who was born in 1957 in Taegu, Korea, and who lives and works in New York, Paris and Seoul, has produced a body of work that inspires viewers to a new way of seeing the world. In recent correspondence with the authors for this book, Kimsooja has said that she sees herself not as an activist, but as a witness. Certainly, witnessing is one of the key ways in which creative people respond to the need to achieve ethical responsibility in their art, and one of the key ways that art connects to contemporary life. Her work is very embedded in contemporary life and in the moment. This is evident in her extended performances (that become video installations), *A Needle Woman*, where she stands motionless and

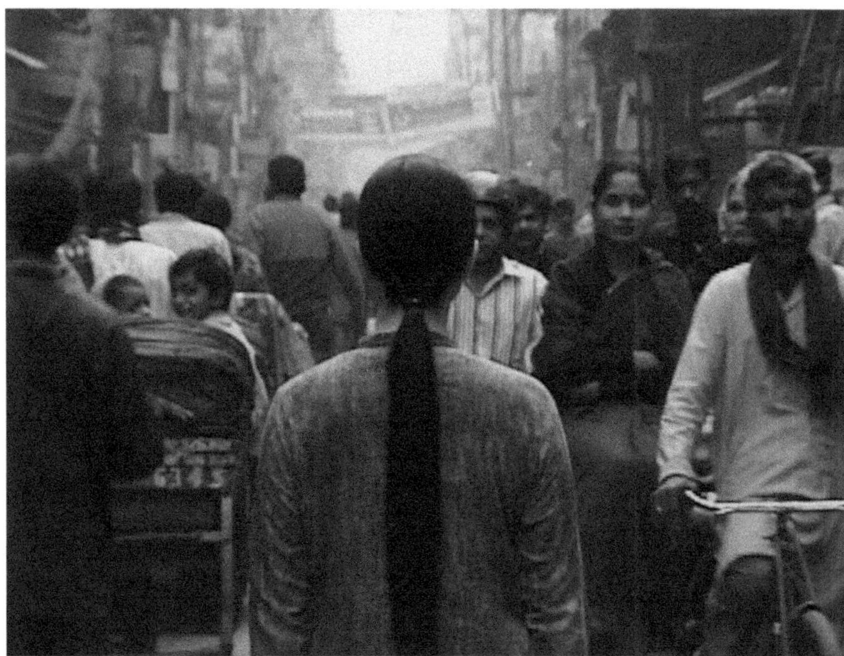

4.1 Kimsooja, *A Needle Woman*, 1999–2001. Video still from Delhi, eight-channel video, 6:33 loop, silent. Collection: National Museum of Contemporary Art, South Korea.

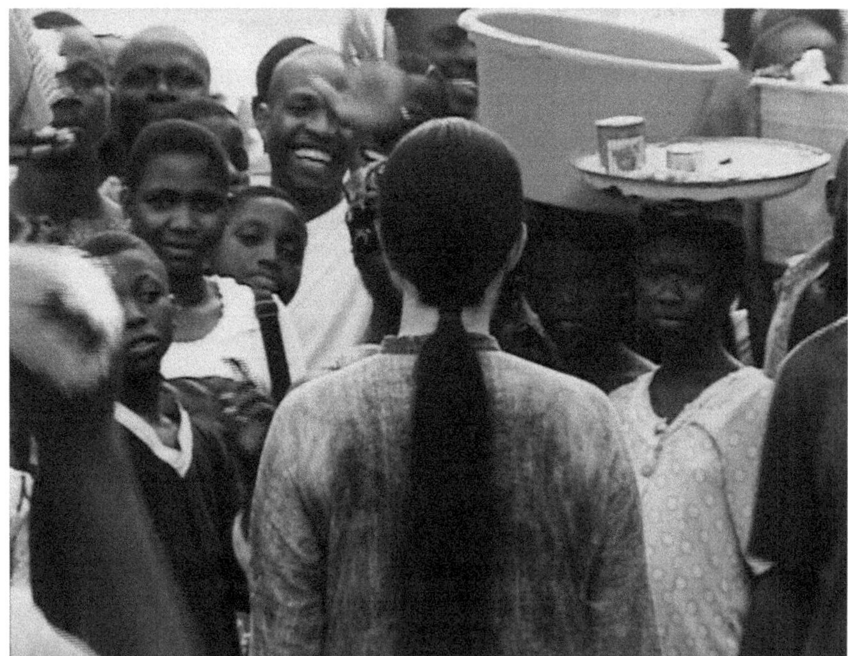

4.2 Kimsooja, *A Needle Woman*, 1999–2001. Video still from Lagos, eight-channel video, 6:33 loop, silent. Collection: The National Museum of Contemporary Art, South Korea.

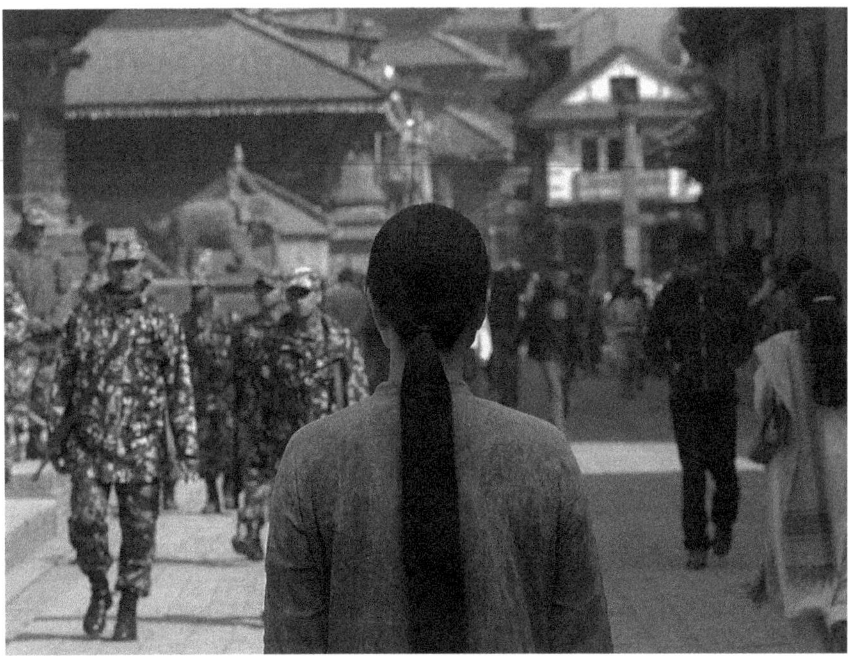

Kimsooja, *A Needle Woman*, 2005. Video still from Patan (Nepal), six-channel video, **4.3**
10:40 loop, silent. Collection: Los Angeles County Museum of Art.

silent in a public space, her back to the camera, which records the reactions of the
crowds as they part and move around her. This recalls the story told by Australian
writer Nicholas Jose of the Chinese ruler who declared as the true artist one who
had turned his back on the world.[29] But to turn one's back on the world is an
impossibility for many artists, especially in Asia today, who think about art in
terms of ethical responsibility to society, to humanity and to future generations;
and Kimsooja's performances pay close attention to these issues. Located in specific places,[30] reacted to by local people in what she has identified as locally specific ways, the videos that record the performances also witness to local identity
in the face of globalisation. Her intention, she has said, is to keep her body in
stillness so that she can create a 'barometer' of the scene, encompassing different
societies and cultures, and coming to understand the world.

René Morales, curator of the Miami Art Museum, argues that *A Needle
Woman* is not specifically about globalism or urbanism, but agrees that these
themes are embedded in, and emerge in, the making of the work. This is primarily because the work 'vividly embodies the struggle to preserve a place for
the individual within society'.[31] As well as the gestures it makes towards the
impact of globalisation, in the record of the samenesses and differences found
in urban communities around the world, it attests to the treatment of identity

in contemporary society. Kimsooja resists the pigeonholing of people on the basis of any elements of identity. As she writes in her Action One, where she explains her decision to name herself as Kimsooja: 'A one word name refuses gender identity, marital status, socio-political or cultural and geographical identity by not separating the family name and the first name.'[32] Setting her name as a single word is, in her terms, anarchism, presumably because it refuses normative processes of nomenclature, and obscures the conventional markers of identity.

Though she does not identify as a 'feminist' artist, she certainly addresses woman-oriented practices and modes of employment: as well as *A Needle Woman* (from 1999), she has produced and exhibited *A Laundry Woman* (from 2000), *A Mirror Woman* (from 2003) and *A Wind Woman* (from 2006). Though her work is not presented as political text, it is 'delicately and essentially about the female perspective in its most universal aspect',[33] and actively engages cultural values and identities. For example, Kimsooja deploys feminised technologies, being perhaps best known for her early works that involve the use of Korean traditional cloths and fabrics. This is sometimes presented in a very direct manner, as in her fabric works where the fabric itself evokes the presence of selves and others, bodies and memories. At other times it is highly metaphorised, as in her *Needle Woman* series, where her body becomes what she calls 'a symbolic needle',[34] stitching her into the social space, making her 'part of the cloth' that is the local social context.[35]

The literal and metaphoric elements of her fabric work are closely aligned: she describes its significance to her art in an interview with curator Mary Jane Jacob, saying:

> One day in 1983, I was sewing a bedcover with my mother and then at the very moment when I passed the needle through the fabric's surface, I had a sensation like an electric shock, the energy of my body channeled through the needle, seeming to connect to the energy of the world. From that moment, I understood the power of sewing: the relationship of needle to fabric is like my body to the universe, and the fundamental relationship of things and structure were in it.[36]

Her connection to fabric predates this charged experience, though: as a child growing up in a nation torn by war, she experienced a nomadic existence that emerged later in art. Her work for the exhibition *Cities on the Move*[37] emerges, she said in the same interview, from that experience of constant relocation, which she now sees as representative of contemporary society:

> We were wrapping and unwrapping bundles all the time; we were endlessly in a new environment, leaving people whom we loved behind and meeting new neighbors, as we passed from one city to another, one village to another. We were, in fact, nomads, and I am continuing the nomadic life as an artist, a

condition which has become one of the main issues in contemporary art and society.[38]

The bundles of fabric, called *bottari* in Korean, have a special resonance in Korea. They are used still in South Korea, writes Annett Reckert, 'like ordinary containers for the safe-keeping or transportation of a family's worldly goods. They are not meant for a family's valuables or heirlooms, but for the most elementary household goods with which to make a start in another place.'[39] In her work for *Cities on the Move*, Kimsooja travelled on a truck loaded with *bottari*, to places where she lived as a child. Her body, she suggests, became 'just another bottari on the move':[40] and by locating her self as fabric, she begins to draw attention to what fabric might witness about human selves. Reckert observes that these bundles of fabric 'are stand-ins for the people whose second skin they once were', that Kimsooja's performance, in stitching the self into the world, is 'linked to the existential themes of flight and migration' and that in consequence, 'the question of freedom and coercion comes into play'.[41]

As we noted above, Kimsooja does not identify as an activist, but because her work focuses on society it necessarily offers ways of seeing that offer an interruption to the dominant, or approved, positions. Sandra Johnston insists that because she places herself physically and visibly in the public sphere, her body 'cannot be perceived as neutral, but always a zone of contention'.[42] Similarly her fabric work introduces zones of contention, primarily by calling up questions about who, and where, the original wearers of the garments and owners of the rolls of fabric might be. This is especially relevant in Korea, a society divided by war and ideology where families have been separated for decades and where the absence of missing relatives is both a reality and a poignant theme in art. In this way her exhibited work often explicitly draws attention to loss and human rights abuse.

One example is the installation she presented at the inaugural Gwangju Biennale in 1995, the site of the May 18th Democratic Uprising in 1980, where demonstrators against martial law were killed by government forces. The reference to this massacre is explicit in the title of Kimsooja's work, *Sewing into Walking: Dedicated to the Victims of Kwangju*, and in her own depiction of the work (see Plate 9). She installed bundles of clothing on the mountainside at the biennale's site, evoking, she said, 'the image of the sacrificed bodies. People could walk on them, listening to the "Imagine" song by John Lennon which, through the audiences' bodies, evoked the confrontation of stepping on bodies and guilty conscience, as well as memorializing the victims' lives.'[43] She left the fabric out to decay in the natural environment, but the local people engaged actively with the bundles of clothes. Kimsooja notes that, of the 2.5 tonnes of fabric in the installation, about 1 tonne were either draped over trees on the mountainside, or taken away by audience members.

Her concerns for human society can also be seen in the work *A Laundry Woman* (2000). For this performance work, Kimsooja stood on the bank of the Yamuna River in India, a place of cremation. Floating by her in the river were burned flowers and other debris (including presumably pieces of bodies) from Hindu cremations. This particular performance she saw as a 'spiritual' experience, related to life and destiny, in which she contemplated the death that must come to all human beings.[44] In *A Beggar Woman*, she extends this concern for others and creates a work about responsibility to other humans by placing herself in the position of a beggar, or a homeless woman – someone in the lowest position of humanity. This series was inspired, she says, by a woman she saw begging in the street in Mexico City; and she reflects on how others responded to her. In most cities, those as different as London and Lagos, people gave her money; only in Cairo did no one give her money, but there one man placed a small living bird in her hand.[45] This act beautifully reflects the effect of Kimsooja's body of work – of 'locating the extraordinary back within the ordinary'.[46] This phrase comes from Philip Fisher's investigation into wonder, but it can equally be applied to Kimsooja's work which, like Fisher's examples, can 'open the fabric of the ordinary and change it forever'.[47]

Alfredo and Isabel Aquilizan: empowering people

Globalisation has had a significant effect on the Philippines, resulting as it did in the high levels of migration by Filipinos to work as household servants and as labourers. Deirdre McKay reports that, by the early 1990s, 'overseas migration had become a definitive part of what it meant to be a Filipino' in this globalised state.[48] By 2006, some 10 per cent of Filipinos had become economic migrants, working in mostly low-skill positions overseas and sending remittances home to support their family members. Philippines art historian Patrick Flores calculates that a third of the population now live abroad, 'sending home around \$USD20 billion a year in remittances, and countless of them coming home as corpses'.[49] For those who have remained at home, class as well as the urban/rural divide continues to determine an individual's life chances, and ethnic minorities remain on the edges of political culture.[50] Despite this situation, McKay's research finds that relational ties are not weakened by globalisation and transnationalism; the identity even of those who are settled elsewhere 'remains relational rather than individuated, and people have a sense of themselves that is at once cosmopolitical and tied to locality yet simultaneously state-oriented'.[51] This is the context from which Alfredo and Isabel Aquilizan have emerged as Filipino and cosmopolitan artists, and the experience of mobility and migration is one they share with many of their fellow citizens.

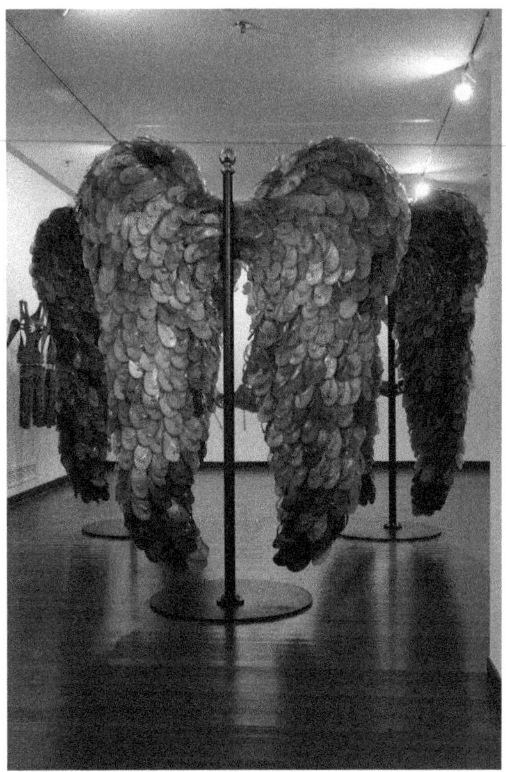

Alfredo Aquilizan & Isabel Gaudinez-Aquilizan, *Wings*, 2009. Installation view.   **4.4**
Collection Singapore Art Museum.

Alfredo, who was born in 1962 in the Cagayan Valley, Philippines, studied at the Norwich School of Art and Design in the UK; Isabel, born in 1965 in Manila, was trained at Assumption College in the Philippines. The artists married, and have worked collaboratively for many years. In 2006 they emigrated to Brisbane where they have continued to make art that speaks to their exploration of cultural traditions and values, and of personal experience and narratives. Artists can, through their work, reflect the most important challenges confronting communities, and like many artists, the Aquilizans have dedicated their work to issues that have significance to their own community, including the issue of journeys, of new forms of connections and of everyday life. The significance of art lies in the fact that it can speak across cultures in ways that no other form of speech or communication can afford: their work, like that of many other artists, is capable of communicating with audiences through global dialogical practices, and through communal projects that are rooted in place and connected to local audiences.

Alfredo and Isabel Aquilizan come out of a long heritage of art in the Philippines which is focused on community and local culture, and they came of age at a time when contemporary art was a vibrant and often contentious domain, challenging not just the systems of political power, but also the enormous influence of the Roman Catholic Church. Artists of the 1970s such as Jaime de Guzman were deeply involved in social activism; those of the 1980s were also concerned with reviving Filipino identity after centuries of colonisation, and art writers such as Alice Guillermo have noted the strong focus on 'people empowerment' in their work.[52] Artists such as Santiago Bose, Roberto Villanueva and Roberto Feleo adopted indigenous art processes, using local materials such as bamboo and twigs. The focus on the nation and its identity, or identities, remains of critical importance to twenty-first-century artists.[53]

For the Aquilizans, this has manifested in two key ways. One is the body of works they have produced that record their own experience of migration and journeying, an experience they hold in common with many of their fellow Filipinos. The second is the focus they have had on community and collaborative work, which allows them to engage organically with local and indigenous traditions, and to find spaces for individual narratives to emerge and be put on record. The former is a contribution to understandings of how art can elucidate some of the impacts of postcolonial nationhood and globalisation; the latter can be seen as a human rights intervention, since the right to know and to narrate one's own story has increasingly been seen as a basic human right.[54] Their work for Hou Hanru's *Zone of Urgency* exhibition at the 2003 Venice Biennale, *Project M201: In God We Trust*, was a vehicle based on the ubiquitous 'jeepney', the old second world war jeep used as public transport since the war in the Philippines, and often held together with made-up parts. Their stainless steel version, loaded with domestic goods, travelled for thirty-two days from Manila to Venice by sea and then on land. This work draws together some of the threads of their practice, referencing objects that speak of everyday life in the Philippines, while exemplifying the common experience of travel and migration.

Their interest in the collective identity of the Philippines, and how that identity is changing in the contemporary world, is evidenced across much of their work. Frequently they explore this through the use of personal possessions, to produce metaphors for human existence in today's world. The materials they employ are usually the most mundane and domestic of objects – used toothbrushes,[55] bedding,[56] clothing, toys and other personal possessions brought by migrants from their home country,[57] books,[58] and even rubber slippers used by inmates in a Singaporean correctional facility (see Figure 4.4).[59] These elements are exemplified by their installation for the sixth Asia-Pacific Triennial, *In-Flight (Project: Another Country)* 2009. This took the form of a giant heap of aircraft, composed of hundreds of little toys put together by adults and children from found scrap materials, which was intended to symbolise the shared

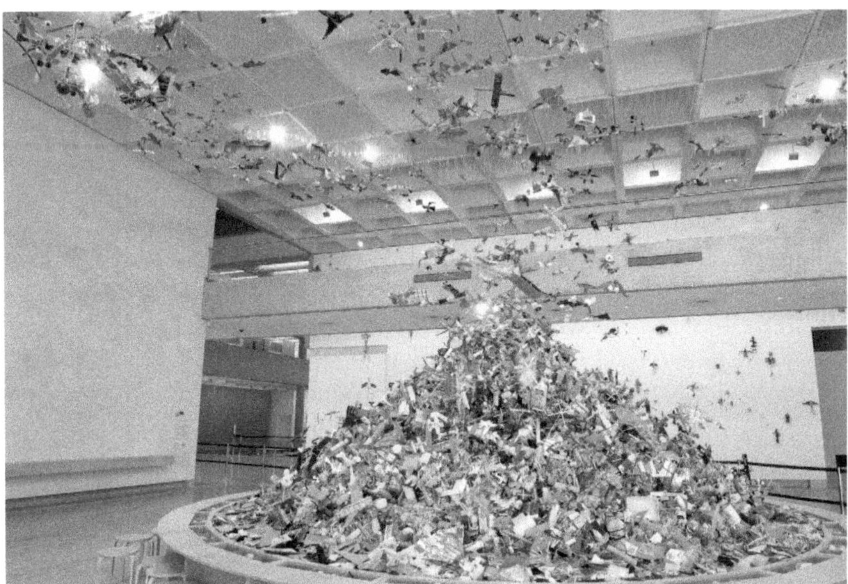

Alfredo Aquilizan & Isabel Gaudinez-Aquilizan, *In-Flight (Project: Another Country)*, **4.5** 2009. Detail. Site-specific installation Queensland Art Gallery. The project for Kids' APT6 asked the audience to make aeroplanes out of found materials which were then suspended from the ceiling of the Queensland Art Gallery.

reality of human existence in a world dislocated by the tensions between points of destination, arrivals and departures. The world may be characterised by new forms of global communication such as air travel and the internet, but it remains the case that people need and want to communicate and connect at local level and with local communities. As eminent human rights lawyer Christine Chinkin reminds us, 'artists are rooted in their own localities and are shaped by local values'. It is in fact 'the depiction of local issues – including local human rights abuse – [that] can relay universal messages and assist in the understanding of human rights violations as a matter of global concern, wherever their location'.[60]

The Aquilizans' practice, which focuses so closely on local issues, focuses their audiences' attention also on specific features of Filipino identity and thereby on more universal qualities of being human, and of human being. This provides opportunities to deliver the sort of awareness of others that historian Wang Gungwu identifies as an effect of the modern world, which 'has made people aware of similarities and differences among themselves to an extent never dreamed of in the past. Being thus aware, people can never be the same again'.[61] The artists contribute to this understanding by the works they produce in collaboration with community and audience members. This approach to artistic practice has a long pedigree and a variety of modes of operation. Homi Bhabha describes as 'conversational art'[62] the democratising practice of artists who organise the participation of others in the production of their works; and the point of this 'conversation' is not necessarily sociopolitical action, but redefining art in a way that provides space for minority or marginalised groups. Claire Bishop is less positive about this approach, due to what she identifies as a tendency to overlook the quality of the art produced because of the political importance of the project.[63] In addition, dialogical art can, she notes, work against Bhabha's ideal when it becomes a matter of artists offering patronage to the community, or exploiting their narratives in the interests of producing work. Grant Kester focuses more on a process of art practice where the artists are committed to openness and listening, and where the work is 'a more reciprocal process of dialogue and mutual education'.[64]

The Aquilizans' approach is more organic and participatory than instrumental or institutional, and can be seen to contribute to a tradition of art that is socially and ethically concerned, and concerned, too, about the views, ideas and narratives of other people. Their reason for involving communities and audience members to participate in artistic projects is, they say, to 'create communal experiences' and thereby 'formulate meaning':

> Our customary practice is to immerse ourselves in the community, employing narratives from the objects and fragments of facts we continuously collect, reconfiguring mundane objects and treating personal gesture as a metaphor of human existence with particular emphasis on contemporary culture … Our interest lies in the works providing a platform for exchange through creative processes, negotiations with the audience, audience members as active participants in the production of the meaning of the work, and the repercussions of the work with respect to the audience.[65]

To this extent, their practice adopts a position that is aligned with Suzanne Lacy's ideal: the project is engaged not necessarily to make political statements, but rather to come to understandings about what might matter to that group, in that place, at that time. In such a model, Lacy suggests, the outcome is more likely to be a genuinely communal act committed to the construction or confirmation of values and identity.[66]

One example of this approach is their work *Project Be-Longing #2* which was included in the Third Asia-Pacific Triennial in 1999. This installation was designed 'to rekindle the spirit of kinship and a sense of belonging/be-longing … evoking memories which help define being part of a particular community'. Elements of the works – household items, mementos and related stories – were provided by members of Brisbane's Filipino community. The objects and stories spoke of 'home' to the expatriate Filipinos involved, and the project took the Aquilizans out of the studio and into the two communities of interest – other artists; other Filipino immigrants.[67]

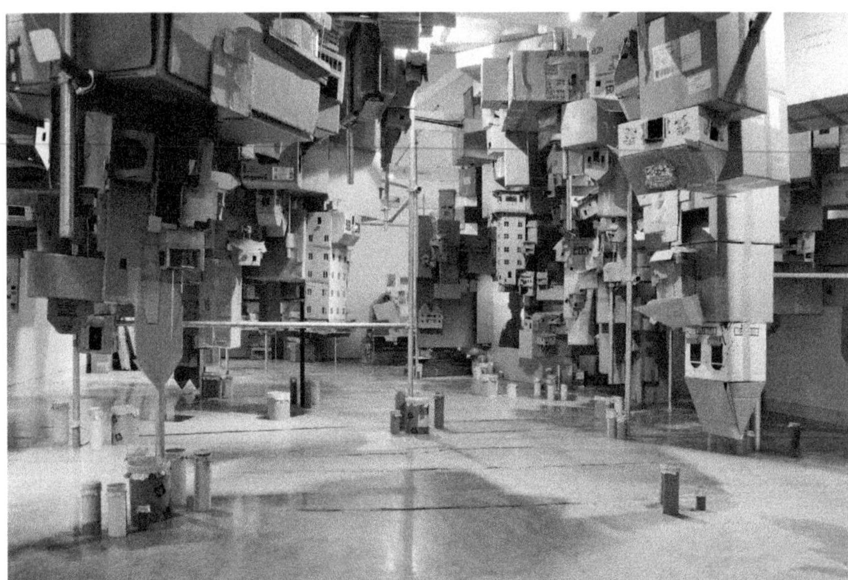

Alfredo Aquilizan & Isabel Gaudinez-Aquilizan, *In-Habit: Project Another Country*,   **4.6**
2012. Installation view. Commissioned by Sherman Contemporary Art Foundation,
Sydney.

Their approach is also, Gene Sherman suggests, predicated on their roles
as 'serious creative researchers'.[68] Discussing one of their collaborative works,
In-Habit: Project Another Country, she notes that 'they returned to their homeland in order to explore the idea of working with, and bearing witness artis-
tically to, the millions of urban poor'.[69] This work emerged out of a trip back
to the Philippines in 2008, when they met members of one of the minority
groups in the Philippines, the Badjao (or 'sea gypsies'). This community has
been relocated from their itinerant ocean life to marginal urban life, and the
children earn money by performing rap music in the streets. The project
involved spending time with the children, learning about their lifestyle, their
values and their ways of getting by. They then filmed the children busking, in
this way recording their particular approach to rap, and to musical expression.
Though rap is, of course, not a traditional practice, the Aquilizans observed
that the Badjao use materials and languages that specifically connect to their
Badjao identity.[70]

The exhibited work was a major installation involving stacks of cardboard
boxes (referencing packaging, transience and ephemerality) mounted on stilts
(referencing the Badjaos' temporary homes), accompanied by a video work of
the Badjao children in their everyday lives (see Plate 8). Gene Sherman says
of this work:

> When we stand before or within the Aquilizans' towering slum dwellings, recycled cardboard boxes precariously constructed on, across and around industrial scaffolding by people we know or imagine, we are faced with a highly poeticised visualisation of imagined personal stories. When, in the video work, we listen to and watch the global/rap chanting of marginalised Badjao children whose parents are no longer able to roam the seas as fisher folk at large, we know that despite intense deprivation, the human spirit somehow strives to live on.[71]

The effect, we suggest, is a work that both addresses Bishop's concern about the quality of the art (because the finished work has high production and aesthetic values), and satisfies Kester's requirement that the work rely on reciprocity and mutual education. Their projects demonstrate what artists can do in collaborations with communities: participating in a long local search for identity in the Philippines, and connecting with local culture in ways that can achieve what art historian Alice Guillermo describes as 'people empowerment'.[72] Like so many other artists in former colonies, and artists in communities struggling with poverty and inequality, they dream that society can be different, and that artists can contribute to making a better society.

Oscar Ho and John Young: contemporary Hong Kong

In the final section of this chapter, we look to Hong Kong for a further way of understanding artists' engagement with the forces of postcolonialism, globalisation and identity. Hong Kong has a very specific history and character, being a city state rather than a nation state, one that has only a degree of autonomy and self-government, but has a long history of discrete cultural norms and mores. Prior to the arrival of the British colonial authorities in 1841, Hong Kong did not have an expressly Chinese character.[73] Although the Hongkongese were, of course, ethnically Chinese prior to the British intervention, the community was a congeries of indigenous groups – farmers and fishermen, Cantonese landowners, and migrant workers travelling between Hong Kong and China proper – who identified more closely with those who shared regional origins and dialects, rather than with the world of China. The effect was a population of people who were flexible as to identity, experiencing a degree of hybridisation because they were at once local and Chinese, and for those closely associated with the colonial enterprise, western as well. Sussman describes the local context as one of 'nested identities' – 'a core Chinese identity surrounded by Western economic and civic values encased in a regional geographic identity'.[74] To this extent, it could be argued, Hong Kong is an exemplar of what Marsha Meskimmon identifies as a new form of cosmopolitanism, one that breaks with the 'masculine-normative, Eurocentric project', and is predicated on 'the possibilities of dialogue and community building which acknowledge the complexities of the intertwining of the local within the global'.[75]

Hong Kong has survived nearly two centuries of external control, first by Britain, and since 1997 by China, perhaps because of the pragmatism it shows in the face of overwhelming external powers. Though there are political incidents from time to time, often attracting very large crowds who gather to protest, Hong Kong is often considered less volatile than some of its neighbours.[76] Some local commentators in fact consider that the community is rather apathetic: Lee and Chan suggest the apparent apathy is in part attributable to the lack of opportunity, and in part to a view held of themselves by Hong Kong residents; though a city where protests are capable of attracting up to half a million people do not indicate genuine political apathy.[77] The concept of freedom of speech has been important to many in the art world in Hong Kong. However, commentators in Hong Kong often identify the city as economically rather than politically motivated, and its people as unaware of the extent to which the mechanisms for repression and censorship, established by the British, remain in place.[78]

Art is well supported by the government, but an effect of this support is that the field is quite bureaucratised, and is managed not by artists and curators, but by public servants. Consequently, and especially when compared with the vitality of the art community in China, the local scene can seem rather tame, with few curators, few spaces in which to make or show art, few artists doing innovative or experimental work, and a limited critical discourse.[79] Though it is still very quiet compared to the Chinese mainland, the economic improvements of the 1980s, which meant more people could travel abroad to art school, have provided a critical mass of trained practitioners on the local art scene. Oscar Ho was part of that first generation who travelled abroad for art education. Born in Hong Kong in 1956, the son of a housewife and a salesman who later became a successful businessman, he became a curator, artist, educator and cultural mediator. Apart from the years he spent at university in Canada and the US, and then a later period as founding director of the Shanghai Museum of Contemporary Art (2004–06), he has lived in Hong Kong all his life, and is a passionate advocate of Hong Kong identity, seeing China as very different in cultural and political terms, and as the source of a different approach to art.

Ho is passionate but not sentimental about art. Though he is very conscious of the role art can play in the social sphere and in helping people adjust to the shifting political identity of their home town, he notes the limits of its capacity. These lie partly in the fact that Hong Kong is a comparatively small community, with few institutions dedicated to training practising artists, and a restricted art sector. His response, on returning to Hong Kong from his studies and beginning to establish his position, was to reconsider the definition of art, and both look beyond Hong Kong for his curatorial work, and expand the definition of art for his own practice. He observed early on that pop art was a strength in

Hong Kong,[80] and this shaped his personal artistic practice as well as his curatorial interventions. His work has steered away from many of the tropes of contemporary experimental art, in his curation and his art practice (frequently his curation is in fact his art practice, the gallery site becoming both palette and canvas), partly because of the inherent resistance he feels towards any form of hierarchy. He makes this clear in his early (1980s) exhibitions, *Living with Art* and *In Search of Art*, which involved public participation in the form of contributions to the exhibition, and were 'deliberate attempts to dismantle this categorisation of art and make it just a human activity'. That 'human' impulse is evident also in his witty *Stories Around Town* series (1991–98), a sequence of about eighty drawings, each accompanied by a written text. These works combine actual news stories with rewritten legends and often absurd fabricated stories to produce a tongue-in-cheek response to what he describes as the 'collective hysteria' triggered by the impending reunification with China.[81]

His own sense that art needs to do something that is of social value means he has little time for art that does not aim to achieve change. He explains this with reference to a participatory art project, *Still Lives: Art by Vietnamese Boat People* (1991), which worked with Vietnamese refugees in camps in Hong Kong. Ho says:

> The community was getting really hostile toward them, so I decided to curate an exhibition of their artworks to just show them as human. We got the adults and the children to do drawings about life in the camp for the exhibitions, and I managed to get some politicians to come to the opening so we got a lot of press, and I think it was successful in terms of sensitising the community. We had got the licenses to bring them out of the camp … and all was wonderful until the moment the opening was over, and then they were all sent back to the camp. So the question is: what is going on here? What have we achieved?[82]

Reflecting on this, he said, he came to realise that community art is just a metaphor for us to deal with our guilt, and so though he continued to do dialogical and relational projects, he changed the fundamental logic of that work. For example, he describes a contract he was offered to teach art appreciation to a group of unemployed men. He took the contract with the proviso that he would teach them to make art, rather than to view it, on the grounds that they need jobs, not the ability to look at art. The form he taught them allows them to paint representational simple works that they can sell at the markets. The point is, he states, that they need an income and dignity, and this comes from learning to paint something their friends can recognise, and for which those friends will praise them. 'So in a sense I look at art from a very functional point of view', he says; 'I don't really believe in kind of abstract kind of absolute value of art. Actually I should be honest, I do believe it, but …' Although Ho is a formally trained contemporary artist who is deeply versed in practice and in

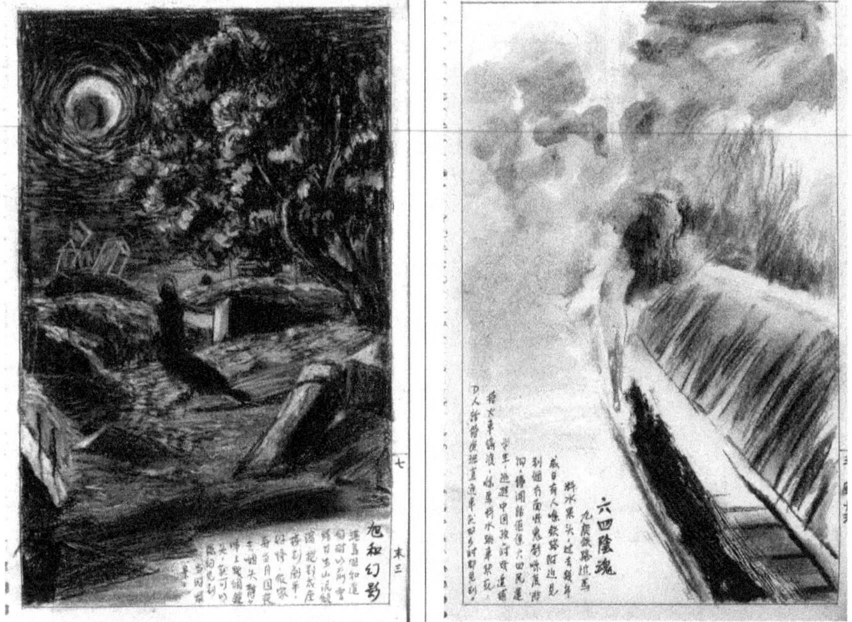

4.7a & 4.7b Oscar Ho, *Shadow of Ghost at Yuk Wo*, 1994. *Phantom of June 4ᵗʰ*, 1995.

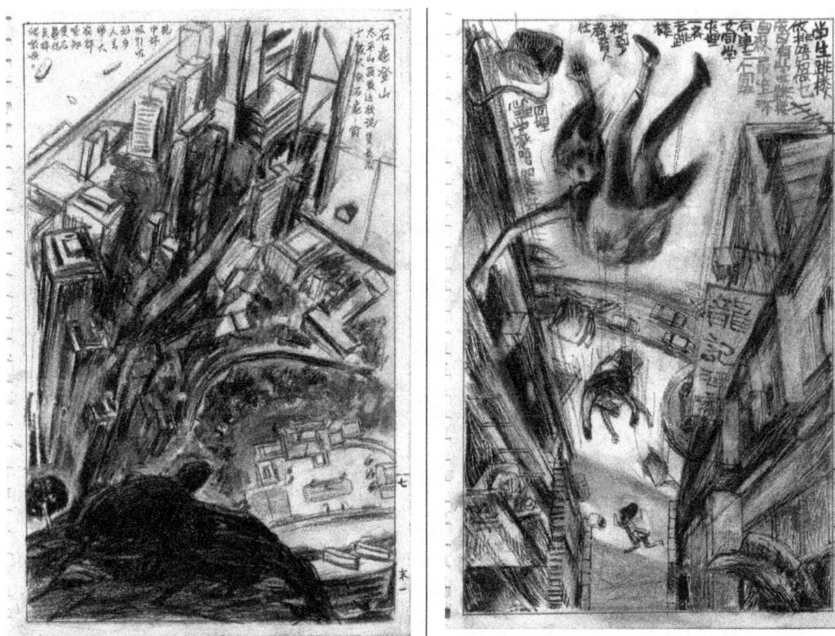

4.8a & 4.8b Oscar Ho, *Turtle Rock reaches the Peak*, 1993. *Students' Suicides*, 1996.

aesthetic principles, as an art worker he considers that the importance of art is to provide people with dignity, a sense of community and, where possible, the chance to earn a living.[83]

His iconoclastic approach to curation and his work as a cultural agent is present in his own artistic practice, particularly his witty exhibitions in the late 1990s where his 'fake history museums' challenged the idea of the museum while interrogating other authoritative discourses, especially those of history and political 'truth'. This attitude to curatorial and art practice could be compared to what Claire Bishop criticises in the 'social turn' in art: a move away from the visual towards the discursive; from the sensory to negotiation; and from art to identity politics and 'political correctness'.[84] However, given his energetic engagement with the task of making art accessible to many people, and his deep commitment to the traditions of practice, we suggest that his work is more aligned with genuine participatory practice, and the pleasures of the form and field, than with political correctness. He says of art that it is 'a final frontier, the last contemplative space in the community where you can engage in something, intellectually emotionally profound'. But still he regrets that when it remains an elite practice, 'art cannot do much; how many people come and see art?'[85] By bringing it to the community, and by bringing the community to it, art's possibilities for political intervention, for the freedom to interrupt traditions and experiment with new modes, and to engender social change are radically heightened. In this respect, as Chang Tsong-Zung comments, 'Perhaps cultural identity is something that cannot be grasped without the intervention of the creative arts. After all, what is kept behind glass in a museum vitrine belongs to a different era; the face of a contemporary can only be truly sketched by another contemporary.'[86] One of Ho's contributions to this is his active involvement in helping form a transnational Asian Curators Network; its purpose is to implement museum models and curatorial approaches that are attentive to Asia's particular cultural contexts, that respect local cultures and initiatives, and that are not dominated by western practices.[87]

Ho's focus on the role of art in constructing and preserving an identity that is generative, productive and socially valuable, especially in times of significant change, points to the importance of community, dialogue and wit as tools for resilience and resistance. John Young Zerunge, too, focuses on art and identity, though his concern is more directly about questions of cross-cultural perception and transexperience. Like Ho, Young was born in Hong Kong in 1956, but his family sent him to Australia, to attend boarding school, in 1967, to escape the rioting and bombings that were crippling the city. He later studied at the University of Sydney and the Sydney College of the Arts, and Australia has been his home. Young has exhibited widely in Australia as well as in Asia, Europe and the US, and has been a leader in developing opportunities for Asian Australian artists, as one of the founders of the Asian Australian Artists' Association and the 4A Centre for Contemporary Asian Art in Sydney.[88] His

Asian identity is, therefore, clearly important to his practice and his public expression, and he has explored this quite extensively. After his studies at the Sydney College of the Arts, and encouraged by his parents, Young travelled to China in 1979, where he undertook a site-specific conceptual work *Manchurian Snow Walk*, partly to reconnect with his Chinese heritage. During the late 1990s, too, Young travelled to Hong Kong and to Guangzhou on a number of occasions. Art historian Carolyn Barnes notes that this had the effect of 'heightening his connections with Asia but also his awareness of being neither western nor eastern'.[89] Not until he connected with the Chinese artists Chen Zhen, Cai Guo-Qiang and Xu Bing, Barnes continues, did he begin to identify as a Hong Kong-Australian artist, 'reflecting the world's view of him, even if it did not necessarily fit his own perception of himself'.[90]

Young's approach to art is deeply informed by his background in western philosophy. At the University of Sydney he studied the philosophy of science and aesthetics, and wrote a thesis on Wittgenstein. His art training and early career also had a western inflection: he was trained in a period in Australia when European-American modernism was the focus of artistic discussion, and from the early 1980s he experimented with conceptual and minimal approaches. He later engaged with newly emerging discourses, including post-modernism, postcolonialism and globalisation, and explored the complexities of transcultural crossings through his art, through writing for seminal post-modern journals such as *Art & Text*, and through his connections with other 'transcultural' artists, particularly Imants Tillers.[91]

This exploration finds visual expression in *The Double Ground Paintings* (1993–2005), a series of multimedia paintings which, for Barnes, is 'informed by Young's situation as insider and outsider to more than one culture simultaneously, [and] took disaporic experience as a model for broader issues of identity and meaning, and their splintering in globalization'.[92] These paintings begin with what Young calls 'underbelly images',[93] images he creates from 'found generic photographs, primarily images of landscape, figures and still lifes from painterly genres', and then places in the foreground of a work. The backgrounds are drawn from secondary, often historical, sources, and have no necessary reference to the foreground. Barnes identifies in this process both a 'cultural flattening and fragmentation' associated with globalisation, in that ownership and origin are dissipated, and an interrogation of the value of innovation in favour of recontextualising previous cultural product. Young has indicated that attending John Clark's 1991 conference, 'Modernism and Postmodernism in Asian Art', at the Humanities Research Centre, Australian National University, was an impetus for exploring Asian modernity and cultural framings.[94] Many of the images in the *Double Ground* series deliberately reflect stereotyped and romantic projections of the transcultural, and their backgrounds contain Asian or 'Oriental' elements, including the work of Giuseppe Castiglioni, an eighteenth-century Jesuit missionary to China, and imagery from Persian art. In the whole series, he also continued his exploration of the syntax of paintings, as well as ideas of affect and historical resonance, and of cultural formations, mergings and collisions. This series forms part of the major retrospective exhibition of his work, 'Orient/ Occident: A Survey of Works by John Young, 1978–2005', presented in 2005–06 by the TarraWarra Museum of Art in Melbourne. Since then he has produced several key series that are related to Asia. One example is *1967 Dispersion* (2008), work that commemorates not only the labour disputes in Hong Kong during 1967, but also the severe floods the city experienced in that year.[95] Its themes relate to Young's work on displaced peoples, and have a visual affinity with his series on refugees, which was completed in the 1990s. *The Macau Days* (2012), shown at 10 Chancery Lane Gallery in Hong Kong in 2012, explores the rich transcultural history of the oldest European settlement in Asia, and has as its epigraph lines from Scottish poet Kenneth White: '*I saw myself disappearing / And it was good / For I was still there*'.[96]

In such ways, his work can be understood as treating the East/West binary, but this is not his core focus. Australian academic Jacqueline Lo in fact questions the way that much writing about Young's work identifies it 'as a signifier of his Chinese-Australian identity' despite that fact that, as both Barnes and Lo point out, the artist has resisted that categorisation.[97] Indeed, Lo makes the point that Young expresses 'unease with the prevailing discourse of diaspora and racialised positions', seeing them as reflecting 'wider concerns in diaspora and critical race studies in Australia and in the USA'.[98] This is an issue of significant importance in the region, given that so many artists are in fact transnational – living as members of a diaspora, or living in their home nation as one cultural group among many.

For Asian artists living in, say, Australia or the US, who are often designated 'Asian-Australian' or 'Asian-American', there is a double-bind: the choice seems to be either to identify with their Asian cultural background and be caught in what is often a ghettoised or restrictive identity, or to adopt the dominant identity and efface the important Asian cultural tradition they possess. As Lo writes:

> The decision to express cultural allegiance outside a performative Australianness was perceived as lacking identification with the nation while encouraging in some factions … excessive production and consumption of ethnic and racial Otherness … as well as overlooking the diversity within Asian Australian cultural practices.[99]

Young has expressed his own concerns about this; although he defines himself as a Hong Kong-Australian artist, his artistic oeuvre is essentially cross-cultural in its qualities, and he insists: 'All my projects today are transcultural, or at least had something to do with the condition of crossing cultures.'[100]

Young's most recent transcultural work is a research project on the Chinese in Australia. In 2012 he was awarded a two-year Fellowship for Senior Artists, funded by the Australia Council for the Arts, to research the Chinese diaspora in Australia from 1850 to the present. This is part of a five-year project that will include a number of creative outcomes. One significant outcome is the *Open Monument – Acknowledging the Chinese Peoples' Contribution to Ballarat*, a contribution to understanding the history of Ballarat, a gold-mining city that attracted many Chinese in the nineteenth century. But Young is not in any sense a political artist, and his art is not essentially about himself or his own identity. Rather, it attends to deeper questions of the condition of humanity, and the role of art and the artist in society. He is interested in moral and ethical dilemmas in confronting catastrophic situations, and his art engages the ambiguities and uncertainties of the human condition and of history, in an attempt to 'reawaken an intrinsic ethical impulse in the present'.[101]

An important work that emerged from that attempt was John Young's installation *Bonhoeffer in Harlem* (2009). It commemorates the sixty-fourth anniversary of the execution of German Lutheran theologian, pastor and finally martyr, Dietrich Bonhoeffer. Originally designed for St Matthauskirche, Kulturforum, Berlin, where Bonhoeffer was ordained, it is now permanently installed in the Evangelische Erlöserkirche in Bamberg.[102] The title derives from the fact that Bonhoeffer travelled to the United States in 1930 to undertake postgraduate study at New York City's Union Theological Seminary. There he was introduced to the Abyssinian Baptist Church in Harlem under Pastor Adam Clayton Powell Sr, a founder of the National Urban League and member of the NAACP, who had made the church a vibrant centre for social justice in the African American community. Bonhoeffer became aware of the levels of discrimination against Black Americans, and also discovered the spirituality of gospel music. 'Through this experience', Young writes, 'Bonhoeffer returned to Germany with the understanding to defend the "marginalized, the vulnerable and the oppressed"'.[103]

Bonhoeffer returned to his homeland in 1931 to find that racial oppression, especially related to Jews, was about to be enforced in its most extreme form. This led him to challenge the principles and practice of the Nazi regime, first openly, then undercover as a committed member of the anti-Nazi resistance. He was eventually arrested by the Gestapo and hanged just weeks before the camp where he had been incarcerated was liberated by the US Army.

Young interpreted this history in a work that responds both to the story and to a stained glass window in the Abyssinian Baptist Church in Harlem: in its vivid purples and greens, he states, it was one from which initially he 'felt very distant … It was a black aesthetic which was as alien as Chinese opera to Western ears.'[104] The glass, though, captures something of the vibrancy of local African American culture in the Harlem renaissance of the 1920s. Young has said that he sees the overcoming of his personal cultural boundaries as an

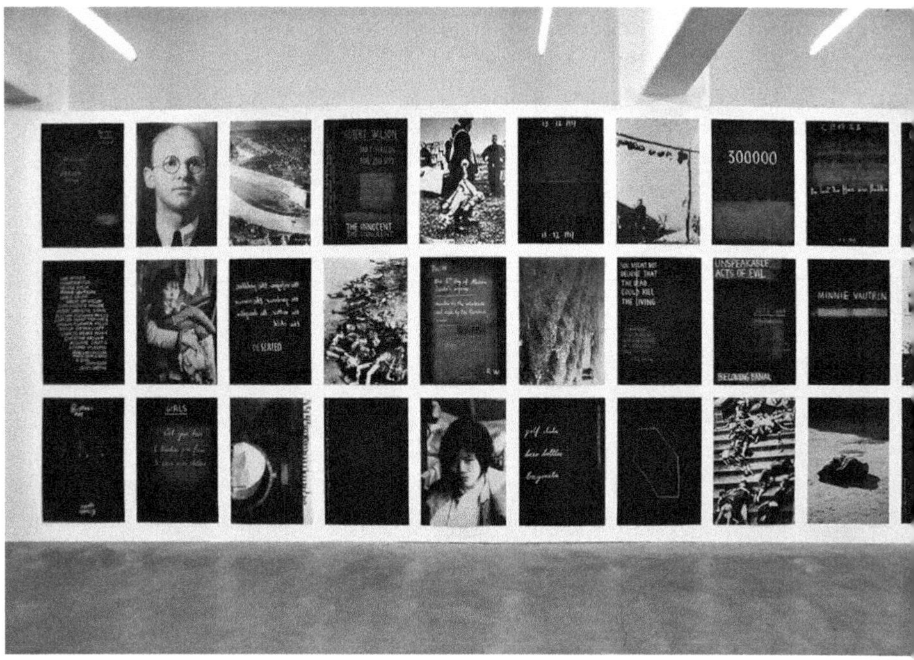

4.9 John Young, *Safety Zone*, 2010. Installation view, Anna Schwartz Gallery, Melbourne.

artist, in finding a way to engage with this effusion of floating colour, was his response to a call from Bonhoeffer 'to see the other. And not only to see the other, but to try to be the other. In other words, to make art not from the point of narcissism, but hopefully from empathy.'[105]

The work is comprised of three discrete parts. One is a series of chalk drawings on paper covered with blackboard paint, and bearing messages – some partly erased, but still legible. These include exhortations in Chinese, such as 'Evil – oppose it directly', and 'responsible action, a highly risky action'; 'Sermon on the Mount' in English; and Bonhoeffer's call to be 'eine Speiche im Rad des Staates'[106] in German. These 'chalkboard' works, which, as Thomas Berghuis points out, have references to the blackboard drawings of Joseph Beuys and Rudolf Steiner's blackboard lectures, are accompanied by inkjet prints that contain biographical details about Bonhoeffer, and include poignant images of Bonhoeffer as an adult, and as a young child with his twin sister. There is also an image of a thrush, a small bird that Bonhoeffer had seen and heard singing from his prison window, and had described in a letter to his fiancée.

The second element is a large silk tapestry that responds directly to the stained glass window (see Plate 10). This was a collaborative and transcultural project involving Young's conception that was then translated by German rug

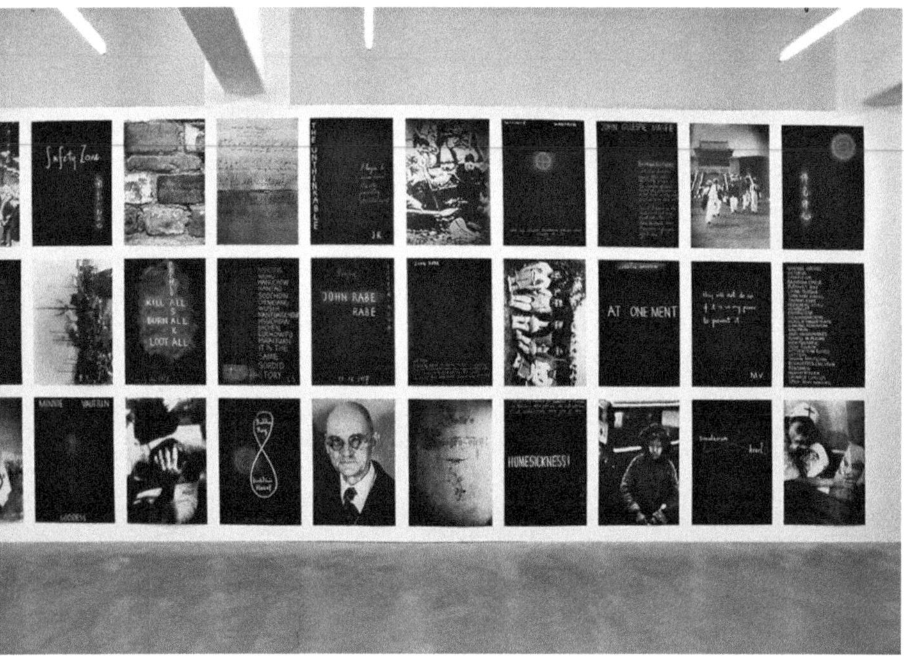

designer Jürgen Dahlmanns, and then finally produced in Nepal by the rug weaver Dolma Lob Sang, daughter of a Tibetan monk. The final element in the work is a pair of abstract paintings created through a computer manipulation of images the artist then transfers in oil to canvas. Sylvia Volz writes of this work, 'the tapestry as well as both abstract works disperse the severity of these works, and in so doing Young leads us back to light and hope'.[107] Certainly this transcultural work – informed by African American sensibility, designed by a Chinese-Australian, and then woven by a Tibetan – contrasts sharply with the monocultural Lutheran church, and significantly changes its cultural frame.

Safety Zone (2010) again responds to a major instance of integrity and humanity. This is an installation of sixty works on paper – chalk drawings – and digital prints, along with several paintings. For Berghuis, these works 'resemble historical reminiscences of human survival by linking experimental contemporary art with investigative visual reports, in historical photographs and documents'.[108] The installation grew out of research and interviews undertaken by Young in Nanjing, Berlin and Heidelberg about an event that took place in 1937, while the Japanese Army was closing in on Nanjing. The Chinese authorities had abandoned the city, leaving an International Committee of fifteen Americans and Europeans to try to establish a safety zone for the protection of the Chinese civilians remaining in the city.[109]

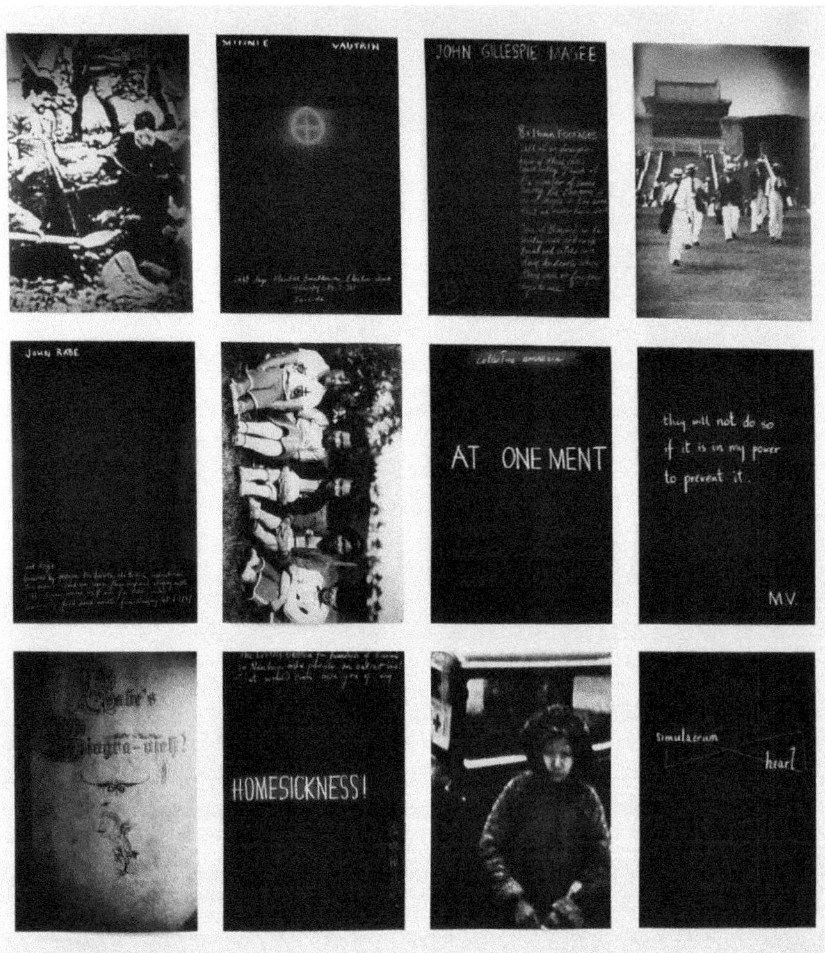

4.10 John Young, *Safety Zone*, 2010. Detail.

The elected chair of the Committee, German businessman John Rabe, was an employee of the German engineering firm of Siemens and a member of the Nazi Party, and it was hoped that this might give him some influence. Rabe indeed protested repeatedly to Japanese authorities in attempts to stop the sustained orgy of rape and murder, with very little success. Tens of thousands of women were raped, and many Chinese civilians were killed.[110] Nonetheless, the International Safety Zone was able to provide protection for some Chinese people.[111]

In 1938 the siege was lifted and Rabe returned to Germany, where he continued to denounce the Japanese outrages. He was poorly treated by history: interrogated first by the Gestapo and again, after the defeat of Germany, first by the Soviet NKVD and then by the British. Denounced as a Nazi, he was

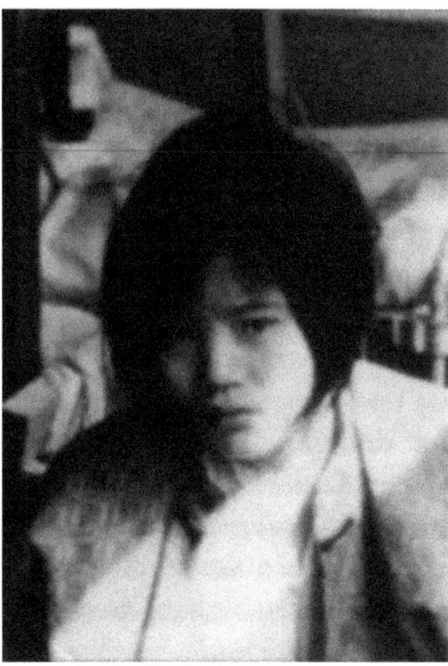

John Young, *Safety Zone*, 2010. Detail, 'Victim'. **4.11**

denied permission to work and, with his family, was quite literally starving to death when a group of citizens in Nanjing learned of their miserable circumstances, and sent them first money and then monthly food parcels. Rabe died in Germany in 1951. A similarly tragic fate was experienced by his Safety Zone colleague, the American missionary Minnie Vautrin: she was so distressed by her inability to protect all those under her care that she lost her faith and committed suicide on her return to the United States.

Young treats this tragedy with empathy and with philosophical reflection. The images in his work are not so much about Japanese atrocities, but about what transcultural individuals did to try to prevent them, and about individuals caught in terrible circumstances. The sixty works on paper, like elements in Young's *Bonhoeffer in Harlem*, bear messages in German, Chinese and English: 'Du hast das Herz einer Buddha';[112] 'This is a drawing for John Rabe' (in Chinese); 'You have saved thousands of poor people from danger and want'; and Rabe's own disclaimer, 'Everyone thinks I am a hero and that can be very annoying. I can see nothing heroic about me or within me.'[113] There are also images that represent victims.

However, the representation of broken branches and shattered tree trunks in the paintings that comprise *The Crippled Tree* obviously symbolise the brutal violence inflicted on the Chinese victims; and Jacqueline Lo writes, 'One of the most horrific photos that I came across was of a female corpse profaned by a large tree branch inserted into her vagina'.[114] One of the paintings, however, *Flower Market (Nanjing 1936)*, deploys a more elusive poignancy. In this work, 'carefully painted spring flowers and bleached corals are superimposed over historical photographs taken in Nanjing a year prior to the massacre'[115] – a reminder, perhaps, that there is beauty and rebirth despite the horrors of history.

Lo observes that what is striking about the extraordinary transcultural empathy of Young's work in both *Bonhoeffer in Harlem* and *Safety Zone* is that 'his work demonstrates the ways in which the transnational memory of both Bonhoeffer and Nanjing have been memorialised from an inter-diasporic perspective'. Because of this, John Young's artwork 'offers a way to grieve' for history: 'not to reify a victim discourse or promote cultural chauvinism but rather to reimagine, reengage and co-exist with others with compassion and empathy'.[116] Young seems to affirm this, writing of his life and his practice: 'When you are crossing cultures, you are in the middle, and you can see both sides, so you are put in a conflictual or a paradoxical situation where something is right and wrong at the same time, depending on which cultural perspective you are looking from.'[117]

Young's work can be identified as part of the active dialogue between what art historian Michael Sullivan calls 'Eastern' art and 'Western' art,[118] one that – as Barnes again notes – engages 'the whole culture in overarching questions concerning the shaping of historical memory'.[119] This points to an impulse very like those of the other artists we discuss in this chapter, whose practice explores memory, identity and responsibility in a postcolonial, globalised world.

Conclusion

Terry Smith described contemporary art as 'truly an art *of* the world. It comes *from* the whole world, and frequently tries to imagine the world *as a differentiated yet inevitably connected whole*'.[120] How this diversity of art, location and identity might be expressed and realised is a matter for each artist involved. As Oscar Ho writes, 'Identity is a fabrication. There are times when such fabrication is meaningful and necessary, and there are also times when it is deceptive and destructive.'[121] The artists we discuss in this chapter possess a strong sense of art that is *of* the world, in Smith's terms, and of the importance of interrogating notions of identity. Rather than attempting to impose a single way of seeing and being, or on the other hand perceiving human culture in binary or bifurcated ways, they are concerned to provide more nuanced accounts with the different ways in which groups and individuals within and beyond Asia might operate, might understand themselves, and connect with others and with their own histories and sociopolitical realities.

We can understand their visions of the world in terms laid out by cultural anthropologist Arjun Appadurai, who suggests that the neighbourhood provides a metaphor for culture more generally. He writes that 'the context-generative dimension of neighborhoods is an important matter because it provides the beginnings of a theoretical angle on the relationship between local and global realities'.[122] Echoing Appadurai's reference to neighbourhoods, Homi Bhabha comments on the ethical function of the right of interpretation among particular people in a particular time and place, writing:

> The universality of Rights lies less, I believe, in the value of the Individual as an end-in-itself. The value of Universality comes with our growing awareness that to fulfil our ends – of equality, freedom, well-being –, or to find a means to survive our fates – of pain, oppression, humiliation, failure – we need to belong to the solidarity and the community of Others, be they Neighbours or Strangers, and through their alterity derive a sense of agency.[123]

Many artists work through and across questions of the relationship between strangers and neighbours, between the local and the global. In the process they often produce art that engages closely with the matter of being: who we are, what might we become, and how we connect with each other. Their investigative, observant, and often dialogical approach to the making of art raises our understandings of identity and of community, and affords a way of seeing that may lead to greater clarity about identity, and to deeper levels of empathy.

Notes

1 Jörn Rüsen, *History: Narration, Interpretation, Orientation* (Oxford: Berghahn Books, 2005), p. 52.
2 bell hooks, *Yearning: Race, Gender and Cultural Politics* (Boston: South End Press, 1990), p. 149.
3 Lily Kong, unpublished paper delivered at *Knowing Asia: Asian Studies in an Asian Century*, the 19th Biennial Conference of the Asian Studies Association of Australia, University of Western Sydney (July 2012).
4 Stuart Hall, 'Cultural Identity and Diaspora', in J. Rutherford (ed.), *Identity: Community, Culture and Difference* (London: Lawrence & Wishart, 1990), pp. 222–37: 225.
5 William Stueck (ed.), *The Korean War in World History* (Lexington: University Press of Kentucky, 2004).
6 For the history of South Korea's political changes, see Robert Bedeski, *The Transformation of South Korea: Reform and Reconstitution in the Sixth Republic under Roh Tae Woo 1987–92* (Milton Park: Routledge, 1994).
7 Alice G. Guillermo, 'Brief Survey of Philippine Art', in Turner (ed.), *Art and Social Change*, pp. 253–66.
8 Eva-Lotta E. Hedman and John T. Sidel, *Philippine Politics and Society in the Twentieth Century: Colonial Legacies, Post-Colonial Trajectories* (London: Routledge, 2000).
9 Interestingly both South Korea and the Philippines have had women presidents in modern times, a very unusual situation in Asia. Corazon Aquino, the first woman president in Asia, ruled the Philippines from 1986 to 1992, and Gloria

Macapagal-Arroyo from 2001 to 2010; Park Geun-hye, elected in 2013 as president of South Korea, is the first woman head of state in modern north-east Asia, and daughter of the assassinated President Park Chung-hee, who ruled South Korea from 1961 to 1979.

10 Quansheng Zhao (ed.), *Future Trends in East Asian International Relations: Security, Politics, and Economics in the Twenty-first Century* (Milton Park: Routledge, 2014).

11 Ming Sing (ed.), *Politics and Government in Hong Kong: Crisis Under Chinese Sovereignty* (Milton Park: Routledge, 2009).

12 Manuel Castells, *The Rise of the Network Society*, 2nd edn (Oxford; Malden, MA: Blackwell, 2000), p. 29.

13 Homi Bhabha, 'On Writing Rights', in Matthew Gibney (ed.), *Globalizing Rights: The Oxford Amnesty Lectures* (Oxford: Oxford University, 2003), pp. 162–83: 162.

14 Tony Schirato and Jen Webb, *Understanding Globalization* (London and New York: SAGE, 2003), p. 88.

15 Chen Zhen, 'Transexperiences: A Conversation between Chen Zhen and Zhu Xian', trans. William Y. Jiang, in *Chen Zhen: Invocation of Washing Fire* (Siene, Italy: Gli Ori, 2003), p. 156.

16 Chen Zhen, 'Transexperiences'.

17 A. D. Smith, 'Towards a Global Culture?', in Michael Featherstone (ed.), *Global Culture: Nationalism, Globalization and Modernity* (London: Sage, 1990), pp. 171–91: 175.

18 Zygmunt Bauman, *Globalization: The Human Consequences* (Cambridge, UK: Polity Press, 1998), p. 64.

19 Dominique Caouette, *Thinking and Nurturing Transnational Activism in Southeast Asia: Connecting Local Struggles With Global Advocacy* (Paris: Institute for Research and Debate on Governance, 2006), names a number of transnational NGOs and activist groups, including Third World Network (TWN) in Malaysia, Focus on the Global South in Thailand, the Asia Pacific Research Network (APRN) in the Philippines, Asian Forum for Human Rights And Development (Forum-Asia), and the Asia Pacific Women, Law and Development.

20 See Dawn Weist, 'Interstate Dynamics and Transnational Social Movement Coalitions: A Comparison of Northeast and Southeast Asia', in Nella Van Dyke and Holly J. McCammon (eds), *Strategic Alliances: Coalition Building and Social Movements* (Minneapolis: University of Minnesota Press, 2010), pp. 50–79. See also Diane Stone, *Knowledge Actors and Transnational Governance: The Private-Public Policy Nexus in the Global Agora* (New York: Palgrave Macmillan, 2013).

21 Michael Hardt and Antonio Negri, *Empire* (Cambridge, MA: Harvard University Press, 2000), p. 308.

22 Hardt and Negri, *Empire*, p. 15.

23 Homi Bhabha, 'On Writing Rights', p. 162.

24 Hou Hanru, 'On the Midground: Chinese Artists, Diaspora and Global Art', *Beyond the Future: The Third Asia-Pacific Triennial of Contemporary Art* (Brisbane: Queensland Art Gallery, 1999), p. 191.

25 Roland Robertson, *Globalization: Social Theory and Global Culture* (London: Sage, 1992).

26 Catherine Diamond, 'The Impossibility of Performing "Asia"', in Fuyubi Nakamura, Morgan Perkins and Olivier Krischer (eds), *Asia Through Art and Anthropology: Cultural Translation Across Borders* (London: Bloomsbury Publishing, 2013), pp. 179–91: 179.

27 Diamond, 'The Impossibility of Performing "Asia"', p. 189.

28 Diamond, 'The Impossibility of Performing "Asia"', p. 191.

29 Nicholas Jose, 'Pulping Herbert Read in a Washing-Machine', *London Review of Books* 21:12 (10 June 1999), pp. 15–18.

30 The locations for the first series of *A Needle Woman* (1999–2001) are Tokyo (Japan), Shanghai (China), Mexico City (Mexico), London (England), Delhi (India), New York (USA), Cairo (Egypt), Lagos (Nigeria); for the second series (2005), she entered locations of conflict and even war: Patan (Nepal), Jerusalem (Israel), Sana' (Yemen), Havana (Cuba), Rio de Janeiro (Brazil), N'Djamena (Chad).

31 Kimsooja and René Morales, Artist Talk, Miami Art Museum (2012), www.youtube.com/watch?v=M3m2T4OojoE, accessed 7 July 2014.

32 Kimsooja, 'Action 1: A One-Word Name is an Anarchist's Name' (14 July 2003), www.kimsooja.com/action1.html, accessed 12 August 2014.

33 Press release, 'Kimsooja: A Mirror Woman', Peter Blum Gallery, 23 February–18 May 2002, *Artnet* (2002), www.artnet.com/galleries/peter-blum/kimsooja-a-mirror-woman/, accessed 12 August 2014.

34 Kimsooja and René Morales, Artist Talk.

35 Paul Duncum and Stephanie Springgay, 'Extreme Bodies: The Body as Represented and Experienced through Critical and Popular Visual Culture', in Liora Bresler (ed.), *International Handbook of Research in Arts Education* (Dordrecht: Springer Press, 2007), pp. 1143–58: 1147.

36 Mary Jane Jacob, 'In the Space of Art: Buddha and the Culture of Now', interview with Kimsooja (2003), www.kimsooja.com/texts/jacob.html, accessed 4 February 2014.

37 'Cities on the Move – Contemporary Asian Art on the Turn of the 21st Century' was curated by Hou Hanru and Hans Ulrich Obrist; it ran from 26 November 1997 to 18 January 1998, at the Wiener Secession, Vienna.

38 Jacob, 'In the Space of Art'.

39 Annett Reckert, 'The Concept of Bottari', *Kimsooja: Texts* (2001), www.kimsooja.com/texts/reckert.html, accessed 12 August 2014.

40 Jacob, 'In the Space of Art'.

41 Reckert, 'The Concept of Bottari'.

42 Sandra Johnston, *Beyond Reasonable Doubt: An Investigation of Doubt, Risk and Testimony through Performance Art Processes in Relation to Systems of Legal Justice* (Zurich: LIT Verlag, 2014), p. 96.

43 Jacob, 'In the Space of Art'.

44 Kimsooja and René Morales, Artist Talk.

45 Kimsooja and René Morales, Artist Talk.

46 Philip Fisher, *Wonder, the Rainbow and the Aesthetics of Rare Experiences* (Cambridge, MA: Harvard University Press, 1998), p. 100.

47 Fisher, *Wonder, the Rainbow*.

48 Deirdre McKay, *Global Filipinos: Migrants' Lives in the Virtual Village* (Bloomington: Indiana University Press, 2012), p. 5.

49 Patrick D. Flores, 'Polytropic Philippine: Intimating the World in Pieces', in Michelle Antoinette and Caroline Turner (eds), *Contemporary Asian Art and Exhibitions: Connectivities and World-Making* (Canberra: ANU Press, 2014), p. 64.

50 McKay, *Global Filipinos*, p. 7.

51 McKay, *Global Filipinos*, p. 198.

52 Alice G. Guillermo, *Protest/Revolutionary Art in the Philippines 1970–1990* (Manila: University of the Philippines Press, 2001).

53 Angelito Junior Huang, 'On Resurfacing: A Case for a Cultural Renaissance' (Master of Architecture dissertation, University of Waterloo, 2013).

54 See Joseph R. Slaughter, 'A Question of Narration: The Voice in International Human Rights Law', *Human Rights Quarterly*, 19:2 (May 1997), pp. 406–30.

55 Used toothbrushes were installed for their work *Erasure and Remembrance* at the sixth Havana Biennial in 1997, and again for *Presences and Absences*, Fukuoka Asian Art Triennale, 1999.

56 *Dream Blanket*, a series of projects installed in Japan and South Korea in 2002, and in the US in 2005, used blankets collected from the community for a highly personal installation.

57 *Project: Be-longing*, a series they developed from 1999, and *Address* (2007–08), both involved the collection and installation of personal items from Filipinos who had migrated to Australia or returned to the Philippines.

58 Australian artist and academic Pat Hoffie tells of spending time in the Philippines as an exchange artist in 1993, when with a group of local artists she came across an abandoned library in the jungle, one of Imelda Marcos's extravagant projects. The artists took the books to a local village high school where Isabel and Alfredo Aquilizan were teaching, and created a community library, an 'igloo in the jungle' (Hoffie, in conversation with Turner, 2005).

59 Used in the works *Flight* (2004–08) and *Wings* (2009).

60 Christine Chinkin, 'The Language of Human Rights Law', in Caroline Turner and Nancy Sever (eds), *Witnessing to Silence: Art and Human Rights* (Canberra: Humanities Research Centre and Drill Hall Gallery, 2003, pp. 13–15: 14.

61 Wang Gungwu, 'Foreword', in Turner (ed.), *Tradition and Change*, p. vii.

62 Homi Bhabha, 'Conversational Art', in Mary Jane Jacob with Michael Brenson (eds), *Conversations at the Castle: Changing Audiences and Contemporary Art* (Cambridge, MA: MIT Press, 1998), pp. 38–47.

63 Claire Bishop, *Artificial Hells: Participatory Art and the Politics of Spectatorship* (London: Verso, 2012), p. 13.

64 Grant Kester, *Conversation Pieces: Community and Communication in Modern Art* (Berkeley: University of California Press, 2004), p. 151.

65 Dolla S. Merrillees, Alfredo + Isabel Aquilizan, 'Interview', Sherman Contemporary Art Foundation, April 2012, www.nelsonmeersfoundation.org.au/alfredo-and-isabel-aquilizan, accessed 15 September 2014.

66 Suzanne Lacy (ed.), *Mapping the Terrain: New Genre Public Art* (Seattle: Bay Press, 1994).

67 'Alfredo and Isabel Aquilizan', in *Artists Work*, Queensland Art Gallery (1999), www. visualarts.qld.gov.au/apt3/artists/artist_bios/alfredo_aquilizan_a.htm, accessed 14 August 2014.

68 Gene Sherman, in *Alfredo Juan Aquilizan and Isabel Gaudinez-Aquilizan, In-Habit: Project Another Country* (Sydney: Sherman Contemporary Art Foundation, 2012), p. 87.

69 Sherman, *Alfredo Juan Aquilizan and Isabel Gaudinez-Aquilizan.*

70 Merrillees, Interview.

71 Gene Sherman, *Alfredo Juan Aquilizan and Isabel Gaudinez-Aquilizan*, p. 87.

72 Alice Guillermo, in 'APT1: Out of the Shadows', ABC TV (1993), http://tv.qagoma. qld.gov.au/mediatype/videos/, accessed 8 July 2014.

73 Nan M. Sussman, *Return Migration and Identity: A Global Phenomenon, A Hong Kong Case* (Hong Kong: Hong Kong University Press, 2011), p. 11.

74 Sussman, *Return Migration and Identity*, p. 18.

75 Marsha Meskimmon, 'The Precarious Ecologies of Cosmopolitanism', in Turner, Antoinette and Stanhope (eds), *The World and World-Making in Art*, pp. 27–45.

76 This was not the case in 1967, when as a result of industrial abuse there was a major workers' strike that developed into riots and bombings. See Oscar Ho Hing-kay, 'China: The Process of Decolonization in the Case of Hong Kong', in Philipp Gassert and Martin Klimke (eds), *1968 Memories and Legacies of a Global Revolt* (Washington, DC: German Historical Institute, 2009), pp. 79–82.

77 Those connected with the democracy movement in particular attract very large crowds, with tens and sometimes hundreds of thousands joining the annual 1 July march that commemorates the Tiananmen Square protests of 1989. Lee and Chan note that Beijing treats these marches as 'a normal part of the politics of public opinion in Hong Kong'. See Francis L.F. Lee and Joseph M. Chan, *Media, Social Mobilization and Mass Protests in Post-colonial Hong Kong: The Power of a Critical Event* (Milton Park: Routledge, 2011), p. 120. This view cannot be extended, though, to the 2014 pro-democracy protests named the Umbrella Movement, a campaign based on the principle of non-violent civil disobedience. It lasted several months, involved up to 100,000 people occupying key parts of Hong Kong, and was marked by sometimes violent attacks on the protestors.

78 Confidential respondents, interviews with authors, Hong Kong, 2005.

79 See Oscar Ho Hing Kay, 'In Search of Art', in Hans Belting, Andrea Buddensieg and Peter Weibel (eds), *The Global Contemporary and the Rise of New Art Worlds* (Cambridge MA: MIT Press, 2013), pp. 303–9.

80 Oscar Ho Hing Kay, interview with the authors, 2005.

81 Ho, interview, 2005. See also Eliza Lai, 'Oscar Ho's *Stories Around Town*', in Irene Ngan and Eliza Lai (eds), *Mapping Identities: The Art and Curating of Oscar Ho* (Hong Kong: Para/Site Art Space, 2004), pp. 95–109.

82 Ho, interview, 2005.

83 Ho, interview, 2005.

84 Claire Bishop, 'The Social Turn: Collaboration and Its Discontents', *ArtForum* (February 2006), pp. 178–83: 181.

85 Oscar Ho Hing Kay, interview with authors, 2008.

86 Chang Tsong-Zung, 'Folk Lore of Current Affairs', in Ngan and Lai (eds), *Mapping Identities*, pp. 78–80: 78.

87 He discusses this in Oscar Ho, ' Under the Shadow: Problems of Museum Development in Asia', in Antoinette and Turner (eds), *Contemporary Asian Art and Exhibitions*, pp. 179–97.

88 For the history and current activities of 4A, see its website: www.4a.com.au/about-4a/, accessed 16 July 2014.

89 Carolyn Barnes, *John Young* (Melbourne: Craftsman House, 2005), p. 61.

90 Carolyn Barnes, 'Aesthetics and Memory Work in the Recent Painting of John Young', *John Young: The Bridge and the Fruit Tree* (Canberra: Drill Hall Gallery, ANU, 2013), pp. 55–65: 61–2.

91 John Young, communication with authors, 2014. See also the John Young Studio website, www.johnyoungstudio.com (accessed 9 January 2015), which list his publications in *Art & Text* (and other journals), and hosts other resources related to his vocation.

92 Barnes, 'Aesthetics and Memory Work', p. 57.

93 Andrew Frost, 'John Young: Ghosts on Canvas', *Australian Art Collector*, 6 (October-December 1998), pp. 40–4.

94 Carolyn Barnes, 'Towards a Layered Imaginary', John Young Studio resources (n.d.), www.johnyoungstudio.com/cms/resources/barnes.pdf (accessed 9 January 2015).

95 Communication with authors 2014. This work was purchased by Hong Kong's new international museum complex, M+.

96 See Kenneth White, 'The House of Insight', in *The Bird Path: Collected Longer Poems* (Edinburgh: Mainstream Press, 1989), p. 145.

97 Jacqueline Lo, 'Diaspora, Art and Empathy', *John Young: The Bridge and the Fruit Tree* (Canberra: Drill Hall Gallery, ANU, 2013), pp. 19–43: 21. The authors are indebted to Lo for her extensive research into the background of the works discussed below, and for drawing them to our attention.

98 Lo, 'Diaspora', p. 23.

99 Lo, 'Diaspora', pp. 22–3.

100 Cited in Sylvia Dominique Volz, 'John Young/Bonhoeffer in Harlem', in Christhard-Georg Neubert and Alexander Ochs (eds), *John Young/Bonhoeffer in Harlem* (Berlin: Edition St. Matthäus, 2009), p. 84.

101 Cited in Thomas J. Berghuis, 'John Young: Situational Ethics', Art & Australia, 48:3 (Autumn 2011), pp. 440–3: 440.

102 The site where, in 1934, members of the Confessing Church had resisted the consecration of this church by pro-fascist German Christians. Young was invited to re-create his installation 'Bonhoeffer in Harlem' in Bamberg as part of an exhibition entitled *Circles*, with a number of international artists including Ai Weiwei and Micha Ullman.

103 Cited in Volz, *John Young*, p. 80.

104 Cited in Volz, *John Young*, p.87.

105 Cited in Volz, *John Young*, p.87.

106 'a spoke in the wheel of the state'.

107 Volz, *John Young*, p. 89.

108 Thomas Berghuis, 'Safety Zone', *John Young Studio, Projects: Safety Zone* (October 2010), www.johnyoungstudio.com/w/safety-zone, accessed 17 October 2014.

109 This group included John Rabe, Minnie Vautrin, John Magee and Robert Wilson – the only surgeon left in the hospital (Lo, 'Diaspora', p. 35).

110 There are no accurate figures, because Japanese records were destroyed or kept secret. The Chinese government's Nanjing War Crimes Tribunal (1947) claimed that 300,000 civilians had been massacred; the International Military Tribunal for the Far East in 1948 asserted 200,000 deaths; and scholars debate the numbers, with estimates ranging from 40,000 to over 300,000 killed. See Bob Wakabayashi (eds), *The Nanking Atrocity 1937–1938: Complicating the Picture* (Oxford: Berghahn Books, 2007). John Rabe, the 'good man of Nanking', estimates that there would have been 50,000 deaths: he estimates a population of 300,000 in the city, with 250,000 protected by the International Safety Zone; those not accounted for, he determines, must therefore have been massacred. See Diana Lary, *The Chinese People at War: Human Suffering and Social Transformation, 1937–1945* (Cambridge: Cambridge University Press, 2010), p. 21.

111 John Rabe, *The Good Man of Nanking: The Diaries of John Rabe*, edited by Erwin Wickert, translated by John E. Woods (New York: Vintage Books, 2000).

112 'You have the heart of a Buddha'.

113 Lo, 'Diaspora', p. 37.

114 Lo, 'Diaspora', p. 35.

115 Thomas Berghuis, 'Safety Zone', Anna Schwartz Gallery (2010), www.annaschwartzgallery.com/works/artist_exhibitions?artist=30&year=2010&work=12542&exhibition=344&page=1&text=1&c=m, accessed 10 July 2014.

116 Lo, 'Diaspora', p. 41.

117 In Volz, *John Young*, pp. 84–5.

118 Michael Sullivan, *The Meeting of Eastern and Western Art* (Berkeley: University of California Press, 1989).

119 Barnes, 'Aesthetics and Memory Work', p. 59.

120 Terry Smith, 'Worlds Pictured in Contemporary Art: Planes and Connectivities', in Turner, Antoinette and Stanhope, pp. 11–26: 12.

121 Oscar Ho, 'My Curatorial Work, My Art', in Ngan and Lai, pp. 42–53: 50.

122 Arjun Appadurai, 'The Production of Locality', in Peter Beyer (ed.), *Religion in the Process of Globalization* (Wurzburg: Ergon Verlag, 2001), pp. 99–123.

123 Homi K. Bhabha, 'On Writing and Rights: Some Thoughts on the Culture of Human Rights', keynote speech at *Our Common Future* congress (Hanover, 2–6 November 2010), www.ourcommonfuture.de/fileadmin/user_upload/dateien/Reden/Bhabha_keynote_final.pdf, accessed 12 September 2013.

5   Worldmaking in art

Introduction

As the previous chapters suggest, individuals and nations bring the past with them into the present. This chapter takes up that issue with reference to the theme of worldmaking, something that is concerned not only with the past, but also with the future, because it begins with the willingness and the ability to imagine a different world. Art is an important element in any worldmaking agenda, because it has always been a means to imagine other possibilities.

In 2011, the Humanities Research Centre at the Australian National University explicitly provided a venue to explore this concept, convening a conference titled *The World and World-Making in Art*. Its focus was 'the significance of connectivities and differences in the field of art: its practices, histories, institutions, inclusions and exclusions, ethical concerns and theoretical and methodological approaches'.[1] Worldmaking was positioned as a way of decentring Euro-American views of the world, and enabling new forms of connectivity. The artists we discuss in this chapter – Pakistan-based Salima Hashmi, India-based Nalini Malani, Chinese-Australian Guan Wei and Chinese-born, now American Cai Guo-Qiang – are worldmakers in this sense: they connect to histories of justice and humanity within and beyond borders, testing assumptions about human rights that extend far beyond the immediate contexts. In this, they provide a vision of art that is rigorous and profound in its ethical focus, but open-ended in the questions it raises about the world, global connectivities and humanity's future.

World is not a concept that is easily expressed, as the character Goldberg, from Harold Pinter's *The Birthday Party* (1957), makes clear.[2] Though Goldberg is 'a veritable mine of plausible phrase and fable', he cannot find a way to explain the world to his associate. Steven Connor reads Goldberg's incapacity as an analogue, not of the limits of language, nor of 'the largeness and variousness of the world', but rather of the world's 'indeterminate finitude' – it *must* be something, but *need not* be any one thing.[3] Perhaps because of this expansive possibility, worldmaking is a concept that has attracted attention from scholars across the disciplines. Philosopher David Hume, for example, writes that 'Numerous universes might have been botched and bungled throughout an eternity, ere this system was struck out; much labor lost, many fruitless trials made, and a slow but continual improvement carried out during infinite ages in the art of world-making'[4] – a stark reminder that there is no clear or direct route to a new world. For Karl Marx, it is through labour that we make the world, 'acting on it and changing it', and in the process being ourselves changed.[5] But the concept of worldmaking was formulated most precisely by Nelson Goodman, who coined the term for his seminal book, *Ways of Worldmaking* (1978),[6] which posits first that we build worlds out of our experiences, our cultural foundations and our imaginations; and next that this is a transformative practice. Goodman specifically identifies art as a zone for worldmaking on the grounds that art does not merely *represent* the world but actually *constructs* our way of knowing it: thus, 'What is at stake is the power of processes of worldmaking to turn chaotic data into culturally significant truths … It is because any and every constructed world serves particular interests that it is so important to defend the plurality of worlds against the desire of homogenisation.'[7]

Goodman's thesis has been discussed, critiqued and developed during the decades since 1978. One of its respondents is academic Frederik Tygstrup, whose work focuses on the cultural values that are inevitably imported into any worldmaking project. Tygstrup argues that worldmaking is both an epistemological and an ontological act because, in making worlds, we both draw on and add to ways of knowing and of being; and that it is a political act because it involves the selection of truths, facts and values in the formulation of that world. It depends, therefore, on 'the precarious relationship' between facts and truths:[8] precarious because facts and truths belong to different domains of thought. Facts are statement, while truths are experiential; facts have scientific validity, while truths relate more closely to belief systems. Although truths need have little if any demonstrable accuracy, they tend to have greater carriage than do facts, which cannot be put to the work of making meanings until they are organised, categorised, and narrativised. Facts, therefore, exist *objectively* in and of themselves, but cannot exist *for us* independent of their description and hence their interpretation.[9]

This becomes a social or political problem because facts are very easily ignored or effaced if they do not fit the truth system that governs a particular frame of reference; different alignments of facts and truths have a significant impact on the actuality of the worlds in which we live, and therefore on the experience and wellbeing of individuals. Many worlds are possible; and, as art shows us, not all are directed towards equity. What is important, then, as Tygstrup argues, is the ability to turn facts into socially significant truths and thus to include them in a shared world of certainties, as well as the ability to acknowledge new facts and changing configurations of facts as novel elements in a dynamic world-view flexible enough to embrace the changing environment for social worldmaking.[10]

The domain of art, or creative expression more generally, is central to this work because art has the capacity to engage the 'truth', or the affectual part of human society, and in this way has a heightened ability to juxtapose fact and truth, and imbue viewers with new understandings – new 'truths'. Maurice Blanchot writes that 'art is useless, even to itself',[11] but he refers here not to fact, but to truth – to the feeling in society that art is not capable of engaging with the great forces of politics and economics. Jacques Rancière, however, makes the point that art 'is a way of doing and making that intervenes in the general distribution of ways of doing and making as well as in the relationships they maintain to modes of being and forms of visibility'.[12] It is, in short, a way of making reality felt and, in that way, of remaking realit(ies).

This is of signal importance in any consideration of human rights problems, and of the interventions that might be able to address them, because the world/s made will determine the capacity of their inhabitants to live lives that are safe and fulfilling. There is, though, no easy solution: the work of worldmaking must begin with the understanding that this is both complex and plural, and predicated on contradictory impulses. As Slavoj Žižek notes, none of us can have all of the rights all of the time; *my* right to freedom of expression is limited by *your* right not to be vilified.[13] The act of juggling relative rights in different contexts requires sensitivity to the alignment between facts and truths, and the acknowledgement that there are no absolutes in rights, or any permanent solutions.[14] Art, in its extraordinary variability, is remarkably effective at capturing plurality, and engaging a range of possible ways of seeing and being – and therefore of worldmaking. The artists we discuss in this chapter are engaged in the making of worlds – those that are directed towards rights and wellbeing, towards the construction of a viable global community, and towards the protection of the planet on which we live. The artists may not be involved in active protest or political action, but their works provide a way of aligning facts and truths, and thus of proferring new ways of living that might be more efficacious than the fraught world we currently inhabit.

Salima Hashmi: keeping hope alive in a state of turmoil

Salima Hashmi is an artist, cultural writer, activist, educator, and human rights campaigner for both women's rights and for peace. Born in New Delhi in 1942, before the Partition of India – instituted by Britain as it withdrew from the subcontinent in 1947 – she is the daughter of Faiz Ahmed Faiz,[15] one of the greatest Urdu poets, and Alys Faiz,[16] a respected journalist and peace activist in the UK where she was born, and in Pakistan. Both her parents were committed to humanist principles, and opposed fundamentalist extremism. Both India and Pakistan wanted Faiz Ahmed Faiz to live in their respective countries after Partition, but the family, as Muslims, chose during the dislocation of Partition to return in 1947 to their family home in the Punjab.

The Partition has been described by Indian author Arundhati Roy as 'Britain's final, parting kick to us', one that 'triggered the massacre of more than a million people and the largest migration of a human population in contemporary history'.[17] Its legacy has included three wars between Pakistan and India (in 1947, 1965 and 1971), and an undeclared war in 1999. In one of his poems, written in a mood of prescience on the very day of independence, Hashmi's father lamented: *'Those tarnished rays, this night smudged light / This is not that Dawn for which, ravished with freedom / we had set out in sheer longing / … / Friends, come away from this false light. Come, we must / search for that promised Dawn'.*[18] His intuition that Partition would not deliver the political and cultural future for which they hoped was accurate. Lawyer, leader of the Muslim League and first Governor-General of Pakistan Mohammed Ali Jinnah had insisted at the time of Partition that religion should be of no concern to the state, but it was the nation's tragedy, as author Pankaj Mishra writes, that he 'died before he could build a civilian – and secular – democracy in what had been India's most feudal regions'.[19] Pakistan was declared an Islamic Republic in 1956. It has experienced, in the nearly sixty years since, over two decades of martial law; a constitution that has been suspended five times; and a revolving series of leaders, with twelve presidents, and twenty-three prime ministers (two of whom were assassinated and one executed).

Faiz himself was arrested and accused of treason in the 1950s for alleged participation in a left-leaning conspiracy to stage a coup, though Hashmi has indicated that her father was never a member of the Communist Party, but rather was a Marxist who believed that a socialist society would be more humane. The sentence was commuted, but later he went into exile. He was, she says, always 'rebellious in the face of injustice and oppression', though it was always done 'with a very mild and sweet voice';[20] and he spoke 'for the "weaker voice" in the square, for religious minorities and the unorthodox, as in his prayer: *Let us too lift our hands, / We who do not remember the customary prayer, / We who do not remember any idol or God except love'.*[21] Above all, 'he celebrated the fact that it was possible to keep hope alive';[22] and in this lies his continuing appeal to young people in the subcontinent. Salima Hashmi has devoted her life to the same principles: her art has a strong humanist and human rights focus, and she has curated exhibitions of art from Pakistan for the UK, Europe, the US, Australia, Japan and India. In her life and work she has aimed to recover the vision of Pakistan's identity that her father, and many of its founders, dreamed of: a Pakistan that encompasses a strong commitment to human rights and humanist values.

She was also one of the Pakistani women who early took on a public and professional role. She studied design at the National College of Arts in Lahore, then continued her studies at the Bath Academy of Art in the United Kingdom and subsequently at the Rhode Island School of Design in the United States. On her return to Pakistan she and her husband, economics professor Shoaib Hashmi, embarked on a different career, starring in a weekly TV comedy show entitled colloquially *Don't Tell Fibs*, inspired by the BBC show *That Was The Week That Was*, dealing with public life in Pakistan. She is a former principal of the National Art School and was a teacher there for over thirty years, and is now Dean at Beaconhouse National University, a private liberal arts institution in Lahore.

Her writing on art in Pakistan has been a major contribution to scholarship.[23] Hashmi's influence has been extensive in Pakistan and internationally, and she has been described as 'one of the most loving, respected and revered personalities of Pakistani art today'.[24] She has, however, she says, 'been in trouble regularly with most Pakistani governments', because of her role as 'an arts activist and activist for human rights and women's rights'.[25] She was at odds with General Zia ul-Haq, who seized power in 1977, suspended the Constitution and imposed martial law together with certain aspects of *shari'a* law (with provisions such as those that decreed that a woman claiming to have been raped should be treated as an adulteress unless she could provide four male witnesses to testify that she had not been a willing participant). He asserted that religion represented the essential identity of Pakistan, declaring, 'Pakistan is like Israel, an ideological state.'[26] It was a rejection of the original vision for Pakistan, and was rejected by Faiz, who refused to believe that only in religion could humanity find its true identity.[27]

For Hashmi, freedom of expression was very important. When she was banned from television and returned to teaching, she was required, like all women government employees, schoolgirls and college students, to wear the chador. 'So because it was decreed,' she says, 'of course we weren't going to do it.'[28] This was a perilous decision under the rule of Zia, a period when artists, and particularly women artists, were at risk. Former Prime Minister Zulfikar Ali Bhutto was hanged and, Hashmi writes, there was enormous pressure placed on cultural practices: 'acceptable codes of dress, behaviour and language were quickly imposed. Dance was eliminated entirely from public view.' While strictures were placed on figurative art, she writes, 'Calligraphy and the genre of landscape painting were swiftly appropriated as being suitable,' but 'not a single woman artist took up calligraphy or changed her mode of working to bring it in line with official State policy.'[29] This assertion by women artists of their rights was the more courageous once Zia's tyranny was guaranteed international support when the Soviet Union invaded Afghanistan in December 1979. Increasingly unfree Pakistan became an invaluable ally of the 'free world', as perceived by Washington. A strong underground resistance, the Movement for Democracy, began to develop in 1981; and ironically, the market for art grew steadily.

Artists were still permitted to paint figurative subjects, including the nude, provided they did so in private. So Hashmi and two architects started a private gallery, believing that in 'a social framework where women's visibility is undesirable, the depiction of the female nude assumes potent political meaning, especially when enunciated by a woman'.[30] Hashmi and other women artists saw the use of the nude as a statement of the presence and the visibility of women in a context where women were increasingly excluded, and thus 'in some of Salima's works from that period, the female body became a gesture defying the decrees of the state'.[31] This growing challenge by Pakistani women to Zia's tyranny abruptly became very visible when, on 12 February 1982, a group of women went to the High Court in Lahore to deliver a petition to the Chief Justice. Hashmi recalls:

> Because there was a law against assembly of more than four persons, the women went in groups of two, like in crocodile fashion. And before they got to the High Court, the police came and the demonstration was very brutally beaten up. Now, this was the first time in Pakistan's history that actually there had been a police action against a women's demonstration. And the photographs became internationally known, and so the Women's Action Forum was set up, which was a loose sort of federation of all women's organisations who came together.[32]

This was followed in 1983 by further action when, during the National Exhibition in Lahore, artists, women activists, journalists, lawyers, writers, performers and poets came together and produced a manifesto. Though this document could not be made public, it 'noted with concern the decline in status and condition of the life of Pakistani women'; 'noted the significant contribution which pioneering women artists have made to the course of arts and art education in Pakistan'; and 'condemned the propagation of the obscurantist and discriminatory laws being enacted'.[33]

Some occasion for hope that constraints might be alleviated came when Zia ended martial law and restored the Constitution on 30 December 1986. Then Benazir Bhutto, daughter of executed former Prime Minister Z. A. Bhutto, returned from exile to lead the Pakistan People's Party. Zia was killed on 17 August 1988 in an aircraft accident and, following national elections, Benazir Bhutto became Pakistan's first woman prime minister, releasing political prisoners, lifting the ban on trade unions and reducing control over the electronic

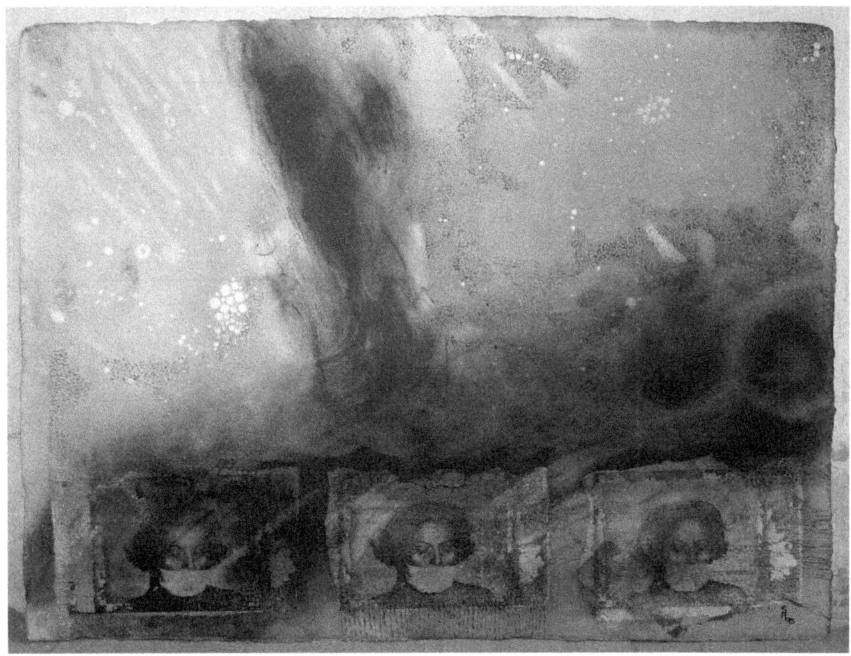

5.1 Salima Hashmi, *A Poem for Zainab*, 1995.

media. But this did not mean that women had gained power, or had become less invisible.[34] After Bhutto was dismissed in 1990 on charges of corruption, she was succeeded by Nawaz Sharif. He continued in Zia's path, planning to have *shari'a* law formally incorporated into the legal code, until he was himself dismissed for corruption in 1993. Benazir Bhutto became prime minister again in 1995, and was dismissed again in 1996. Sharif again became prime minister in 1997 and attempted to secure his position by imposing emergency measures, but was dismissed yet again in 1999 following a military coup engineered by Chief of Army General Pervez Musharraf.

Despite this political turmoil, Salima Hashmi was able to continue with her work. 'It's odd', she reflected later, 'that the worse things are, the better the art becomes … the human spirit or the resilience of creative people is challenged and comes to the fore.'[35] She also continued to resist the oppression of women in art and in social action. These two impulses were combined in the case of an imam who brutally assaulted his own wife. Hashmi's work *A Poem for Zainab* (1994), a semi-abstract acrylic and collage work that includes a representation of a gagged woman, references this violence, and is described by Neluka Silva as 'particularly daring' in its treatment of such an act.[36] Action by women's groups, including the Women's Action Forum in which Hashmi was prominent, led to the imam's imprisonment. In its sensitivity, the painting exemplifies her approach, which is based on a great respect for the ordinary people, for artistic traditions including craft traditions, for nature, and for human rights. Her works reflect the elegance of court manuscripts and the essence of Urdu and Persian poetry, combined with western art traditions. She uses allusive images – open windows, caged birds and symbols of fragile short-lived flowers, such as hyacinth and lilies – to represent the heroic moment in the face of brutality.

She was commissioned by the Bradford Museums and Galleries in the UK to produce *Zones of Dreams* (1996) (see Plate 11) as part of their project for social cohesion in Britain. This work is a triptych, depicting an image of the Indo-Pakistan subcontinent, embellished with gold leaf and collage, and layered with symbols of history and culture. As one commentator indicates, it is a profound work, where the geographical reality of the subcontinent, bordered by seas and mountains, adopts an almost mythical presence. Sri Lanka is engulfed in an emerald sea, and a lotus is painted over Bangladesh.[37] Hashmi painted 'clouds over Kashmir since I didn't want to carve it up in my map'.[38] This artwork celebrates the interconnectedness of the subcontinent, its physical beauty and rich traditions, as well as the geographical, historical and cultural links between its peoples.

Two other series of works made in 2003 and 2006 revolved around major calamities: the Taliban's destruction, in 2001, of the Bamiyan Buddhas in Afghanistan; and the 2005 earthquake that devastated large areas in Northern Pakistan, including the areas near the disputed border with Indian Kashmir.[39] The intensity of the natural calamity brought together, very briefly, Kashmiris on both sides of the border: authorities allowed the first phone calls to take place between families who had been divided for five decades.[40] The magnitude of this disaster is evident in the works that emerged from Hashmi's studio at the time: her *October 8* series comprises dark, sharp, almost savage charcoal works. These are very different from the meditative, delicately lyrical series that marked the destruction of the monumental Bamiyan Buddhas. Titled *Pursuing Radiance*, and rendered in paper in pigment, collage, tea wash and ink, the mood in this series is 'a tribute to the persistence and survival of Buddha's teachings. The mountains stood firm, the remaining void indicating what had been lost, but would be forever remembered.' Hashmi sourced the imagery of hands in these works from the hands of Buddha in the 'teaching mudra' position, as seen in Gandhara sculpture of the period.[41]

Hashmi is concerned not only with the condition of the cultural and political world, but also the physical environment: she is a known activist who protests against the development of nuclear weapons, and condemned the nuclear tests conducted by India and Pakistan in 1998. After Pakistan exploded its bomb, she said, 'I had people calling me up and saying, "We have done it. We have gone into the nuclear age". Her response was: 'We will live to weep this dawn.'[42]

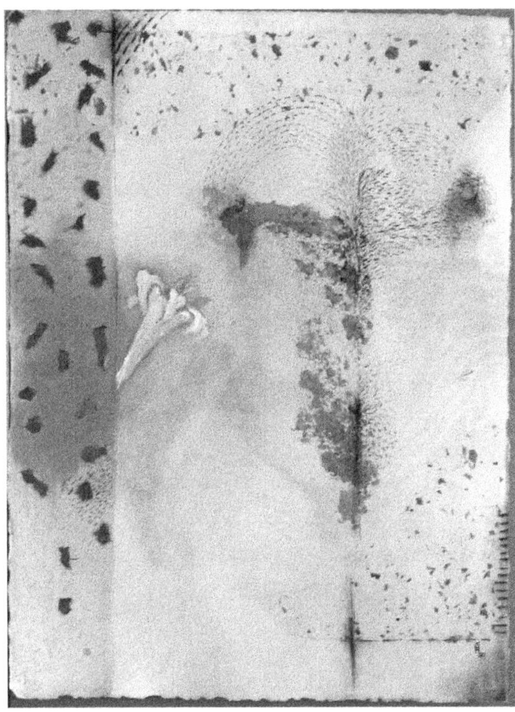

5.2   Salima Hashmi, *The People Wept at Dawn*, 1994.

The People Wept at Dawn, created in response to those tests, and included in the 2000 National Millennium Art Exhibition at Alhamra Art Gallery, Lahore, presents a flower emerging from a damaged structure – an image, perhaps, of hope.

In 2003 she published her seminal book, *Unveiling the Visible: Lives and Works of Women Artists in Pakistan*. She was also one of twelve curators who organised the inaugural programme of exhibitions, *Moving Ahead* (2007), for the new National Art Gallery, a programme that included nude studies and figurative sculptures despite the 'contested terrain' this comprised.[43] In this year, though, Benazir Bhutto returned from exile, and a suicide bomber immediately attempted to assassinate her. Bhutto was unhurt, but 136 people were killed, and Musharraf responded to the mounting turmoil by suspending the Constitution and dismissing the Chief Justice. It was in this situation that her father's poem '*Bol* [Speak]' – written in 1941 while his country was still under British control – was revived.[44] In acts of resistance, people across the country began to mark the word *Bol* on their clothing, cars and buildings.[45] Hashmi has affirmed her own belief that people must speak out against extreme views and injustice, and that art is an important part of speaking out, and forging resilience in troubled times.

Musharraf restored the Constitution on 18 December, but Bhutto was assassinated a week later. He resigned in 2008 under the threat of impeachment for eroding the trust of the nation, and in 2013 was charged with complicity in the murder of Bhutto. Hashmi records how, on 'a bleak January morning in 2008, artists Naiza Khan, Faiza Butt, and I were huddled around a small gas fire in Gallery Rohtas 2 in Lahore, still stunned by the trauma of Benazir Bhutto's assassination just days before'.[46] But more was to be destroyed: a suicide bombing in the Marriott Hotel in Islamabad killed fifty-three people; and a further 166 died in an attack by Pakistan-based militants on the Taj Mahal Hotel in Mumbai in 2008. It was in these circumstances that Hashmi launched the first exhibition in the US devoted to the contemporary art of Pakistan, *Hanging Fire*, at the Asia Society in New York in September 2009, saying that her intention was to give her country a new identity in the perception of the world outside.

Her work extends beyond her own creative vision and sociopolitical action, to her role in helping to build the careers of other artists who can take up the multiple challenges of the contemporary world. In the course of her substantial career, Hashmi has been a pivotal figure in supporting the art of a number of students who became significant Pakistani artists – Rashid Rana, Shahzia Sikander, Imran Qureshi, Faiza Butt, Aisha Khalid, Nusra Latif Qureshi. As one of her students, Faiza Butt, has said, 'At NCA, (Lahore) under the mentoring of Prof. Salima Hashmi, we were encouraged to dwell deeper into the influences surrounding us, rather than make work derivative of western history'.[47] She has encouraged her students to be involved with the community, with education, to go into villages and support craft work by women and to help with relief work during natural disasters. She indicates that a number of artists who had left Pakistan have since returned because they believe they are needed, not least because the majority of the population in Pakistan do not hold extremist beliefs and artists can work to combat the extremists.[48]

The building of a community of artists is increasingly important, as crisis continues to surround many aspects of life in Pakistan: a crisis for women which encroaches on a woman's right to be herself and to choose what she wants to do with her life, with her body and with her future; a crisis for minorities or religious groups; an urban/rural clash; the devastation of large areas of Pakistan by environmental change and natural disasters; and the crisis of borders. In the face of this complexity, Hashmi says, 'I think that you find artists and their work can reflect some of these [crises], but it is also about the celebration of survival, and the fact that you are living to tell the tale today'.[49] It is, as her father would have said, a matter of 'keeping hope alive'.

Nalini Malani: 'In Search of Vanished Blood'

Nalini Malani was born in 1946 in Karachi, just prior to independence and Partition in 1947. Her website describes her as a 'refugee of the Partition of India,'[50] because her family was forced to flee from what was to become Pakistan to settle in India – the opposite route from that taken by Salima Hashmi. She later studied art at the Sir Jamsetjee Jeejebhoy School of Art in Mumbai (1964–69), and had a studio at the Bhulabhai Memorial Institute in Bombay – a mix of artists, dancers and theatre people. Malani accepted a French Government scholarship for 1970–72 and studied in a Paris that was still defined by the 1968 radical movements. Her work is very well received and respected in her home country of India and internationally, and has been exhibited internationally in major exhibitions, including the Asia-Pacific Triennial in 1996 and 2002; *Traditions/Tensions* in New York, 1996; *Century City* at the Tate Modern (2001); the Venice Biennale in 2005 and 2007; *Paris, New Delhi, Bombay*, Centre Pompiduo, 2011; Documenta in Germany (2012); a major retrospective at the Kiran Nadar Museum of Art (New Delhi, 2014); and *Scenes for a New Heritage* (MoMA, NY, 2015).

Malani shares with Salima Hashmi that early childhood experience of Partition and relocation, but their two countries have had quite different political histories. India is the world's largest democracy, and has a commitment to being a secular republic, though it has faced challenges, including the assassinations of prominent leaders, and major sectarian violence. Malani has been one of those Indian intellectuals who have spoken out against fanaticism and violence. She also has an interest in poetry, and particularly in the poetry of Hashmi's father, Faiz Ahmed Faiz, having taken his *In Search of Vanished Blood* (translated into English by poet Agha Shahid Ali), as the title of her major art work for *Documenta 13* in Germany in 2012. That poem, written after the Indo-Pakistani War in 1965, reads in part:

> But, unheard, it still kept crying out to be heard.
> No one had the time to listen, no one the desire.
> It kept crying out, this orphan blood,
> but there was no witness. No case was filed.
> From the beginning this blood was nourished only by dust.
> Then it turned to ashes, left no trace, became food for dust.[51]

Responding to the poem, Malani produced a multimedia installation in the form of what she terms 'a video/shadow play' (see Plate 12). The work is presented in a darkened space, and contains large revolving Mylar cylinders that seem to reference Buddhist prayer wheels. Projected as shadows on the walls are images of human and animal figures – in many cases, with what appear to be the bodies of humans, carried by animals. In one sequence, words from

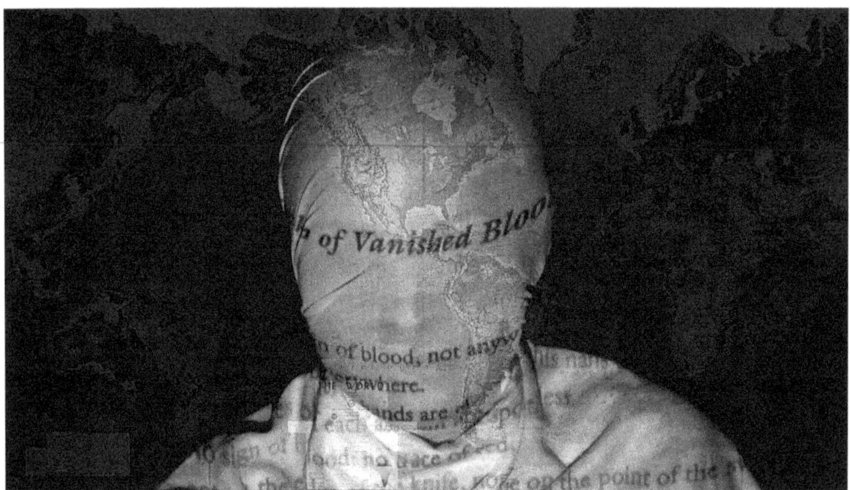

Nalini Malani, *In Search of Vanished Blood*, 2012. Detail. Single-channel video/play,   **5.3**
sound, 11 minutes. Installation view at Kochi-Muziris Biennale, 2012. Another version
of the six-channel video/shadow play, shown at Documenta 13. Collection: Auckland
Art Gallery.

Faiz's poem are projected onto the face of a veiled female figure. The imagery is
accompanied by a haunting soundtrack of music and voices. One of the voices
says, 'This is Cassandra speaking', while the chorus quotes lines from Joseph
Conrad, Heiner Müller and Samuel Beckett, including one who says, 'In the
name of the victims'.[52] Malani has said, 'for me that particular poem *In Search
of Vanished Blood* epitomizes the Partition in every possible way. And every
time there have been sectarian problems and violence this poem completely
comes to mind'.[53]

While her practice is often placed in the postcolonial context of today's India,
her work also quotes from the discourses and traditions of western art,[54] and in
this way reflects global rather than purely local crises. As Andreas Huyssen
argues, 'Malani's work since the 1990s must be seen in the context of a vast, and
by now worldwide culture of memory politics – memories of historical trauma,
dictatorships, genocide, rape, and structural violence'.[55] While we suggest that
her work is as committed to the present as to historical violence, Huyssen's view
is very pertinent to her *In Search of Vanished Blood*. This work not only directly
cites Faiz's poem, which is itself a cry against war on the subcontinent, but also
incorporates European contexts in its reference to the tragedy of the prophet
Cassandra, daughter of King Priam of Troy, who was cursed to know the future,
but not to be believed by those she attempted to warn.[56]

Inspired by her reading of Christa Wolf's 1984 novel *Cassandra*, Malani
has often incorporated into her art powerful female figures from western

and Indian literature and mythology, including Cassandra, Medea and Sita because, she says, 'Mythology is a universal language; it forms a link to the viewer. Many myths are still widely known. Whether I refer to Vishnu or Shiva or Cassandra or Medea, people know the stories.'[57] For her, the Cassandra figure is an invocation to take action, though with little confidence that it will have effect:

> There is a Cassandra in all of us; we have insights, instincts, we know what is right and what is wrong. But how many of us speak out? Scores of people die in Iraq every day. Considering our technological progress, such loss of life is insane. We hear things, but we don't listen. We know things are wrong, like depleting the earth's resources, but we continue to do them. And that is Cassandra; she warned her father about the Trojan horse.[58]

Her art, which reflects on the silences in history, particularly in relation to violence against women, is ultimately not a vision of hope, but rather a witness for those – and especially women – whose vanished blood has been forgotten. This raises the question of whether contemporary women artists display particular empathy in communicating issues of human rights that relate to women and children, who are the more marginalised and less protected members of society. A number of scholars have debated this point,[59] and Malani offers her own thoughts on the topic:

> Following feminist philosophers like Luce Irigaray and Judith Butler, I believe that the intuitive part of the mind is coded as female. But this is not a female prerogative; it exists in all of us. Why don't we listen to that? After all, in the aftermath of war or violence it's women who take care of the wounded and mourn for the dead. Maybe if men performed these roles, there would be fewer deaths.[60]

Whether empathy is inherently connected to gender, or an effect of social role, it is not a question that can be answered in an evidentiary manner. It is clear, however, that Malani identifies with those who have a less reliable access to social and cultural rights. As Srimoyee Mitra notes, her works 'include the points of view of national minorities and global migrants'.[61]

The question remains: what can art do in the face of brutality, violence and human rights abuses? Malani says only:

> Well, I don't know what art can really do. All it can do is put forward issues and questions while probably not delivering all the answers. As an artist one has to avoid falling into the area of propaganda and sloganeering. In turn one must find a particular area called art where what one proposes continues to be art, which will contain many different aspects of a problematic, while addressing urgent issues.[62]

This is a sort of coda to her *In Search of Vanished Blood*, a work that has broad universal meaning and directly treats oppression and trauma both local and global, historical and of the present. Much of her earlier work engages with the same problem. *Hamletmachine* (1999/2000), for example, based on a 1977 play by influential East German writer Heiner Müller, is at one level overtly about issues in India, and particularly Hindu fundamentalism and the destruction of the sixteenth-century Ayodhya mosque, Babri Masjid.[63] But it is also about fanaticism and fascism in Europe and Asia, as Geeta Kapur and Ashish Rajadhyaksha suggest: 'As sounds and images from the fascist movement in Europe and Japan overlap, the threat of suppressed fascism in India surfaces.'[64]

The work is a video play, with three videos projected onto the walls, and a fourth projected onto a layer of salt on the floor in what the art historian Johan Pijnappel describes as 'a reference to Gandhi's salt march'.[65] As artist and academic Pat Hoffie writes, it 'is neither a cynical proposition nor an idealistic call for moral and ethical piety – rather the work invents a space and time-span where witness becomes an essential first response'.[66] *Hamletmachine* contains elements similar to those later rehearsed for *In Search of Vanished Blood*, such as the projection onto a human body (in this case, the Butoh dancer Harada Nobuo) and the staining effect of the coalescing of images that bleed together, within a haunting enveloping soundtrack of voices. It is one of Malani's most beautiful works, more intimate than *Remembering Toba Tek Singh* (1998–99), but just as disturbing. And in her use of video, it becomes more accessible to an audience beyond the community of contemporary arts, as she suggests:

> Even if they are free, art galleries are daunting for the middle class, who feel that they are elite spaces. But video is seductive and draws people in. The shadow plays are similar. They are mesmerizing; you can watch the different images – painted, projected, shadows – overlap and combine. However, once I draw people in, I want to tell my own stories.[67]

Malani began to tell such stories very early, for example in her 1969/76 experimental film installation *Utopia* that reflects on the concept of and challenges in a modernistic utopian future for India.[68] She has had a long-term commitment to work with ordinary people; an early example is seen in a project she conducted in a slum area of Mumbai in 1973, before the emergency (1975–77). This was, she says, a community of Muslims where '[e]verybody was gainfully employed … and very proud of it'. She spent time with them, and did some filming in their homes, and then arrived one morning to find that the whole area had been cleared by the authorities, 'and the entire community could not be traced'. Similar incidents of the forced relocation of people have also triggered her concern, including the dispossession of tribal people in India from their lands, and she has long been actively involved in the artists' group

SAHMAT (discussed in Chapter 1), which exists to speak out for freedom of speech and against violence.[69]

The treatment of colonialism and neocolonialism remains central in much of Malani's work, and particularly where it involves environmental threats to the developing world. *The Mutants* (1995–96) is a series that began as a response to US nuclear programmes at Bikini atoll in 1954, and the deformed babies born to Micronesian mothers as a consequence. The drawings on paper and on the wall not only comment on this violence against nature, but also gesture towards the effect of such violence on women's bodies. Malani states: 'The woman as de-gendered mutant, violated beyond imagination, has been an ongoing pre-occupation in my work',[70] and *The Mutants* refers to other catastrophes, including the infamous Bhopal disaster in India in 1984 when a gas leak from the US-owned Union Carbide factory killed thousands of people, and affected the long-term health of many more. She extended this work, and its concerns, for the second Asia-Pacific Triennial of Contemporary Art at the Queensland Art Gallery in 1996, when she created *Body as Site*. This installation involved two elements: a series of six large-scale fabric dye paintings on milk carton paper from the *Mutant* series, and *Woman*: three mixed media charcoal and chalk drawings made directly onto the Gallery wall, dissolving and distorted figures that are more beautiful than hideous. Significantly, at the end of the exhibition, and at the artist's request, the wall paintings were washed away with milk as an act of erasure and of respect.

Malani's opposition to nuclear testing – in this case, the 1998 Indian and Pakistan nuclear tests – emerged again in her powerful video play *Remembering Toba Tek Singh* (1998–99), a work that, as Malani notes, related to India as a nation committed to non-violence and the Gandhian way, and which 'was an indictment against India's underground nuclear testing'.[71] It is based on the story *Toba Tek Singh* by Saadat Hasan Manto, about a mental patient who, during Partition, was to be released from the institution and sent to India, but refused to go because he believed that his village, Toba Tek Singh, was in what became Pakistan. He was forcibly removed but died, trapped in no man's land between the two countries. The gap in understanding between Pakistan and India, and the vulnerability of ordinary people in the face of geopolitical moves, are manifest in Malani's installation. It includes a number of large tin trunks representing migration and refugees; the trunks contain video monitors that show archival images from the dropping of the atomic bombs in Japan in 1945. A sound track enfolds the audience in the darkened space, and the video incorporates imagery of bomb blasts, figures that melt and reform, and animated versions of the earlier mutant drawings to indicate the effects of the blasts on humans. A key visual element included two videos of birth, showing 'a white child and an Indian child' being born and then, in a reversal, drawn back into the womb. On opposite sides of the room is a projection of

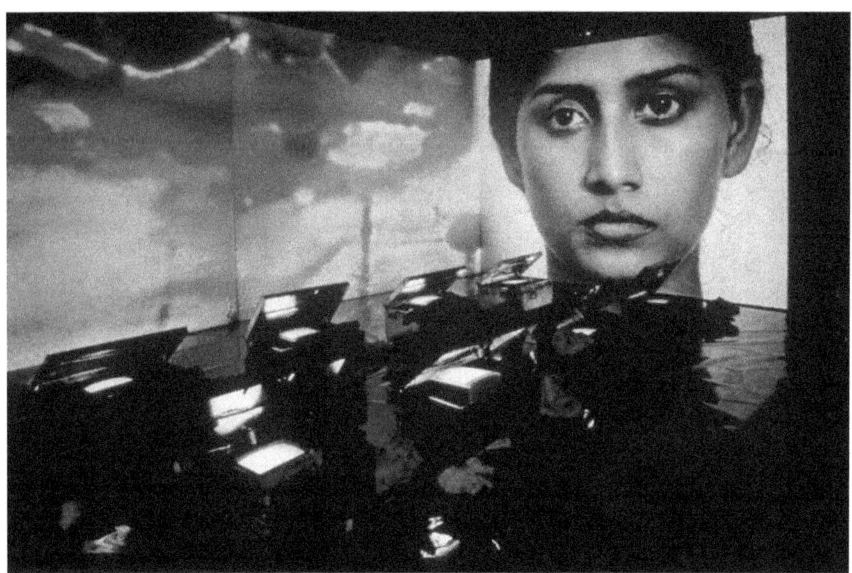

Nalini Malani, *Remembering Toba Tek Singh*, 1998. Installation view at Prince of   **5.4**
Wales Museum, Bombay (Mumbai). Four-channel video/play, 12 monitors, sound,
20 minutes. Collection: Queensland Art Gallery. Foundation Grant 2000.

two women futilely trying to fold a sari; as Victoria Lynn writes, 'The billowing
smoke swallows the image and each poetic configuration of the sari takes on
metaphoric connotations: the veil, the mushroom cloud, nature, earth.'[72]

Remembering Toba Tek Singh was the beginning of a new series of works
that warn ever more insistently about the threat of nuclear and environmental
catastrophe on a global scale. This is not surprising, as the potential for conflict with Pakistan remains (the Islamist terrorists who launched the Mumbai
attack in 2008 came from Pakistan) and global tensions and environmental
disasters appear routinely in the news. Malani was awarded the prestigious
Arts and Culture Fukuoka Prize Japan in 2013 for her 'consistent focus on such
daring contemporary and universal themes as religious conflict, war, oppression of women and environmental destruction.'[73] But she remains conscious
of the challenges inherent in the Cassandra role, wondering, 'How then to
militate one's way from historical sites to contemporary episodes that run in
repetitively compulsive cycles?'[74]

Perhaps it is not possible to escape, but it is possible to reconsider and to
incorporate alternative frames of reference and, by overlaying those historical sites, to observe the possibility of a more effective intervention. Her video
play *Unity in Diversity* (2003), for example, is based on the painting *Galaxy of
Musicians* by the nineteenth-century Indian painter Raja Ravi Varma, where

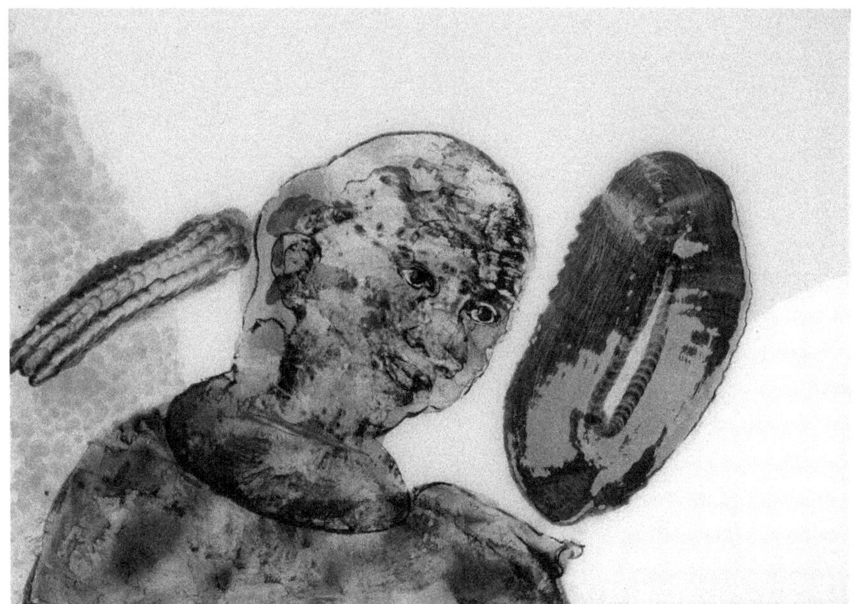

5.5 Nalini Malani, *Cassandra*, 2009. Detail. 30 panel reverse painting on acrylic sheet. Collection: Kiran Nadar Museum of Art. (Full image at: http://www.nalinimalani. com/painting/cassandra.htm)

eleven musicians, each clad in the costume of a different part of India, perform 'in unity'. Malani's work shows the hollow nature of imposed unity by incorporating later histories of violence into that image. Chaitanya Sambrani observes the references in her video to the Gujarat riots of 2002, and her critique of the 'primary motto of cultural policy' in modern Indian culture: 'Unity in diversity'. This, he writes, 'is one of the foundational myths of the modern, secular democracy that was mobilized to support the creation of a sovereign state out of the disparate remnants of British colonialism'.[75]

From a similar perspective, the video play *Mother India: Transactions in the Construction of Pain* (2005) challenges the effects of British colonialism and the Partition it enforced, and particularly its effect on women. In this enormous work (which is projected onto five screens totalling twenty metres), a plethora of images of nation and of Indian culture are presented, intercut with images of a woman's body. An important element in this work is a map on which a woman's body is superimposed. The effect, curator Macushla Robinson writes, is of nation inscribed onto the female body: 'borders and place names read as wounds and scars on the surface of the body. This image makes the violence involved in establishing these national boundaries palpable, and relates it back to the violence against individual bodies.'[76] Though she does not identify herself with the term 'feminism', she consistently attends to the representation of women in her video installations and her paintings, which often focus on strong female figures taking centre stage among collections of mythological animals. *Splitting the Other* (2007), for example, features an unfolding narrative of disaster across the fourteen panels of the painting, where explosions and germ-like ectoplasms merge in a dream-like blending. Her thirty-panel painting *Cassandra* (2009) presents a world of violence swirling around the terrifying bald figure of Cassandra and her ignored prophecies.

Though Malani's work does not necessarily rely on a sense of hope for a different world, she does engage the possibility of renewal. She believes human beings can find solutions and has said, 'I cannot be pessimistic about the human race.' Arjun Appadurai writes that her work

> is a bold answer to the conundrum of the global and the local … her work is a deep critique of the nation-form which seeks always to find the old in the new – timeless essences, universal abstractions, rote formulae of loyalty. Malani's work does just the reverse, by seeking the new in the old, even in the forms and techniques of violence, which she turns into places of discovery in the heart of darkness.[77]

Guan Wei: imagining new worlds

Guan Wei's art connects very explicitly to human rights, encompassing the need for shared understandings between peoples. His art also has treated critical themes of refugees, war and global crisis. He was born in Beijing in 1957, the son of an actor who played the roles of high-ranking military officers in the Beijing Opera and the descendant of the Manchu aristocracy who ruled China under the Qing Dynasty, from 1644 until the fall of the Empire in 1911. As sinologist Linda Jaivin writes, his great-great-grandfather was Comptroller of the Summer Palace under the last Empress Cixi, and his great-great-aunt was the mother of the last Emperor of China.[78] She notes Geremie Barmé's observation that Guan Wei 'not only has the typical stature and accent of a Manchu nobleman, but he is heir to that culture's fascination with diversions and entertainments, including poetry, painting and opera', and is widely read in fields as diverse as genetics and alchemy as well as western and Chinese history and art history.[79] He is, we suggest, one of those contemporary Chinese artists who in recent times have sought to move beyond the art of the Mao era, to reconnect to China's much older intellectual and artistic traditions, and to explore ways of bringing those traditions and western art together.[80]

Guan Wei graduated from Beijing Capital University in 1986, and became a high school art teacher. By this time China had emerged from the Cultural Revolution (1966–76), which had so disrupted his generation's education. New ideas, particularly from the west, were creating an environment of experimentation. Guan Wei has said that he and his fellow students at university 'painted their way through the last century of western art history'.[81] He came to Australia at the beginning of 1989 to take up a residency at the Tasmanian School of Art, returning to China just as the protest movement there was reaching a climax. His response to the events of 1989 was to produce his *Two Finger Exercises* (1989), a series of forty-eight pieces in which 'figures frolic with their fingers extended in the V-for-victory sign adopted by the demonstrators. It communicates the sense of rowdy innocence and exuberance on the streets of Beijing before the tanks moved in'.[82] The series also opens questions as to whether the figures understand the potential repercussions of what they are doing, and is an enduring record of the emotions of that era and of the individuals caught up in its events.

Guan Wei described himself and his Beijing friends as 'underground artists' who showed their art in private apartments and to foreigners, including Australian writer and diplomat Nicholas Jose, who encouraged him to go to Australia.[83] Of the reform movement in China he told Jeremy Eccles, 'Artists were in the middle, between the students and the government. We wanted society improved, but we were worried that it might be broken'.[84] These limitations, along with the effect of witnessing the events at Tiananmen Square in 1989, and the failure of the democratic movement, persuaded him to accept further residencies in Australia, returning there in 1990. He spent time at the Museum of Contemporary Art in Sydney and the School of Art at the Australian National University in Canberra, and in 1993 became an Australian citizen under the Distinguished Talent scheme.

Guan Wei has said of his journey to Australia, 'Consciously or unconsciously, I embarked on a journey of exploration of my own identity … In my first few years here, I regarded myself as an outsider looking in and maintaining a feeling of detachment … I floated freely between two cultures, fascinated by my role as an outsider'.[85] However, he gradually found Australia to be a familiar place – a place where he could make 'attempts to transform Western and Eastern culture. I am using my own particular visual language to see how I can express Western culture, history and society'.[86] Guan Wei has had a major impact in his adopted country and, as he told the authors, he now feels sufficiently at home to comment on Australian life, history and politics. He has produced a series of art works about the history of Australia related to Europeans taking possession of a continent inhabited by Aboriginal people, thus opening up the question of how Australians can reconcile their past and present. In recent years he has also produced work that takes up Australia's treatment of refugees. His art is, however, broader in philosophical scope, encompassing issues of global war, forced migrations and potentially the future of the planet; and it reflects our theme of worldmaking in the sense of providing alternative visions and histories for humanity.

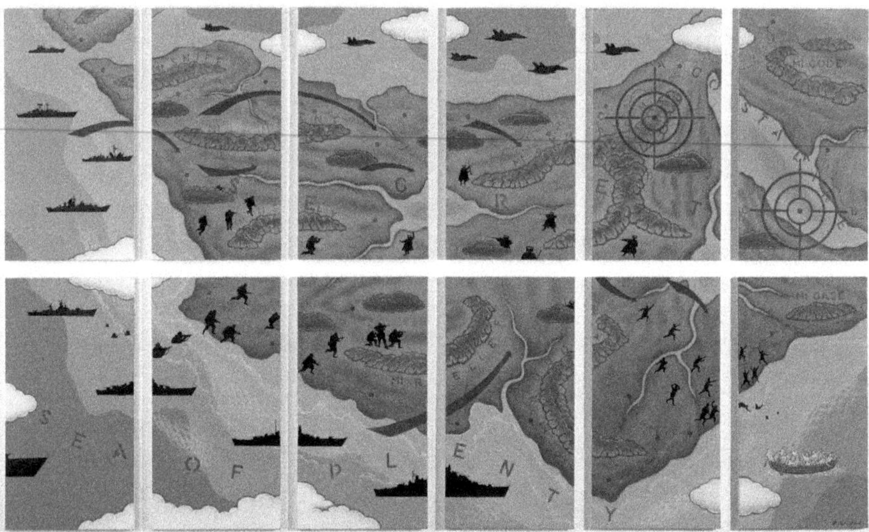

Guan Wei, *Where's Ned Kelly*, 2004.   **5.6**

The first of the works he produced in Australia treated themes such as travel and science: for example, a series of paintings on test tube babies (1992), the *Efficacy of Medicine* (1995) and *The Great War of the Eggplant* (1994), which, he has indicated, was about cultural crossings, and was a response to the first Gulf War. He also created a number of works which aim to bring together eastern and western concepts, such as *Zodiac* (2008), whose elements reference planetary and star maps, the western zodiac, Chinese views of the heavens, acupuncture and Taoist philosophy. In *Zen Garden* (1999) and the *Buddha's Hand* series (2010) he drew on Buddhist philosophy, while *Les Vents* (1998), a painting about the winds, includes scientific symbols for chemical compounds – for example, sulphur dioxide – suggesting perhaps acid rain and global pollution.

The colours in his art were initially cool, even monochrome. Later he started to make installations and sculptures. The works displayed from the outset what were to be his prevailing and unique qualities of a playful tongue-in-cheek humour. Since coming to Australia he has had over fifty solo exhibitions in Australia and overseas, and has been awarded many prizes, including the prestigious Sulman Prize from the Art Gallery of New South Wales. He has been included in major international exhibitions, including the Osaka Triennial, the Gwangju Biennale, the Havana Biennale, the Shanghai Biennale and the Asia-Pacific Triennial in Brisbane, as well as solo and group exhibitions in Berlin, Beijing, Paris, Hong Kong, Taipei, Oxford, Singapore,

Mexico City and The Hague. He also served as a curator in 1996 for Chinese art for the Asia-Pacific Triennial.

Guan Wei is not only an artist whose identity is shaped by his personal experiences of migration, but one whose world view is defined by a genuine ability to think across cultures and to speak to audiences in cities as diverse as Beijing or Sydney. His art brings together a personal vocabulary of rich, multi-layered symbolic (and sometimes fantastical) representations, complex myths and stories, in imagining a world that crosses boundaries between east and west, and it raises profound questions about human existence. Many of the symbols in his art are cross-cultural and have the accessibility of a story narrative and an aura of universality; and though his art exudes humour, there is a strong underlying moral and ethical focus. He says:

> I try to emphasize three elements in my work: wisdom, knowledge and humor. I believe people need wisdom to choose from the many different cultural traditions that confront us everyday; knowledge is the key to open our minds to the diversity of the world; and humor is necessary to comfort our hearts.[87]

These qualities were manifest in the emergence of the most immediately recognisable of his artistic symbols: pink nude figures, endearingly plump and disconcertingly featureless, sometimes without mouths or with only one eye. Guan Wei's explanation for these idiosyncrasies was, he told Jeremy Eccles, that: 'When I was painting in China, people didn't have the right to speak, so I didn't give them mouths … And since what they saw was ugly, I had the figures close one eye.'[88] When the mouths are there, they are often vacant openings, as if their owners are unable to speak, or have been stopped in midst of uttering screams. While Guan Wei has on occasion portrayed the pink figures cavorting happily around swimming pools, moving, as Philippa Kelly put it, 'in a hapless, playful way through life',[89] there is usually a deep seriousness in the message of the works.

One of those messages is the importance of history and different ways of constructing and understanding it. In 2006, for the Powerhouse Museum in Sydney, Guan Wei created *Other Histories* (curated by Claire Roberts), which he described as a 'Fable for the Contemporary World'. Using artefacts from the Museum's collection combined with wall paintings, he created an imaginary history of Chinese discovery of Australian shores long before the Europeans' arrival. Some historians have suggested that this could indeed have happened, even if the physical evidence is now lost. The paintings are filled with fantastical sea creatures, ships and maps, and allusions to voyaging as well as to the habitation of the continent by Indigenous peoples. In this world the Museum functions, in the artist's words, as a 'floating, poetic corridor in which history and memory, fact and fiction are blurred'.[90]

They are blurred again in a later series, where Guan Wei blends fields as different as cartography and Australian folklore. In *Where's Ned Kelly* (2004) (see Figure 5.6) he relocates the iconic Australian nineteenth-century bushranger and outlaw/folk hero Ned Kelly to a fantastic landscape, with the addition of elements of modern war equipment and even a small refugee boat. In his *Reflection* works (also 2003), a series of drawings on maps of Australia, he presents a world in which the settler culture spreads across the country, regardless of the presence of Indigenous peoples. Indigenous warriors defend their home against the assault, sometimes against, or possibly with the assistance of, modern soldiers supported by swooping helicopters.

This blending of past and present, reality and the imaginary world, and the challenge of cross-cultural relations reappears in his 2005 work *Echo*. For this work Guan Wei appropriates elements from *Jiu Ri Shi Cheng Tu Juan*, an esteemed landscape painting by Wang Yuanqi (1641–1715), and *Landing of Captain Cook at Botany Bay 1770*, by Australian painter E. Phillips Fox (1865–1915). The harmony and balance of the Chinese landscape provides an ironic background for the image of the initially elegant British in the foreground, who in the midground seem to be behaving, in Guan Wei's words,

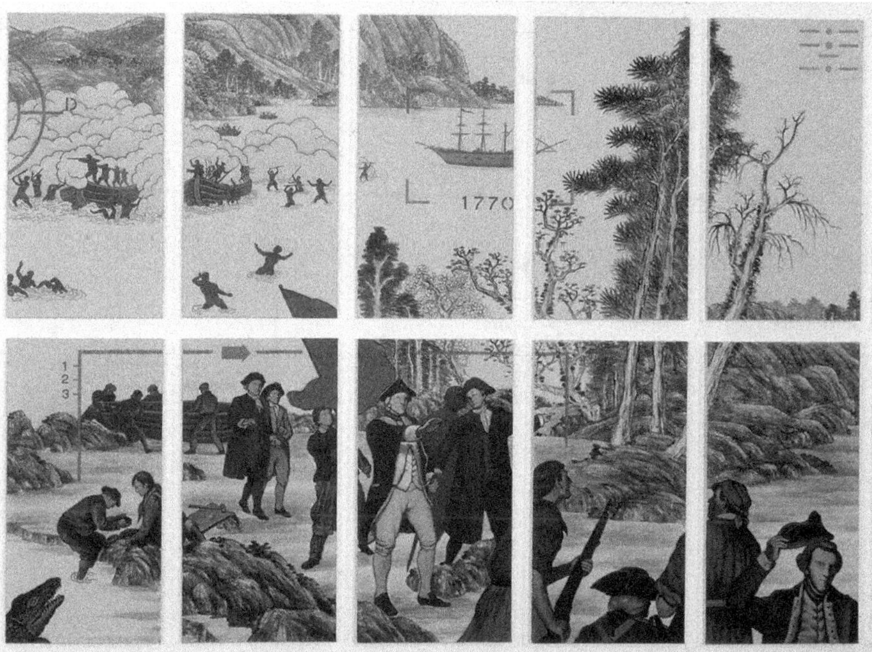

Guan Wei, *Echo*, 2005. 42 panels. Detail of central panels. Collection: Queensland   **5.7**
Art Gallery. The Queensland Government's Gallery of Modern Art Acquisitions
Fund. Purchased 2006.

'like a group of brutal bandits'.[91] Here Guan Wei evokes a past that historians have also begun to emphasise – a history filled with violence and which, from the perspective of Indigenous people, was an invasion by the white settlers.

He has also produced a powerful series of art works related to immigration and the contemporary waves of refugee boat people coming to Australia. The multi-panel painting *Dow Island* (2002), a key work shown in the exhibition *Witnessing to Silence: Art and Human Rights* at the Australian National University in 2003, was later bought by the National Gallery of Australia. Here large numbers of little pink people appear to be seeking in anguish to escape from the islands of Calamity and Trepidation. The figures in this work have no discernible national or racial characteristics, and thus could be any or all of us. Most are attempting to make their way in pathetically inadequate boats to the Enchanted Coast in the south, which bears a rough but sufficient resemblance to the north coast of Australia. All the boats seem to be in trouble, one has sunk, and the refugees are falling into a sea that harbours sinister monsters and a still more sinister submarine. None seems to have actually reached the Enchanted Coast, which is patrolled by vicious-looking black birds. 'In China', as former Director of the ANU School of Art Professor David Williams noted:

> black birds signify bad luck and all indications are this will be an inhospitable land. Dotted around the larger islands are many smaller ones hardly big enough on which to get a toehold. In any event they are inhabited by huge solitary birds or mythical creatures, which at a single glance leave no room for any intruder or boat landing.[92]

The painting was inspired by the true story of the 460 refugees, men, women and children, mostly from Middle Eastern countries, who were rescued from their sinking boat near Indonesia by a Norwegian freighter, the *Tampa*, in 2001. The Australian government refused the ship entry to Australian waters, and in the lead-up to an election the then prime minister, John Howard, declared boat people from the *Tampa* would never set foot on Australian soil. Australian commentator Glen Barclay notes:

> Successive Australian governments have employed all available resources to ensure that the Enchanted Coast is rendered inhospitable to the point that no one attempting to land by boat can succeed in doing so, and Guan Wei's imagery of the smaller islands provides excellent imagery for the various 'Pacific Solutions' attempted by Australian governments as a technique for resettling refugees anywhere but in Australia, however unpromising the prospects for resettlement in those venues might be.[93]

The series *Looking for Enemies* (2004) was created after a residency in New York in the aftermath of the 9/11 trauma. Guan Wei uses computer game-style

icons – fighter planes, warships and gun sights – overlaid onto one of his familiar sea- and landscapes, where his equally familiar characters, both pink and
black, are fighting and fleeing. The paintings leave wholly ambiguous the question of whether the soldiers depicted in the paintings are invading Australia
or rescuing it from invasion, or indeed what country or countries the soldiers
might represent.[94]

Guan Wei's *Journey to Australia* (2013) (see Plate 13) was commissioned
as a mural for the entrance of the Museum of Contemporary Art on Sydney's
Circular Quay. It is also the place where the British, under Arthur Phillip, first
landed to start a colony on Gadigal land in 1788: 'a place', Guan Wei said, 'where,
in the past, many immigrants have landed – a place which links the past with
the present, you with me, and Australia with the world'.[95] In this art work, we
suggest, Australia can be conceptualised as a testing ground for issues of global concern, human rights and worldmaking. The work is very consciously
focused on immigration and refugees, and deploys the full panoply of Guan

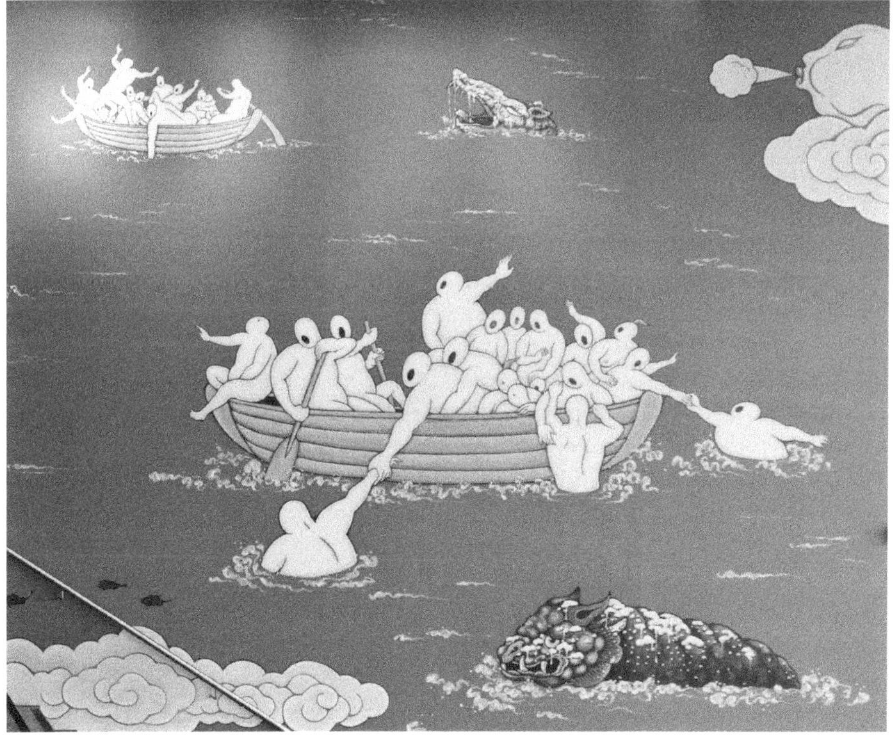

Guan Wei, *The Journey to Australia* 2013. Detail of installation view. Commissioned   **5.8**
by the Museum of Contemporary Art, Sydney, Australia.

Wei's worldmaking imagination. It depicts Indigenous people living their lives, unconcerned about the ships that are coming to change their existence forever. Legions of his little pink people – whom he painted, he said, to have a deliberate fragility – are desperately attempting a sea voyage in hopelessly overcrowded boats, some of them sinking already, with the bodies falling into the sea. It is created in dramatic scale on a major wall at the Museum's entrance in a very public place at Circular Quay in Sydney, and the endearing native animals and birds incorporated in the mural cause visitors to pause and take photographs of themselves and their children against the backdrop of what at first sight appears to be a storybook vision. It is a storybook, but the narration includes multiple layers of meaning.

Guan Wei's intention in these art works, we suggest, is not confined to commentary on Australian history. His work also points to the potential for war on a global scale and to the large-scale displacement of people due to human and natural disasters. Perhaps the most consistent message of his works is the need to find ways to live together. The world, he suggests, is full of beauty, and of things that hold a strange fascination. It is full, too, of people who come from different cultural backgrounds, and who need to better understand one another, connect with one another and seek friendships with one another. As Guan Wei says, 'It is imperative that we find a shared set of values to ensure our survival.'[96]

Cai Guo-Qiang: the seen and unseen worlds

Cai Guo-Qiang was born in 1957 in Fujian province in China, and studied stage design at the Shanghai Theater Academy. In 1986 he moved to Japan, which had a dynamic contemporary art scene engaged internationally with western art. He returned to China briefly in 1989, just before the events at Tiananmen Square, to lecture at the central art college in Beijing, which was then a centre of new democratic ideas. He made his reputation in Japan in the early 1990s, and moved to the US in 1995. His personal journey has therefore taken him from China in the years of the Cultural Revolution, to become a twenty-first-century global superstar artist engaging with world issues, and with a worldmaking vision extending across the planet. Cai is a philosopher. His art is also, we argue, highly committed to people and to communities, and the many volunteers who work on his projects are fundamental to their realisation. His art has direct references to historical and contemporary events, both local and global.

Cai's work could not be at once more comprehensively Asian, and more global. Introducing his work at the Museo Guggenheim Bilbao in 2009, art historian and Director of the Guggenheim, New York, Thomas Krens, wrote:

Cai Guo-Qiang has literally exploded the accepted parameters of art making in our time. He draws freely from ancient mythology, military history, Taoist cosmology, Maoist revolutionary tactics, Buddhist philosophy, pyrotechnic technology, Chinese medicine, and methods of terrorist violence. His art is a form of social energy, constantly mutable, linking what he calls 'the seen and unseen worlds'.[97]

A number of the elements identified by Krens are manifested in his fireworks events and installations. It is perhaps not surprising that he so frequently uses this medium, given that his home province, Fujian, is famous for its firecrackers. But fireworks are also a key signifier of the focus of his work. His use of gunpowder works analogically in this respect. It is a reminder that China, which discovered the agent, elected to use it more for the production of fireworks than for warfare (as opposed to western nations, which used it to develop ever more effective means of destruction). It is a reminder, too, that, as Cai insists, gunpowder always had constructive as well as destructive connotations in China, and was associated in China with 'every significant social occasion of any kind'.[98] It was thus wholly appropriate that he should have celebrated the end of apartheid and the dawn of freedom in South Africa by blowing up an old factory as a symbol of the birth of a new nation and an undeniable triumph of human rights.

Cai's art has a serious underlying connection to themes of human existence and to human conflicts. His concern for humanity and his resistance to conflict were given uncompromising expression in one of his earliest works, *Shadow: Pray for Protection* (1985–86), painted before he moved to Japan. It depicts in sombre shades of grey and beige almost vaporised figures dispersed under the shadow of an American B-29 bomber, the type of aircraft that carried the atomic bombs to Hiroshima and Nagasaki. A clock in the far left of the picture is stopped at 11:02, the moment of the Nagasaki blast. A dove in the right of the painting flutters above the figure of Cai himself, his face expressing despair at the massive destruction of human life, and of the environment.[99]

He resumed the theme on a massive scale five years later with *45.5 Meteorite Craters Made by Humans on Their 45.5 Hundred Million Year Old Planet: Project for Extraterrestials No. 3* (1990). For this work Cai, with his team and local volunteers, excavated 45.5 craters over a 10,000-square-metre area of grassland in Aix-en-Provence. All the craters were filled with gunpowder, and detonated simultaneously at dusk. It was designed as a salutary reminder of the fact that, in Cai's words, 'the earth we have cultivated from the beginning of human existence can be destroyed in a matter of seconds'.[100]

Another early work, *Project to Extend the Great Wall of China by 10,000 Meters: Project for Extraterrestrials No. 10* (1993), moved beyond the earth to a cosmic dimension: it rested on the assumption that the Great Wall is the only

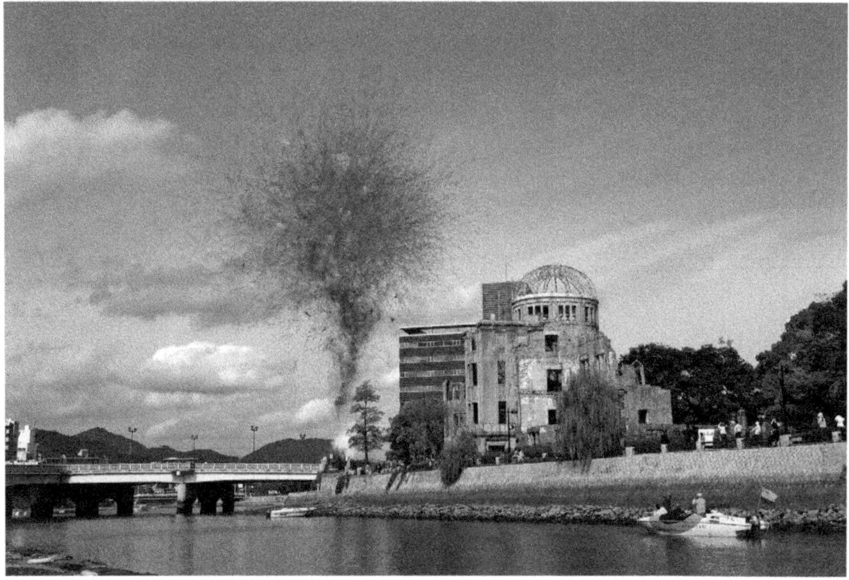

5.9 Cai Guo-Qiang, *Black Fireworks: Project for Hiroshima*, 2008. Realized at Motomachi Riverside Park near the Atomic Bomb Dome, Hiroshima, October 25, 2008, 1:00 p.m, 60 seconds. Commissioned by Hiroshima City Museum of Contemporary Art.

built structure on the planet that is visible from outer space, and invoked the idea that the Wall contains its own cosmic energy. This work involved the laying of a ten-kilometre fuse along the Wall from Jiayuguan in Gansu Province, the western boundary of the Ming dynasty. It took fifteen minutes for the explosion to travel the full ten kilometres, and is reported to have been seen by 40,000 people.[101] As well as being a spectacular event, the work was, curator Takashi Serizawa writes, 'an expression of our times; it was our expression of hope; it was an expression of union extended to the universe as a whole.'[102] But beyond the cosmic dimension there was a human dimension, in that the project involved the assistance of hundreds of volunteers from both China and Japan to lay the gunpowder trail along the 10,000 metres. The whole project reflected Cai's concern with the human predicament: the Great Wall had some success over the centuries in repelling or resisting invasion but its construction may have cost the lives of up to a million workers.

These explosions are, of course, emphatically temporal, existing only in the moment of the event, and in the memories of those who witness it, or now through recordings and social media. Sometimes his explosions continue as part of history on YouTube, such as the fireworks displays he presented at the opening and closing ceremonies of the 2008 Beijing Olympic Games.[103] He also uses explosive processes for more delicate works that are, effectively, drawings. For these, he lays gunpowder across paper, applies stencils and wooden blocks to disperse the impact of the explosion, and then ignites it. The dual effect of smoke and burning leaves startlingly beautiful patterns on the paper: traces, or 'a print on reality'.[104] Art historian Alexandra Munroe suggests Cai uses explosives 'to directly manifest the pure force of energy';[105] the Guggenheim likens this work 'to the practice of a shaman who invokes agents of a spirit world to cause a reaction in the material realm'.[106] Cai perceives his art as connecting to the invisible forces of the universe and says of his own work that it 'is like a dialogue between unseen powers, like alchemy';[107] and certainly, in the sheer scale of his imagination and of the works he produces, he seems to navigate between the material and immaterial worlds.

In 1995 he exhibited, in the Museum of Contemporary Art in Tokyo, a work titled *The Orient (San Jō Tower)*. This is a tower made of timber salvaged from a sunken boat, with seismographs at its base and, symbolically, three 'jō' (999 cm) in height. The tower embodies the principles of 'heaven and earth, eternity and moment',[108] and as with all Cai's work it references ancient philosophies and belief systems from China and Japan. It was first shown at Iwaki City, in Fukushima Prefecture, a place with which Cai has had strong ties over the past twenty years. The community has been involved in many of his projects, providing volunteer work and financial contributions. Since the 2011 tsunami and nuclear disaster, he has returned to create art related to recovery from those devastating events, including the *Project to Plant Ten Thousand Cherry Blossom Trees*.[109] For this project, Cai worked with the Iwaki community to build what he terms 'the Snake Museum of Contemporary Art (SMoCA)', a corridor of trees contaminated by the disaster, winding through the countryside to create a space where cherry trees can be planted and that, Cai hopes, 'will become a space where the residents of Iwaki can bond with their children and let their dreams fly free'.[110]

Cai thus works on a local as well as a global, or even cosmic, scale. One example of this is his work *The Century with Mushroom Clouds: Project for the 20th Century* (1996), a series of small mushroom-shaped explosions above significant locations, including the atomic test site in Nevada. Clouds, of course, are ephemeral, but a nuclear cloud is not such an innocent object. It was the precariousness of human existence that he symbolised with this work. He treated the theme of war again in his *Cry Dragon/Cry Wolf: The Ark of Genghis Khan* (1996), an installation composed of a serpentine trail of 108 sheepskin bags, their form suggesting the spine of a dragon, and powered by three roaring Toyota engines. The deliberate humour of this work heightened the efficacy of its commentary on fears in the west of the rise of Asia, and also the truly catastrophic potential for superpower conflict between the United States and a newly emergent Asian military capacity. It can, however, also be read as a sobering historical reminder, since Genghis Khan's invincible armies used sheepskin bags to contain their drinking water, and as flotation devices when crossing rivers, in their invasion of the west.

No effort of historical memory was required to appreciate the contemporary significance of Cai's remarkably provocative works *Golden Missiles* and *No Destruction, No Construction: Bombing the Taiwan Museum of Art*, both 1998. The first involved launching 200 small gold-painted rockets above Taipei, timed to detonate 150 metres above the city and then descend by means of parachutes; these had an obvious reference to the tensions between China and Taiwan. The second began with explosions in the sky above the museum; these travelled down into the building through skylights, and coiled around the two pillars flanking the entrance, before exiting onto the plaza, blasting the museum with light and noise. It has been likened to a fiery Chinese dragon, the charred traces of which remain on the columns of the museum, and have been accessioned as part of its permanent display.[111]

Such works can be appreciated and enjoyed for their artistry, ingenuity and humour, which provide some relief from their prophetic admonitions; and it is important to remember that Cai's work is as likely to celebrate as to critique, and that it focuses on the possibility of connectedness between people. As the world watched the time tick over to a new millennium in December 1999, for example, Cai launched an extraordinary work, *Dragon Sight Sees Vienna: Project for Extraterrestrials No. 32*. This was a gunpowder explosion that created in the sky over Vienna the outline of a Chinese dragon, heralding what many commentators term the Asian century. Again in 1999, for the Third Asia-Pacific Triennial, Cai produced perhaps his most compelling image of the possibility of achieving harmony among peoples – one that did not involve the use of gunpowder, but is a reminder that cultural crossings and exchanges are not easy. For this work, *Bridge Crossing* (1999), a twenty-three-metre-long bamboo bridge was built across the water mall in the Queensland Art Gallery. At the bridge's centre point, where people crossing from different directions would meet, those who made the encounter were sprayed by a shower of water.

By contrast, the messages of *Clear Sky Black Cloud* (2006), presented at New York's Metropolitan Museum of Art, and *Black Fireworks: Project for Hiroshima* (2008), were unrelievedly stark and menacing. Small symbolic black explosions over New York City need no interpretation. But nothing conjures apocalyptic visions of the ultimate horror of human conflict so effectively as the word 'Hiroshima'. This was the work he produced for the Hiroshima City Museum of Contemporary Art, after being awarded the seventh Hiroshima Art Prize. He was selected for the award, which acknowledges artists whose work has contributed to peace, because his works 'are not only based on a unique vision of the universe rooted in traditional Chinese culture and thought but his art offers a penetrating view of human history and civilization'.[112] His creative

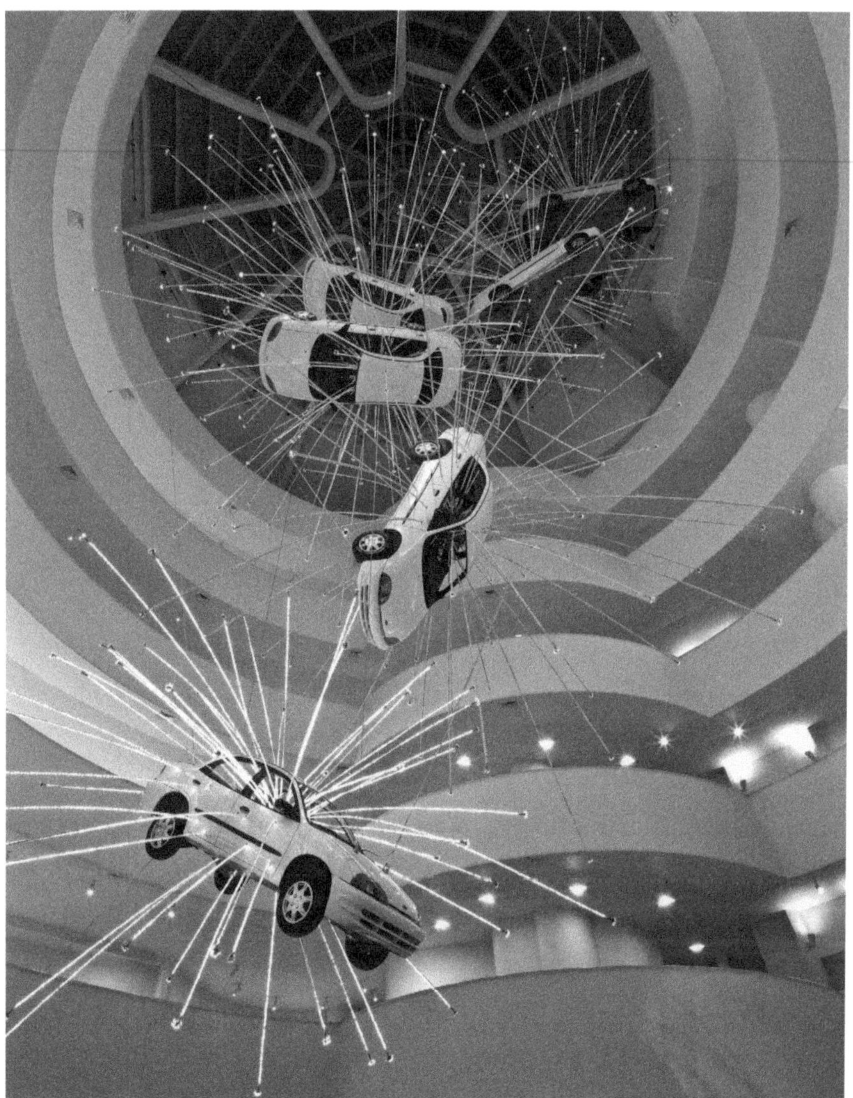

Cai Guo-Qiang, *Inopportune: Stage One*, 2004. Collection: Seattle Art Museum. Gift **5.10**
of Robert M. Arnold, in honor of the 75th Anniversary of the Seattle Art Museum,
2006. Exhibition copy installed at Solomon R. Guggenheim Museum, New York,
2008. © Solomon R. Guggenheim Foundation New York.

activity in this case was displayed by a truly frightening series of black explosions in the sky over the Peace Park in Hiroshima, on the site of the explosion of the first atomic bomb used in war (see Figure 5.9).

The ultimate threat of nuclear holocaust seems to have receded, but it has been replaced by the more random threat of indiscriminate terrorism, of which the car bomb has become the most immediately identifiable symbol. This is a symbol to which Cai gave dramatic artistic expression with *Inopportune Stage One* (2004). This was his largest installation to date, depicting nine white American-made cars falling through the air, while electric light rods inserted in the cars radiate progressively more vivid flashing lights. He has also treated terrorist threats more explicitly, as in his video installation *Illusion* (2004), which displays an exploding car moving through Times Square, apparently ignored by pedestrians and traffic. Cai states:

> I make explosions, so I pay attention to explosions. I can imagine the methods used and the mental state of the suicide bombers … Before igniting an artwork, I am sometimes nervous, yet terrorists face death unflinchingly. Along with the sympathy we hold for the victims I also have compassion for the young men and women who commit the act. Artists can sympathise with the other possibility, present issues from someone else's point of view.[113]

While this is a very confrontational perspective to offer in a world that is currently prosecuting a 'war on terror', Cai's political perceptions are conveyed cogently by his installation *Head On*, first realised in 2006 at the Deutsche Guggenheim, Berlin. This might be, historically, the ideal city in which to display an art work that symbolises the tragic implications of unexamined ideological commitment. The installation involves ninety-nine replicas of wolves that leap through the air in a triumphal trajectory to crash, head on, into a glass wall – originally the exact height of the Berlin Wall. They pick themselves up, return to where they began their leap to futility and presumably start all over again. The integer '9' is one of the luckiest in Chinese numerology, signifying fulfilment and eternity, as well as other good things. But in this case, it seems calculated to induce a sense of total despair regarding the survival of the human race and in consequence of the planet.

Cai has presented the fatally flawed wolves again in the exhibition *Falling Back to Earth* (2013) at the Queensland Art Gallery. As well as the ninety-nine wolves heading constantly for disaster, he has produced another ninety-nine animals for the work *Heritage* (2013), commissioned by the Gallery (see Plate 14). Here the integer '9' achieves its positive identity, presenting as a symbol of hope for the future. *Heritage* is an installation comprised of ninety-nine replicas of animals from around the world, placed around a blue lake on clean white sand, their heads peacefully bowed as they 'drink' from the water. The spectacle of predators and prey animals gathered calmly in the same place, and

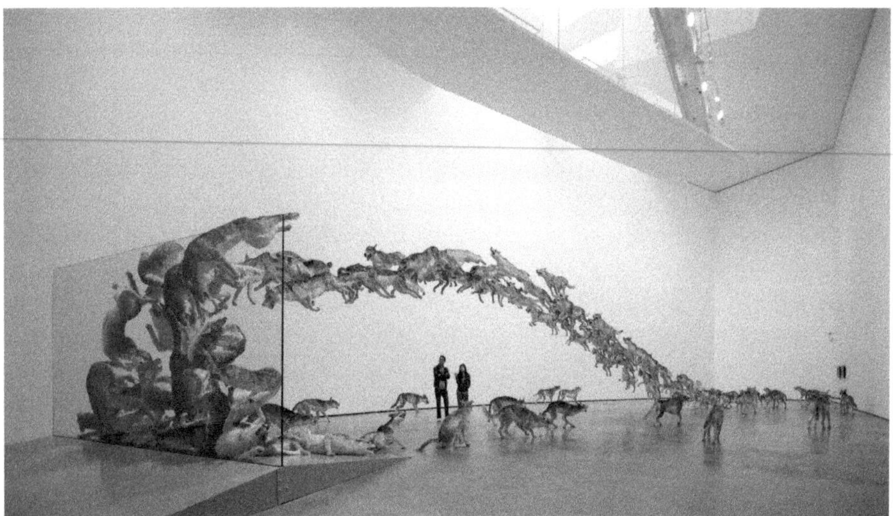

Cai Guo-Qiang, *Head On*, 2006. Deutsche Bank Collection ©FMGB, Guggenheim   **5.11**
Bilbao Museoa, 2009.

the quiet of the installation, act as a counterpoint to *Head On*'s frenetic violence: a utopian vision of a world without conflict or competition.

The third piece in the exhibition, *Eucalyptus*, is another large installation,
this one clearly directed at a conception of the natural world, and of our connection to that world. Much as the water and sands used in *Heritage* reference the islands off the coast of Southern Queensland, and their pristine lakes
and white sand, so too *Eucalyptus* responds to the natural environment of
Southern Queensland. To make this work, Cai first took some research trips
to the Lamington National Park, with its reserves of Gondwanan rainforest,
and then, with the Gallery's help, secured a tree that was already scheduled for
removal.[114] The eucalyptus tree is aesthetically lovely, calmly filling the space;
and it also speaks to the urgency required to treat each living being as something that is an individual, and of value; and thereby to reverse the effects of
urbanisation and environmental degradation. As part of the work and again
reflecting his concern for transcultural meetings, concerts were held with
Taiwanese musician Wang Xinxin and Aboriginal didgeridoo player William
Barton.

Cai says of his own work, 'I ignore the boundaries between different cultural heritages and freely navigate between Chinese, Eastern, and Western,
or whatever world culture there is. I can take one out of context and put it in
another, ignoring all boundaries and socially constructed constraints.'[115] For
Nelson Goodman, 'universes of worlds as well as worlds themselves may be

built in many ways'.[116] Cai's way allows new understandings of these 'universes of worlds', and the possibility of making new, and more sustainable, worlds.

Conclusion

The western conception of world and worldmaking effectively begins with Plato's argument about the co-presence of two worlds: the phenomenal world, which we cannot know, but can only experience; and the ideal world, the domain of Form.[117] This is the foundation for a line of thought in western intellectual history that privileges language and discourse, so that 'world' has come to mean the conceptual rather than the material domain.[118] While this can lead to a lack of care of the planet on which we live, it also provides a way of thinking that gives scope to those who are committed to achieving positive change. The artists we discuss in this chapter seem very alive to the possibilities of making the lived world anew – of finding new ways for human beings and humanity as a whole to live together. In their art works, they 'not only provide a permanent record of how the world was, but also a blueprint for how things might be. And that wistful power is perhaps what is at the heart of worldmaking in art – the attempt to re-examine the "what is", and to make it into something that is genuinely new.'[119]

Notes

1 For details, see *The World and World-Making in Art* conference, Humanities Research Centre, Australian National University, http://hrc.anu.edu.au/node/141/, accessed 14 September 2014.

2 Pinter writes that in *The Birthday Party* he allowed 'a whole range of options to operate in a dense forest of possibility before finally focusing on an act of subjugation'; see Harold Pinter, *Art, Truth and Politics: The Nobel Lecture* (London: Faber & Faber, 2006), p. 21.

3 Steven Connor, 'I Believe that the World', in Vera Nünning, Ansgar Nünning and Birgit Neumann (eds), *Cultural Ways of Worldmaking: Media and Narratives* (Berlin: Walter de Gruyter GmbH, 2010), pp. 29–46: 42.

4 David Hume, *Dialogues Concerning Natural Religion* (Indianapolis: Hackett Publishing, 1980 [1779], p. 36.

5 Karl Marx, *Capital: A Critique of Political Economy 1.1* (New York: Cosimo Press 2007), p. 198.

6 Nelson Goodman, *Ways of Worldmaking* (Indianapolis: Hackett Publishing, 1978).

7 Ansgar Nünning and Vera Nünning. 'Introduction', in Vera Nünning, Ansgar Nünning and Birgit Neumann (eds), *Cultural Ways of Worldmaking: Media and Narratives* (Berlin: Walter de Gruyter GmbH, 2010), pp. 1–25: 4.

8 Frederik Tygstrup, 'The Politics of Symbolic Forms', in Nünning, Nünning and Neumann, pages 87–99: 88.

9 Goodman, *Ways of Worldmaking*, p. 113.

10 Tygstrup, 'Politics', p. 89.

11 Maurice Blanchot, *The Space of Literature*, trans. Ann Smock (Lincoln and London: University of Nebraska Press, 1982), p. 215.

12 Jacques Rancière, *The Politics of Aesthetics: The Dimension of the Sensible*, trans. Gabriel Rockhill (New York: Continuum, 2004), p. 13.

13 Slavoj Žižek, 'Human Rights and its Discontents', lecture presented at Bard College, New York (15 November 1999), www.bard.edu/hrp/Zizekevent.htm, accessed 23 September 2004. See also Slavoj Žižek, 'Against Human Rights', *New Left Review*, 34 (July–Aug. 2005), pp. 115–31.

14 Hans Seigfried, 'We the People/s: Bloody Universal Principles and Ethnic Codes', *Philosophy & Social Criticism*, 27:1 (2001), pp. 63–76: 69.

15 Faiz Ahmed Faiz, a humanist, educator and intellectual, founder of Pakistan's Progressive Writers Movement and editor of *The Pakistan Times*. He was awarded the British Empire medal for service in the British Indian Army in the second world war, won the Lenin Peace Prize from the Soviet Union in 1962 and was nominated for the Nobel Prize in poetry. See www.poets.org/poetsorg/poet/faiz-ahmed-faiz, accessed 14 August 2014.

16 Alys Faiz, née George, journalist, human rights campaigner for UNICEF and the Pakistan Human Rights Commission, www.theguardian.com/media/2003/mar/25/pressandpublishing.guardianobituaries, accessed 16 August 2014.

17 Arundhati Roy, 'The Monster in the Mirror', *The Guardian* (13 December 2008), www.theguardian.com/world/2008/dec/12/mumbai-arundhati-roy, accessed 3 July 2014.

18 Faiz Ahmed Faiz, 'The Dawn of Freedom, August 1947', trans. Agha Shahid Ali, in Muhammad Umar Memon (ed.), *An Epic Unwritten: The Penguin Book of Partition Stories* (New Delhi: Penguin, 1998), p. 3.

19 Pankaj Mishra, 'Pakistan's Writers: Living in a Minefield', *New York Review of Books* (13 October 2011), pp. 37–39.

20 In Christopher Lydon, 'Salima Hashmi: In the Worst of Times, the Alchemy of Art', Radio Interview, *Arts, Ideas and Politics*, Radio Open Source (7 September 2011), http://radioopensource.org/salima-hashmi-in-the-worst-of-times-the-alchemy-of-art/, accessed 14 August 2014.

21 Faiz Ahmed Faiz, 'Doo-a [Prayer]', trans. Azfar Hussain, in Lydon, 'Salima Hashmi'.

22 In Christopher Lydon, 'Salima Hashmi: In the Worst of Times'.

23 For example, her major study on women artists: Salima Hashmi, *Unveiling the Visible: Lives and Works of Women Artists in Pakistan* (Lahore: Sang-E-Meel Publications, 2003).

24 *ArtNow*, 'Salima Hashmi: Multiple Views', *ArtNow: Contemporary Art of Pakistan* (August 2013), www.artnowpakistan.com/Profile/SalimaHashmiMultipleViews-330.html, accessed 14 August 2014.

25 Lydon, 'Salima Hashmi', 2011.

26 Zia ul-Haq, in 'An Engaging Dictator Who Wants to Stay That Way', *The Economist* (12 December 1981), p. 48.

27 Lydon, 'Salima Hashmi'.

28 Hashmi, interview with authors, 2011.

29 Hashmi, *Unveiling the Visible*, pp. 8–9.

30 Hashmi, *Unveiling the Visible*, p.11.

31 *ArtNow*, 'Salima Hashmi: Multiple Views'.

32 Hashmi, interview with authors, 2011.

33 Yashodhara Dalmia and Salima Hashmi, *Memory, Metaphor, Mutations Contemporary Art of India and Pakistan* (New Delhi: Oxford University Press, 2007), p. 44.

34 Asif Noorani, 'Courageous Women's Palette', *Dawn* (2 November 2013), http://indpaedia.com/ind/index.php/Salima_Hashmi, accessed 5 August 2014.

35 Lydon, 'Salima Hashmi'.

36 Neluka Silva, *The Gendered Nation: Contemporary Writings from South Asia* (New Delhi: Sage, 2004), p. 181.

37 Nima Poovaya-Smith 'Keys to the Magic Kingdom: The New Transcultural Collections of the Bradford Art Galleries and Museums', in Tim Barringer and Tom Flynn (eds), *Colonialism and the Object: Empire, Material Culture and the Museum* (London: Routledge, 1998), pp. 111–25: 116.

38 Renuka Nerayanan, 'All We Want is to Know Each Other', *Hindustani Times* (22 January 2009), www.hindustantimes.com/india-news/all-we-want-is-to-know-each-other/article1-369946.aspx, accessed 5 August 2014.

39 Halvorson and Hamilton describe the area as 'a territorial battleground between Pakistan and India. This disputed zone has been at the heart of three wars between the two countries and continues to be riddled with political uncertainty' (187). See Sarah J. Halvorson and Jennifer Parker Hamilton, 'In the Aftermath of the Qa'yamat: The Kashmir Earthquake Disaster in Northern Pakistan', *Disasters*, 34:1 (2010), pp. 184–204.

40 Salima Hashmi, communication with authors, December 2014.

41 Hashmi, communication with authors, December 2014.

42 Hashmi, interview with authors, 2011.

43 Murtaza Vali, 'Salima Hashmi: Paradise Found and Lost', *ArtAsiaPacific*, 57 (March/April 2008), http://artasiapacific.com/Magazine/57/ParadiseFoundLost SalimaHashmi, accessed 12 July 2013.

44 Faiz Ahmed Faiz, 'Bol [Speak]', trans. Azfar Hussain, in Lydon, 'Salima Hashmi'. Lines that are important for that movement include: '*Speak, your lips are free. / Speak, it is your own tongue. / … / Speak, 'cause the truth is not dead yet, / Speak, speak, whatever you must speak*'.

45 Riz Rahim, *In English, Faiz Ahmed Faiz: A Renowned Urdu Poet* (Bloomington: Xlibris Corporation, 2008), p. 93.

46 Salima Hashmi, *Hanging Fire: Contemporary Art from Pakistan* (New York: Asia Society Museum, 2009), p. 13.

47 Faiza Butt, 'Diaspora: Of Beards and Bodies', interview in *ArtNow: Contemporary Art of Pakistan* (November 2011), www.artnowpakistan.com/Profile/DiasporaOf BeardsandBodies-214.html#.U-7nXMIcSpo, accessed 7 August 2014.

48 Hashmi, interview with authors, 2011; see also Lydon, 'Salima Hashmi'.

49 Lydon, 'Salima Hashmi', 2011.

50 Nalini Malani, 'Biography' (n.d.), www.nalinimalani.com/bio.htm, accessed 2 August 2014.

51 Faiz Ahmed Faiz, 'In Search of Vanished Blood', trans. Agha Shahid Ali, *Selected Poems of Faiz Ahmed Faiz* (n.d.), www.faizcentenary.org/poems_in_english.htm, accessed 21 August 2014.

52 Nalini Malani, 'In Search of Vanished Blood' (video), *dOCUMENTA 13*, 2012, www.youtube.com/watch?v=6uK9iRoPds8, accessed 21 August 2014.

53 Daniel Kurjaković, 'Quarries of Blindness and Shadows of Hope: Interview with Nalini Malani', *Torrent* magazine (pilot edition, 2014), pp. 11–28: 17.

54 Carolyn Christov-Bakargiev, 'Introduction' in Carolyn Christov-Bakargiev, Arjun Appadurai and Andreas Huyssen (eds), *Nalini Malani: In Search of Vanished Blood* (Ostfildern: Hatje Catz and Kassel: DOCUMENTA und Museum Fridericianum, 2012), pp. 8–11.

55 Andreas Huyssen, 'Shadow Play as Medium of Memory', in Christov-Bakargiev, Appadurai and Huyssen (eds), *Nalini Malani*, pp. 46–59.

56 See Aeschylus, *Agamemnon*, trans. H. W. Smyth, lines 1212–14.

57 Murtaza Vali, 'Her Cassandra Complex', *ArtAsiaPacific* (May/June 2009).

58 Vali, 'Her Cassandra Complex'. Cassandra's father thought she was insane.

59 See, for example, Hilary Charlesworth and Christine Chinkin, *The Boundaries of International Law: A Feminist Analysis* (Manchester: Manchester University Press, 2000); Geeta Kapur, *When Was Modernism: Essays on Contemporary Cultural Practice in India* (New Delhi: Tulika, 2000), p. 30.

60 Murtaza Vali, 'Her Cassandra Complex'.

61 Srimoyee Mitra, 'Naked Bodies as Site of Social Change', *WRECK: Graduate Journal of Art History, Visual Art, and Theory*, 2:2 (2008), pp. 67–77. This includes tribal peoples in India in their fight to protect their land against mining.

62 Kurjaković, 'Quarries of Blindness', p. 14.

63 Nalini Malani, 'Hamletmachine' (2004), www.nalinimalani.com/video/hamlet.htm, accessed 6 September 2014.

64 Geeta Kapur and Ashish Rajadhyaksha, 'Bombay/Mumbai 1992–2001', in Iwona Blazwick (ed.), *Century City: Art and Culture in the Modern Metropolis* (London: Tate Publishing, 2001), p. 36. See also the discussion of religious violence in India, the rise of the Hindu Right and the identification of Muslim citizens in India with Pakistan and the wider Muslim world, rather than with India, in Arjun Appadurai, *Fear of Small Numbers: An Essay on the Geography of Fear* (Durham, NC, and London: Duke University Press, 2006), p. 69.

65 Johan Pijnappel, 'Doomsday Oracle', *ArtAsiaPacific*, 30 (2001), p. 52.

66 Pat Hoffie, 'Nalini Malani: Hamletmachine', in Caroline Turner and Nancy Sever (eds), *Witnessing to Silence: Art and Human Rights* (Canberra: Humanities Research Centre and Drill Hall Gallery, 2003), pp. 41–3.

67 Vali, 'Her Cassandra Complex', 2009. In the same way she placed Toba Tek Singh in the Prince of Wales Museum, Mumbai, where it was seen by as many as 3,000 people a day in 1999.

68 The first part of *Utopia* is a stop motion animation in 8mm colour stock made in 1969, which shows an abstract urban landscape. The second part is about the desire of a young woman from the slums to have her own home, but in her reflections she sees the dream falling apart (Nalini Malani, conversation with authors, December 2014). The films were recently rediscovered and shown in her 2014 retrospective *Nalini Malani: You Can't Keep Acid in a Paper Bag*, Kiran Nadar Museum of Art, New Delhi.

69 Nalini Malani, conversation with authors, December 2014.

70 Johan Pijnappel, 'Interview with Nalini Malani', in *iCon India Catalogue*, 51st Venice Biennale (2005), www.nalinimalani.com/texts/venice.htm, accessed 4 September 2014.

71 Pijnappel, 'Interview with Nalini Malani', 2005; and interview with authors, 2014. The work was shown in the Prince of Wales Museum, Mumbai, to a large audience of ordinary citizens.

72 Victoria Lynn, 'Profile: Nalini Malani', in Russell Smith and Sarah Tutton (eds), *Experimenta Mesh 17, New Media Art in Australia and Asia* (2004), www.experimenta.org/mesh/mesh17/nalini.htm, accessed 14 August 2014.

73 Arts and Culture Prize, 'Nalini Malani', *Fukuoka Prize: Laureates* (2013), http://fukuoka-prize.org/en/laureate/prize/cul/nalinima.php, accessed 5 August 2014.

74 Pijnappel, 'Interview with Nalini Malani', 2005.

75 Chaitanya Sambrani, 'Apocalyse Recalled: The Recent Works of Nalini Malani' (2004), www.nalinimalani.com/texts/chaitanya.htm, accessed 2 September 2014.

76 Macushla Robinson, *Mother India: Transactions in the Construction of Pain*, www.artgallery.nsw.gov.au/collection/works/338.2011.a-f, accessed 4 September 2014.

77 Arjun Appadurai, 'Foreword: Vanishing Violence', in Christov-Bakargiev *et al.*, *Nalini Malani: In Search of Vanished Blood*, pp. 6–7.

78 Linda Jaivin, 'Guan Wei: Paint Me', *Art Collector*, 20 (2002), www.artcollector.net.au/GuanWeiPaintMe, accessed 14 August 2014.

79 Jaivin, 'Guan Wei: Paint Me'.

80 Reconciliation of traditions is a challenge faced by artists: for example in Taiwan, where ancient traditions and modern western art were also explored by artists from the 1950s. Pan An-Yi *et al.*, *Jie (Boundaries): Contemporary Art from Taiwan* (Cornell University: Herbert F. Johnson Museum of Art, 2014).

81 Philippa Kelly, 'Thinking About Guan Wei', *Artlink*, 20:4 (2003).

82 Jaivin, 'Guan Wei: Paint Me'.

83 Guan Wei and Anna Davis, 'In Conversation' (podcast), Museum of Contemporary Art, Sydney, www.mca.com.au/artists-and-works/building-commissions/guan-wei-journey-australia-2013/, accessed 3 September 2014.

84 Jeremy Eccles, 'The Eye of a Banner Man', *Asiaweek* (2000), http://edition.cnn.com/ASIANOW/asiaweek/99/0702/feat2.html, accessed 12 August.

85 Larry Strange (ed.), *Openings: A Celebration of the 30th Anniversary of Diplomatic Relations between Australia and China* (Sydney: Asia-Australia Institute, University of New South Wales; and Office of the Community Relations Commission for a Multicultural New South Wales, 2002), p. 80.

86 Strange, *Openings: A Celebration*.

87 Guan Wei, artist's statement, in Jennifer Hardy (ed. and curator), *Ways of Being* (Sydney: Ivan Dougherty Gallery, University of New South Wales, 1998), p. 56.

88 Eccles, 'The Eye of a Banner Man'.

89 Kelly, 'Thinking about Guan Wei'.

90 Powerhouse Museum, 'Other Histories: Guan Wei's Fable for a Contemporary World', *Exhibitions* (2006), www.powerhousemuseum.com/exhibitions/Guan_Wei.php, accessed 5 December 2006; Claire Roberts (ed.), *Other Histories: Guan Wei's Fable for a Contemporary World. Documentation of an Exhibition.* (Sydney: Wild Peony, 2008).

91 Queensland Art Gallery, 'Guan Wei: Echo' (2005), *QAG Collection*, http://collection.qagoma.qld.gov.au/qag/imu.php?request=display&port=45001&id=83d3&flag=ecatalogue&offset=1&count=default&view=details, accessed 4 June 2014; the entire painting is illustrated here.

92 David Williams, 'Guan Wei: *Dow Island 2002*', in Turner and Sever (eds), *Witnessing to Silence*, pp. 50–1.

93 Glen Barclay, communication with the authors, 2014.

94 Caroline Turner and Pat Hoffie, *Future Tense: Security and Human Rights* (Brisbane: Griffith University Art Gallery, 2005).

95 ArtsHub, 'MCA Taps into Immigration Debate for New Foyer Launch', *ArtsHub* (9 May 2013), http://visual.artshub.com.au/news-article/news/museums/mca-taps-into-immigration-debate-for-new-foyer-launch-195288, accessed 5 February 2014.

96 Powerhouse Museum, 'Other Histories'.

97 Guggenheim Museum, 'Cai Guo-Qiang: I Want to Believe' (press release, 21 February 2008), www.guggenheim.org/new-york/press-room/releases/press-release-archive/2008/1805-the-guggenheim-museum-presents-cai-guo-qiang-i-want-to-believe, accessed 8 February 2013.

98 Octavio Zaya in Dana Friis-Hansen, Octavio Zaya and Takashi Serizawa, *Cai Guo-Qiang* (New York: Phaidon Press, 2002), p. 14.

99 See Alexandra Munroe, 'Gai Guo-Qiang', in Thomas Krens and Alexandra Munroe (eds), *Cai Guo-Qiang: I Want to Believe* (New York: Guggenheim Museum, 2008), pp. 84–5.

100 Cai Guo-Qiang, 'Artist's Writings', *Cai Guo-Qiang*, in Friis-Hansen, Zaya and Serizawa, *Cai Guo-Qiang*, p. 122.

101 Takashi Serizawa, 'Going Beyond the Wall: *Project to Extend the Great Wall of China by 10 000 Meters: Project for Extraterrestrials No. 10*', in Friis-Hansen, Zaya and Serizawa, pp. 102–10: 110. See also artist website: www.caiguoqiang.com/.

102 Serizawa, 'Going Beyond the Wall', p.110.

103 See Cai Guo-Qiang, 'Fireworks for the 2008 Beijing Olympic Games', http://www.caiguoqiang.com/exhibition/fireworks-2008-beijing-olympic-games, accessed 14 December 2014.

104 Valerie Portefaix, 'Traces and Other Impacts: The Work of Cai Guo Qiang', *tofu-magazine*, 3 (Fall 2000), www.tofu-magazine.net/newVersion/pages/cai_guo_qiang.html, accessed 15 January 2014.

105 Munroe, 'Cai Guo-Qiang', p. 20.

106 Guggenheim Museum, 'Cai Guo-Qiang: I Want To Believe' (press release, 2008), www.guggenheim.org/new-york/press-room/releases/press-release-archive/20 08/1805-the-guggenheim-museum-presents-cai-guo-qiang-i-want-to-believe, accessed 5 April 2013.

107 QAGOMA, 'Cai Guo-Qiang: *Falling Back to Earth*' (video, 23 November 2013), http:// tv.qagoma.qld.gov.au/2013/11/07/qagoma-presents-cai-guo-qiang-falling-back-to-earth/, accessed 15 January 2014.

108 Yasuo Kamon, *Art in Japan Today, 1985–1995* (Tokyo: Museum of Contemporary Art, 1995), p. 48.

109 See Cai Guo-Qiang Studio Blog, https://caiguoqiang.wordpress.com/2014/04/25/ yatai-museum-of-contemporary-art-20th-anniversary-of-cai-guo-qiang-and-iwaki/, accessed 10 January 2015. In 2012 Cai won the Praemium Imperiale Lifetime Achievement award in the Arts (Painting) – the first Chinese artist to do so – and donated the money from this award to establish scholarships for young Japanese artists, and to support the *Project to Plant Ten Thousand Cherry Blossom Trees*.

110 Cai Guo-Qiang Studio Blog.

111 Dana Friis-Hansen, 'Towards a New Methodology in Art', in Friis-Hansen, Zaya and Serizawa, *Cai Guo-Qiang* (New York, Phaidon Press, 2002), p. 83.

112 Hiroshima City, '7th Hiroshima Art Prize', www.city.hiroshima.lg.jp/e/overview/ add/hap/hap7winner.html, accessed 15 January 2014.

113 Munroe, 'Cai Guo-Qiang', pp.37–8.

114 Russell Storer, 'How Did the Tree Get into GOMA?', *QAGOMA Blog* (8 April 2014), http://blog.qag.qld.gov.au/how-did-the-tree-get-into-goma/, accessed 12 August 2014.

115 In Thomas Krens and Alexandra Munroe (eds), *Cai Guo-Qiang: I Want to Believe* (New York: Guggenheim Museum, 2008), p. 25.

116 Goodman, *Ways of Worldmaking*, p. 5.

117 Plato, *Republic* [*c.* 380–350BCE], trans. Benjamin Jowett (New York: Barnes and Noble, 2004), Book VII. We point here to the many twentieth-century theorists whose work analyses the relationship between materiality and meaning, including Wittgenstein, Heidegger, Cassirer and Lyotard. This perspective does not refute the material presence of the world of things, but rather indicates the limited extent to which human beings can access the world of things, mediated as it is by language and signification.

118 Goodman, *Ways of Worldmaking*, p. 5.

119 Jen Webb and Lorraine Webb, 'Making Worlds: Art, Words and Worlds', in Turner, Antoinette and Stanhope (eds), *The World and World-Making in Art, Special Issue of Humanities Research*, 19:2 (2013), pp. 61–80: 78.

At the end of this book we find ourselves unable to offer any conclusive explanations for the past thirty years of art in Asia, and particularly of art motivated by issues of social justice, concern for humanity's future and for human rights: like Amelia Jones, reaching the end of her treatise on identification and the arts, we can offer only 'concluding thoughts, without final conclusions'.[1] This is in part because, of course, the story has not concluded: many of the artists whose work can be categorised within the frame of reference of this book are still practising, and inevitably changing their voice and their focus as their context changes. We can say, however, that each of these artists, like other artists in their cohort, has a very specific history, nationality, aesthetic and set of values, but each has acted as a 'circuit breaker' in the international art world, allowing new modes of thinking and seeing, and new modes of communication between peoples and cultures. They are all, in effect, worldmakers, because in their various ways they look closely at the contemporary order of things, and speak out – in their works, and/or in their political or cultural activism – about those discourses, practices, traditions and legal structures that cause suffering or oppression, or that prevent individuals from achieving a good life. Meskimmon describes this as a kind of worldmaking because it is a 'precarious ecology' that involves

> the sustainable, yet evolving, systems of relation that engender a generous intersubjectivity and an openness to difference. These ecologies are risky, subject to change, premised upon negotiation with others and, I would argue, absolutely critical to an ethical way of inhabiting a global world – to engendering a cosmopolitan imagination.[2]

This cosmopolitan imagination is perhaps the defining feature of those Asian artists whose work erupted onto the scene, as far as western museums and audiences were concerned, late last century. Their insistence on ethics and equity, their humour and passion, and their iconoclastic approach continue to inform ways of making art as well as engaging with questions of human value and rights. As the decades have passed, many have begun to turn their attention to environmental issues.

Among them is Taiwanese Wu Mali, who has built a lifetime's work and an international reputation involving creative and critical responses to social and political issues.[3] From the early works she produced and exhibited in the context of Taiwan's transition from martial law to democracy,[4] Wu Mali has consistently focused on political concerns within the framework of the personal. Linda Jaivan points out that the early works included acts of cultural rebellion, and blended regional gender politics into single works.[5] Later works (such as *Formosa Club*, about the sex industry, shown in the 1998 Taipei Biennale) directly engage gender politics, as does what Wei Hsiu Tung describes as her 'ethnographic' art[6] – such as the local projects involving artistic collaborations with village communities – and her work with the women's rights organisation, the Taipei Awakening Association. As she says, 'Despite the various subjects, I am really dealing with only one core issue in my works: how does a person exist comfortably in an environment? … How does a person live happily in despite of one's identity, gender, background, or social class?'[7]

One way to explore this question is to consider the relation of the self to both socioeconomic and natural environments, and she increasingly attends to the national, and indeed global work of environmental action.[8] Wu Mali began active involvement in environmental work after living in the Danshui area for some years; here she built relationships with other creative practitioners, and together they began a process involving eco education and community involvement to make people aware of the polluted local stream of Plum Tree

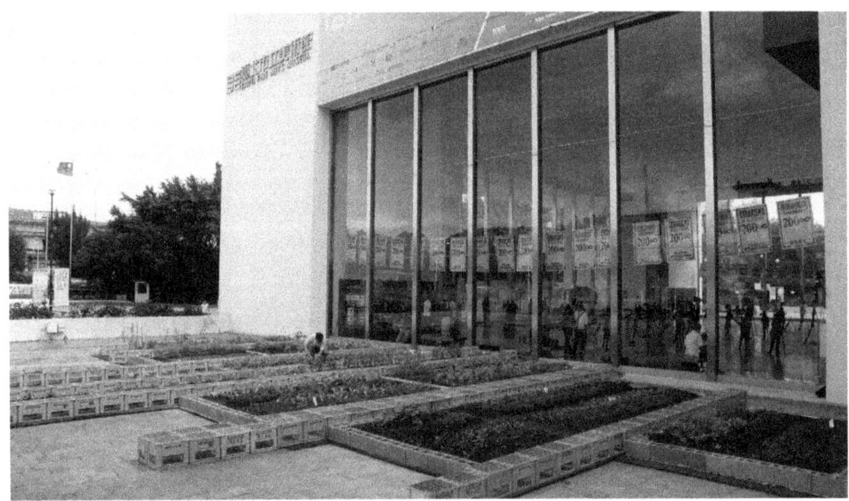

6.1 Wu Mali, *Taipei Tomorrow as a Lake Again*, 2008. Installation showing garden at Taipei Biennial.

Creek in their living environment. She draws a very definite line between artists and activists, one that may be relevant to other modes of practice engaged by artists who operate in the broad domain of human rights:

> I think art stimulates the mind, but I wouldn't compare an artist to an environmentalist. They have different focuses in their roles, but one can simultaneously be an artist and an environmentalist. Environmentalists are focused in making changes; artists, on the other hand, tell the same story with a different medium, they also give the mind an alternative suggestion – this, I think, is the only difference between the two. I think that environmentalists are more proactive than myself, they invest a lot. I, on the other hand, provide an alternative pathway, platform, as I work towards the same goal.[9]

For her, the art work must achieve a satisfying aesthetic outcome; but ideally it will also shift practices, raise consciousness, and ameliorate suffering in society. This is a perspective shared by other artists in our study: one example is the SAHMAT group in India, as discussed in Chapter 1, where artists band together to educate communities across political, religious and cultural boundaries of violence and intolerance.

Cultural crossings and community involvement have been a clear focus in the work of Mella Jaarsma and Nindityo Adipurnomo. In 1988 – during the Suharto years – they founded Cemeti Art House/Gallery in Yogyakarta, Indonesia.[10] Many artists associated with Cemeti created art about political issues: a key example is Moelyono's 1993 exhibition about the murder of a woman trade union leader, Marsinah.[11] Moelyono has spent much of his career teaching poor villagers, especially children; Adipurnomo and Jaarsma,

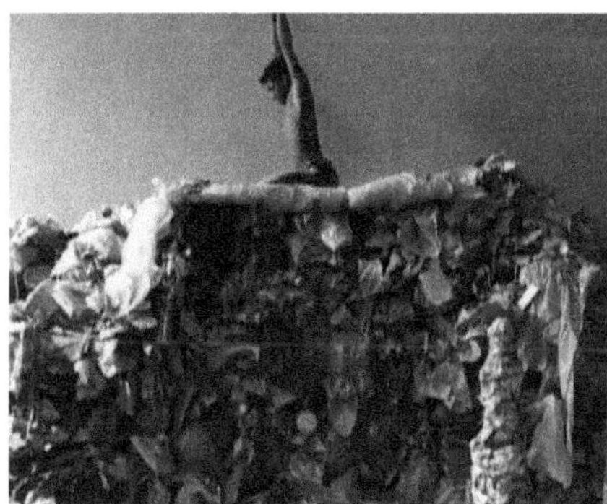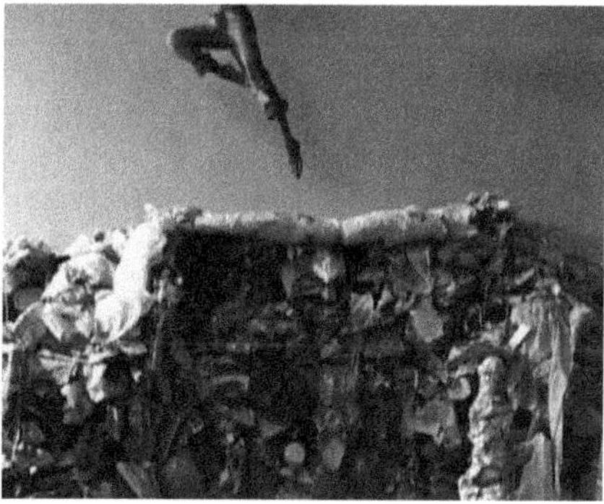

Vivan Sundaram, *The Brief Ascension of Marian Hussain*, 2005 (from the series   **6.2**
'*Trash*'). Video stills. The '*Trash*' series uses recycled rubbish as a statement regarding the social environment. In this work also using the figure of a teenage rag picker. The artist has been a major figure in SAHMAT.

too, have always been concerned with supporting the local community, such as providing relief facilities and workshops for children after the tsunami in 2004. They have also provided a seedbed for art: as Alia Swastika notes, 'All the Indonesian "superstars" who actively joined the global art circuit at the time had started their artistic careers here, from Agus Suwage and Heri Dono to Eko Nugroho and Jompet Kuswidananto.'[12] Cemeti has been enormously influential in Asia, connecting many artists and groups and providing an inspiration for innovative artist-run exhibitions and projects – many focused on the community – for which they have won many international awards.

Adipurnomo's and Jaarsma's own art examines the complexities of changing identity in a globalising world and new ways of seeing that world. Their art has been shown in numerous international exhibitions beyond Asia. Adipurnomo has explored issues such as power, tradition, gender and religion in Javanese society (which is his heritage), working with materials such as hair, traditional Javanese daggers and furniture, in order 'to reconfigure our perception towards the accepted interpretations of society and culture'[13] (see Figure 1.2). Jaarsma's work, suggests Enin Supriyanto, symbolises tensions between human beings and their social environment.[14] Jaarsma was born in the Netherlands but has made Indonesia her home, and has produced artworks that examine the ways human beings communicate across cultural boundaries. Her costumes made of different skins and materials, for example, challenge people to think about the reality of being in another person's skin or culture. In this way both artists are challenging the constraints of culture, and making art that also reconfigures our ways of seeing the world.

Ai Weiwei, who is often described as 'the most powerful artist in the world',[15] is yet another who continually renews his work and his perspective. Though a number of critics doubted the validity of his 'powerful' title,[16] there is fairly universal agreement that he is an artist who has made significant achievements. Indeed, curator Hans Ulrich Obrist, director of International Projects at the Serpentine Gallery, London, writes that Ai Weiwei

> keeps extending the notion of art: he is an artist, a poet, an architect, a curator, an expert on ancient Chinese craft-work, a publisher, an urbanist, a collector, he has his own blog, and so on … Ai Weiwei's broad interest in art, architecture and writing reminds me of the great renaissance artists.[17]

His achievement is the more impressive when one remembers that those great artists created their masterpieces with the support of great and powerful patrons, whereas, his art can also be seen as opposition to the physical manifestations of global power.[18] He does, however, seek to work collaboratively with artists and artisans in China, and elsewhere. One of his better-known works is his *Sunflower Seeds* (2010), shown at Tate Modern, which curator Mark Stevens describes as 'a work of hallucinatory intensity that … consists of

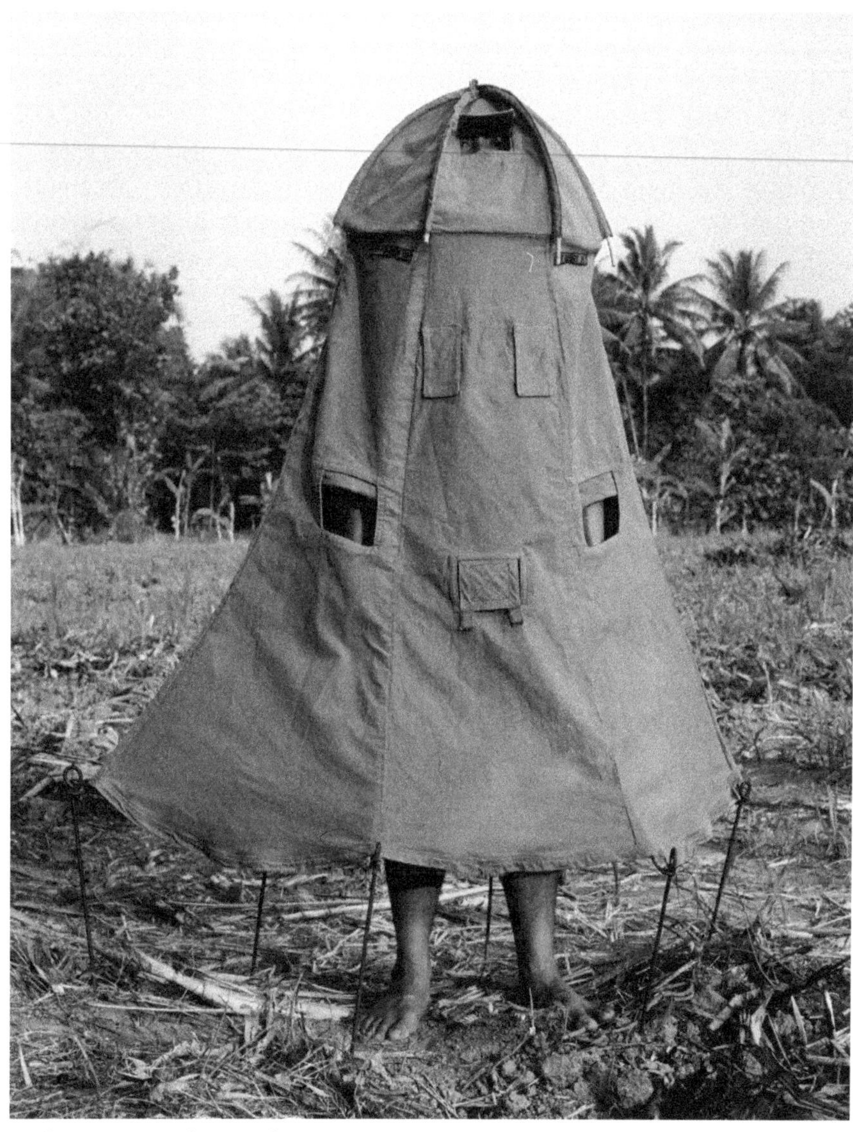

Mella Jaarsma, *Refugee Only*, 2003.   **6.3**

100 million pieces of porcelain, each painted by one of 1,600 Chinese craftsmen to resemble a sunflower seed'.[19] Porcelain, of course, is a very important
luxury product in China, and sunflower seeds are simply an everyday snack.
The combination of these could result in an oxymoron, but instead it is a profoundly moving installation, all the more so once the viewer is informed that

Ai's sunflower project brought employment to the village of Jingdezhen – a community of artisans who, for over a thousand years, made the imperial porcelain. It speaks of poverty, of memory, of nourishment, and inevitably of Chairman Mao, who was presented in propaganda images as the sun towards whom the people – sunflowers – necessarily turned. As such it is a political work, one that draws attention to the individuals that together comprise the mass, and with the question of what it means to be a single person in contemporary society.[20]

The period of art practice we have documented in this book in, through and out of Asia inaugurated a new way of making art, thinking art and seeing art. Though it clearly builds on the work of artists from earlier periods in the twentieth century, and often looks much further back, into local traditional practices, it is an art that is of the contemporary globalised era. It is also an art of people who have become citizens – of their own nations, and of the world. With citizenship comes civic responsibility; and, as Ai Weiwei notes, 'If artists betray the social conscience and the basic principles of being human, where does art stand then?'[21] It may be that art is perfectly capable of being for art's sake only, and has no responsibility to social conscience or the principles of being human; but the artists themselves, it seems, cannot evade this duty. Those artists who emerged into the global museum culture in the latter part of the twentieth century, and whose work has galvanised both art and exhibition practice, have not evaded that duty, but have maintained a steady and critical gaze on their societies, and on what we need to be human.

Notes

1 Amelia Jones, *Seeing Differently: A History and Theory of Identification and the Visual Arts* (Abingdon: Routledge, 2012), p. 218.

2 Marsha Meskimmon, 'The Precarious Ecologies of Cosmopolitanism', in Turner, Antoinette and Stanhope (eds), *The World and World-Making in Art, Special Issue of Humanities Research*, 19:2 (2013), pp. 27–45: 37.

3 For a discussion of Wu Mali's art see Sophie McIntyre, 'Imagining Taiwan: The Making and the Museological Representation of Art in Taiwan's Quest for Identity (1987–2010)', (PhD thesis, Australian National University, 2012); Natalie Seiz, 'The Emergence of Contemporary Women's Art in Taiwan (1970s–2000s)', (PhD thesis, University of Sydney, 2013).

4 Taiwan was under martial law for thirty-eight years, from 1949 to 1987: so long that it seemed a 'permanent imposition of martial law'. The effects were stifling, particularly at periods like the 'White Terror' of the 1950s, which was marked by mass arrests and executions of those identified as political activists. Denny Roy, *Taiwan: A Political History* (Ithaca, NY: Cornell University Press, 2003), pp. 70, 90. Since the 1980s, Taiwan has developed a dynamic and internationally engaged art scene.

5 Linda Jaivin, 'Mali Wu: Profile Consuming Texts: The Work of Mali Wu', *n-Paradoxa*, 5 (November 1997), pp. 54–7: 56.

6 Wei Hsiu Tung, *Art for Social Change and Cultural Awakening: An Anthropology of Residence in Taiwan* (Lanham, MA: Lexington Books, 2013), p. 107.

7 Larry Shao, 'Interview with Wu Mali', *Asiart Archive Diaaalogue* (November 2010), www.aaa.org.hk/Diaaalogue/Details/931, accessed 15 September 2014.

8 Wei Hsiu Tung, *Art for Social Change*, p. 149.

9 In Larry Shao, 'Interview with Wu Mali'. On the project at Plum Tree Creek see http://weadartists.org/plum-tree-creek-action What Olivier Krischer has called 'creative activism' and Tessa Morris-Suzuki has called 'living politics' is often in Asia today related to the environment and connected to transnational networks. See papers by both presented at the conference 'Survival Politics in East Asia: Socio-Environmental Crises and Grassroots Responses', Australian National University, 4–6 March 2015.

10 The Cemeti website notes that in recent years a Foundation (the Indonesian Visual Art Archive IVAA) has been formed to support documentation and education, and that Cemeti is also focusing on reinventing 'Art and Society', 'emphasizing more alternative art practices that honour the "process", rather than the "promotion" of artists and art making'. See www.cemetiarthouse.com/index.php?page=about&lang=en, accessed 28 September 2014.

11 M. Taufiqurrahman, 'Moelyono: The Arts and Social Responsibility', *Jakarta Post* (3 February 2006), www.thejakartapost.com/news/2006/02/03/moelyono-arts-and-social-responsibility.html. See also 'Moelyono: Profile', *Artistspeak*, University of South Australia (2008), http://w3.unisa.edu.au/artarchitecturedesign/events/artistspeak/docs/2007–2009/profilemoelyono2008.pdf.   This work was not done as part of Cemeti's programs, and his exhibition was banned by the authorities.

12 Alia Swastika, 'Postcard from Yogyakarta: 25 Years of Cemeti Art House', *Frieze* (15 March 2013), blog.frieze.com/postcard-from-yogyakarta-25-years-of-cemeti-art-house/, accessed 24 September 2014.

13 Nindityo Adipurnomo, *Indonesian Eye: Fantasies and Realities* (2011), www.indonesianeye.com/artist/nindityo-adipurnomo, accessed 25 September 2014.

14 Cited in Bambang Muryanto, 'Mella Jaarsma: A Guardian of Arts', *Jakarta Post* (16 April 2014), www.thejakartapost.com/news/2014/04/16/mella-jaarsma-a-guardian-arts.html, accessed 25 September 2014.

15 See, e.g., BBC News, 'At-a-glance: Art's most Powerful People', *Entertainment and Arts* (13 October 2011), http://www.bbc.com/news/entertainment-arts-15286754, accessed 24 September 2014.

16 See, e.g., Mark Stevens, 'Is Ai Weiwei China's Most Dangerous Man?' *Smithsonian Magazine* (September 2012), http://www.smithsonianmag.com/arts-culture/is-ai-weiwei-chinas-most-dangerous-man-17989316/, accessed 24 September 2014.

17 Hans Ulrich Obrist, *Ai Weiwei Speaks with Hans Ulrich Obrist* (London: Penguin Books, 2011), pp. vii–ix. In architecture, Ai Weiwei co-designed with Swiss

architects Herzog & de Meuron the Olympic (Bird's Nest) Stadium for the 2008 Olympics.

18 Charles Merewether, 'The House of the People: Forms of Collaboration', in Deborah E. Horowitz (ed.), *Ai Weiwei: According to What?* (Hong Kong: Hirshhorn Museum and Sculpture Garden, the Mori Art Museum, including essays by Mami Kataoka; Kerry Brougher; Charles Merewether, 2012), pp. 22–37. Merewether's reference to Ai's holding up his finger (to Tiananmen Square, the White House, the Eiffel Tower and the Reichstag Building, Berlin) comes from the documentary film *Never Sorry* (2012), directed by Alison Klayman.

19 Mark Stevens, 'Is Ai Weiwei China's Most Dangerous Man?'

20 Tate, 'Ai Weiwei: Sunflower Seeds' (Interpretation text), *The Unilever Series* (2010), http://www.tate.org.uk/whats-on/tate-modern/exhibition/unilever-series-ai-weiwei/interpretation-text, accessed 24 September 2014.

21 Hans Ulrich Obrist (ed., and interviewer), *Ai Weiwei Speaks* (London: Penguin Books, 2011), p. 27.

Index

Note: page numbers referring to illustrations are in *italic*.

EU authorised representative for GPSR:
Easy Access System Europe, Mustamäe tee 50,
10621 Tallinn, Estonia
gpsr.requests@easproject.com

www.ingramcontent.com/pod-product-compliance
Ingram Content Group UK Ltd.
Pitfield, Milton Keynes, MK11 3LW, UK
UKHW062200060726
6981IPUK00009B/101